Contents

Preface

Walt Whitman, born in 1819 on Long Island (the Paumanok of many of his poems). He was arguably America's most influential and innovative poet, was born into a working class family in West Hills, New York, a village near Hempstead, Long Island, on May 31, 1819, just thirty years after George Washington was inaugurated as the first president of the newly formed United States. Walt Whitman was named after his father, a carpenter and farmer who was 34 years old when Whitman was born.

During his early years he trained as a printer, then became a teacher, and finally a journalist and editor. A few of his popular works include "The Inca's Daughter." Long Island Democrat 5 May 1840: "The Love That is Hereafter." Long Island Democrat 19 May 1840: "We All Shall Rest At Last." Long Island Democrat 14 July 1840: "The Spanish Lady." Long Island Democrat 4 August 1840: "The End of All." Long Island Democrat 22 September 1840: "The Columbian's Song." Long Island Democrat 27 October 1840.

Author

Chapter 1

Introduction

Walt Whitman was born in 1819 on Long Island (the Paumanok of many of his poems). During his early years he trained as a printer, then became a teacher, and finally a journalist and editor. He was less than successful; his stridently radical views made him unpopular with readers. After an 1848 sojourn in the South, which introduced him to some of the variety of his country, he returned to New York and began to write poetry.

In 1855 he self-published the first edition of Leaves of Grass, which at the time consisted of only twelve poems. The volume was widely ignored, with one significant exception. Ralph Waldo Emerson wrote him a congratulatory letter, in which he offered his "greet... at the beginning of a great career." Whitman promptly published another edition of Leaves of Grass, expanding it by some twenty poems and appending the letter from Emerson, much to the latter's discomfort. 1860 saw another edition of a now much larger Leaves—containing some 156 poems—which was issued by a trade publisher.

At the outset of the Civil War Whitman volunteered as a nurse in army hospitals; he also wrote dispatches as a correspondent for the New York Times. The war inspired a great deal of poetry, which was published in 1865 as Drum Taps. Drum Taps was then incorporated into an 1867 edition of Leaves of Grass, as was another volume of wartime poetry, Sequel, which included the poems written on Lincoln's assassination.

Whitman's wartime work led to a job with the Department

of the Interior, but he was soon fired when his supervisor learned that he had written the racy poems of Leaves of Grass. The failure of Reconstruction led him to write the best known of his prose works, Democratic Vistas, which, as its title implies, argues for the maintenance of democratic ideals. This volume came out in 1871, as did yet another edition of Leaves of Grass, expanded to include more poems. The 1871 edition was reprinted in 1876 for the centennial. Several other prose works followed, then a further expanded version of Leaves of Grass, in 1881.

Whitman's health had been shaky since the mid-1870s, and by 1891 it was clear he was dying. He therefore prepared his so-called "Deathbed" edition of Leaves of Grass, which contained two appendices of old-age poems as well as a review essay in which he tries to justify his life and work. The "Deathbed Edition" came out in 1892; Whitman died that year.

Whitman's lifetime saw both the Civil War and the rise of the United States as a commercial and political power. He witnessed both the apex and the abolition of slavery. His poetry is thus centered on ideas of democracy, equality, and brotherhood. In response to America's new position in the world, Whitman also tried to develop a poetry that was uniquely American, that both surpassed and broke the mold of its predecessors. Leaves of Grass, with its multiple editions and public controversies, set the pattern for the modern, public artist, and Whitman, with his journalistic endeavors on the side, made the most of his role as celebrity and artist.

When Walt Whitman published his first edition of Leaves of Grass on or around the fourth day of July in 1855, he believed he was embarking on a personal literary journey of national significance. Setting out to define the American experience, Whitman consciously hoped to answer Ralph Waldo Emerson's 1843 essay, "The Poet," which called for a truly original national poet, one who would sing of the new country in a new voice. The undertaking required unlimited optimism, especially considering the fact that Whitman had published only a small handful of poems prior to 1855; however, Whitman felt confident that the time was ripe and that the people would embrace him. This optimism and confidence resulted largely from his awareness of the tremendous changes in the American literary world that had taken place during his lifetime.

At the time of Whitman's birth in 1819, the Constitution and the democratic ideas upon which this country was founded were only a generation old; America was a land of seemingly unlimited space, resources, and possibilities, yet a land with no cultural roots to call its own. In 1820, a year after Whitman's birth, Sydney Smith of Britain's Edinburgh Review was prompted to ask, "In the four quarters of the globe, who reads an American book?" But the period between Smith's remark and the publication of Whitman's first edition of Leaves of Grass in 1855 was one of remarkable and unprecedented change in America, particularly in the world of books.

By 1855, America could boast one of the world's largest and most advanced publishing industries, producing distinctly "American" books by authors such as Poe, Hawthorne, Melville, Stowe, Fuller, Thoreau, and Emerson. The amazing growth of American literature and of the supporting publishing industry was the result of a self-conscious effort by authors and publishers to establish for America a literary culture of its own. The resulting increase in, or rather the sudden appearance of, authorship in this country was made possibly only through American ingenuity, innovation, and technology in pulbishing. In short, the advent of modern pulbishing practices during this period brought books to the peopl in heretofore unimaginable numbers, spawning as a result one of the greatest periods in the history of American literature.

Working as a printer, editor, jounalist, and publisher during the years of the publishing industry's phenomenal growth, Whitman became keenly aware that the tools necessary for his emergence as the new, democratic poet were at his disposal. He believed he could bring poetry to the common people, and with the publication of his 1855 Leaves of Grass, he assumed for himself the role of the American Poet, referring to himself as "one of the roughs," a common man. Whitman carefully continued to cultivate his literary personality throughout his career, especially through the relatively new field of photography. As he revised and enlarged Leaves of Grass (8 editions and numerous printings would appear between 1855 and 1891), Whitman's goal as the self-styled national poet became more clearly defined. Leaves of Grass is essentially a poem in process, with each succeeding edition representing a unique period in the poet's life as well as the nation's. This is perhaps best illustrated by Whitman's Civil War poetry. Originally published in 1865 as a separate volume entitled Drum Taps, these poems were later integrated into Leaves of Grass, growing in importance in the book as the war's historical significance became clearer in Whitman's mind. He would eventually claim that Leaves of Grass "revolves around that four year's war, which, as I was in the midst of it, becomes, in "Drum-Taps," pivotal to the rest entire."

Today, more than a century after the publication of the final edition of Leaves of Grass, Whitman's place in American literary history often seems as nebulous and enigmatic as the ideas upon which America was founded. Numerous poets since Whitman have consciously either placed themselves in the wake of his tradition or reacted violently against him, and the aesthetic value of Whitman's poetry continues to be a controversial subject. The intention of this exhibit is not to make a critical appraisal of Whitman's work; instead, it is hoped that the materials assembled here will help explain the phenomenon which was Walt Whitman. While the subject matter and themes present in Whitman's poetry reflect the historical attitudes and concerns of his day, the books themselves are also artifacts of a fascination and extremely dynamic period of American publishing history.

Chapter 2

Biography

Family Origins

Walt Whitman, arguably America's most influential and innovative poet, was born into a working class family in West Hills, New York, a village near Hempstead, Long Island, on May 31, 1819, just thirty years after George Washington was inaugurated as the first president of the newly formed United States. Walt Whitman was named after his father, a carpenter and farmer who was 34 years old when Whitman was born. Walter Whitman, Sr., had been born just after the end of the American Revolution; always a liberal thinker, he knew and admired Thomas Paine. Trained as a carpenter but struggling to find work, he had taken up farming by the time Walt was born, but when Walt was just about to turn four, Walter Sr. moved the family to the growing city of Brooklyn, across from New York City, or "Mannahatta" as Whitman would come to call it in his celebratory writings about the city that was just emerging as the nation's major urban centre. One of Walt's favourite stories about his childhood concerned the time General Lafayette visited New York and, selecting the six-year-old Walt from the crowd, lifted him up and carried him. Whitman later came to view this event as a kind of laying on of hands, the French hero of the American Revolution anointing the future poet of democracy in the energetic city of immigrants, where the new nation was being invented day by day.

Walt Whitman is thus of the first generation of Americans who were born in the newly formed United States and grew up assuming the stable existence of the new country. Pride in the emergent nation was rampant, and Walter Sr.—after giving his first son Jesse his own father's name, his second son his own name, his daughter Mary the name of Walt's maternal great grandmothers, and his daughter Hannah the name of his own mother—turned to the heroes of the Revolution and the War of 1812 for the names of his other three sons: Andrew Jackson Whitman, George Washington Whitman, and Thomas Jefferson Whitman. Only the youngest son, Edward, who was mentally and physically handicapped, carried a name that tied him to neither the family's nor the country's history.

Walter Whitman Sr. was of English stock, and his marriage in 1816 to Louisa Van Velsor, of Dutch and Welsh stock, led to what Walt always considered a fertile tension in the Whitman children between a more smoldering, brooding Puritanical temperament and a sunnier, more outgoing Dutch disposition. Whitman's father was a stern and sometimes hot-tempered man, maybe an alcoholic, whom Whitman respected but for whom he never felt a great deal of affection. His mother, on the other hand, served throughout his life as his emotional touchstone. There was a special affectional bond between Whitman and his mother, and the long correspondence between them records a kind of partnership in attempting to deal with the family crises that mounted over the years, as Jesse became mentally unstable and violent and eventually had to be institutionalized, as Hannah entered a disastrous marriage with an abusive husband, as Andrew became an alcoholic and married a prostitute before dying of ill health in his 30s, and as Edward required increasingly dedicated care.

A Brooklyn Childhood and LongIsland Interludes

During Walt's childhood, the Whitman family moved around Brooklyn a great deal as Walter Sr. tried, mostly unsuccessfully, to cash in on the city's quick growth by speculating in real estate—buying an empty lot, building a house, moving his family in, then trying to sell it at a profit to start the whole process over again. Walt loved living close to the East River, where as a child he rode the ferries back and forth to New York City, imbibing an experience that would remain significant for him his whole life: he loved ferries and the people who worked on them, and his 1856 poem eventually entitled "Crossing Brooklyn Ferry" explored the full resonance of the experience. The act of crossing became, for Whitman, one of the most evocative events in his life—at once practical, enjoyable, and mystical. The daily commute suggested the passage from life to death to life again and suggested too the passage from poet to reader to poet via the vehicle of the poem. By crossing Brooklyn ferry, Whitman first discovered the magical commutations that he would eventually accomplish in his poetry.

While in Brooklyn, Whitman attended the newly founded Brooklyn public schools for six years, sharing his classes with students of a variety of ages and backgrounds, though most were poor, since children from wealthy families attended private schools. In Whitman's school, all the students were in the same room, except African Americans, who had to attend a separate class on the top floor. Whitman had little to say about his rudimentary formal schooling, except that he hated corporal punishment, a common practice in schools and one that he would attack in later years in both his journalism and his fiction. But most of Whitman's meaningful education came outside of school, when he visited museums, went to libraries, and attended lectures. He always recalled the first great lecture he heard, when he was ten years old, given by the radical Quaker leader Elias Hicks, an acquaintance of Whitman's father and a close friend of Whitman's grandfather Jesse. While Whitman's parents were not members of any religious denomination, Quaker thought always played a major role in Whitman's life, in part because of the early influence of Hicks, and in part because his mother Louisa's family had a Quaker background, especially Whitman's grandmother Amy Williams Van Velsor, whose death—the same year Whitman first heard Hicks—hit young Walt hard, since he had spent many happy days at the farm of his grandmother and colorful grandfather, Major Cornelius Van Velsor.

Visiting his grandparents on Long Island was one of

Whitman's favourite boyhood activities, and during those visits he developed his lifelong love of the Long Island shore, sensing the mystery of that territory where water meets land, fluid melds with solid. One of Whitman's greatest poems, "Out of the Cradle Endlessly Rocking," is on one level a reminiscence of his boyhood on the Long Island shore and of how his desire to be a poet arose in that landscape. The idyllic Long Island countryside formed a sharp contrast to the crowded energy of the quickly growing Brooklyn-New York City urban centre. Whitman's experiences as a young man alternated between the city and the Long Island countryside, and he was attracted to both ways of life. This dual allegiance can be traced in his poetry, which is often marked by shifts between rural and urban settings.

Self-Education and First Career

By the age of eleven, Whitman was done with his formal education (by this time he had far more schooling than either of his parents had received), and he began his life as a laborer, working first as an office boy for some prominent Brooklyn lawyers, who gave him a subscription to a circulating library, where his self-education began. Always an autodidact, Whitman absorbed an eclectic but wide-ranging education through his visits to museums, his nonstop reading, and his penchant for engaging everyone he met in conversation and debate. While most other major writers of his time enjoyed highly structured, classical educations at private institutions, Whitman forged his own rough and informal curriculum of literature, theater, history, geography, music, and archeology out of the developing public resources of America's fastest growing city.

In 1831, Whitman became an apprentice on the Long Island Patriot, a liberal, working-class newspaper, where he learned the printing trade and was first exposed to the excitement of putting words into print, observing how thought and event could be quickly transformed into language and immediately communicated to thousands of readers. At the age of twelve, young Walt was already contributing to the newspaper and experiencing the exhilaration of getting his own words published. Whitman's first signed article, in the upscale New York Mirror in 1834, expressed his amazement at how there were still people alive who could remember "the present great metropolitan city as a little dorp or village; all fresh and green as it was, from its beginning," and he wrote of a slave, "Negro Harry," who had died in1758 at age 120 and who could remember New York "when there were but three houses in it." Even late in his life, he could still recall the excitement of seeing this first article in print: "How it made my heart double-beat to see my piece on the pretty white paper, in nice type." For his entire life, he would maintain this fascination with the materiality of printed objects, with the way his voice and identity could be embodied in type and paper.

Living away from home—the rest of his family moved back to the West Hills area in 1833, leaving fourteen-year-old Walt alone in the city—and learning how to set type under the Patriot's foreman printer William Hartshorne, Whitman was gaining skills and experiencing an independence that would mark his whole career: he would always retain a typesetter's concern for how his words looked on a page, what typeface they were dressed in, what effects various spatial arrangements had, and he would always retain his stubborn independence, never marrying and living alone for most of his life. These early years on his own in Brooklyn and New York remained a formative influence on his writing, for it was during this time that he developed the habit of close observation of the ever-shifting panorama of the city, and a great deal of his journalism, poetry, and prose came to focus on catalogs of urban life and the history of New York City, Brooklyn, and Long Island. Walt's brother Thomas Jefferson, known to everyone in the family as "Jeff," was born during the summer of 1833, soon after his family had resettled on a farm and only weeks after Walt had joined the crowds in Brooklyn that warmly welcomed the newly re-elected president, Andrew Jackson. Brother Jeff, fourteen years younger than Walt, would become the sibling he felt closest to, their bond formed when they traveled together to New

Orleans in 1848, when Jeff was about the same age as Walt was when Jeff was born. But while Jeff was a young child, Whitman spent little time with him. Walt remained separated from his family and furthered his education by absorbing the power of language from a variety of sources: various circulating libraries (where he read Sir Walter Scott, James Fenimore Cooper, and other romance novelists), theaters (where he fell in love with Shakespeare's plays and saw Junius Booth, John Wilkes Booth's father, play the title role in Richard III, always Whitman's favourite play), and lectures (where he heard, among others, Frances Wright, the Scottish radical emancipationist and women's rights advocate). By the time he was sixteen, Walt was a journeyman printer and compositor in New York City. His future career seemed set in the newspaper and printing trades, but then two of New York's worst fires wiped out the major printing and business centers of the city, and, in the midst of a dismal financial climate, Whitman retreated to rural Long Island, joining his family at Hempstead in 1836. As he turned 17, the five-year veteran of the printing trade was already on the verge of a career change.

Schoolteaching Years^

His unlikely next career was that of a teacher. Although his own formal education was, by today's standards, minimal, he had developed as a newspaper apprentice the skills of reading and writing, more than enough for the kind of teaching he would find himself doing over the next few years. He knew he did not want to become a farmer, and he rebelled at his father's attempts to get him to work on the new family farm. Teaching was therefore an escape but was also clearly a job he was forced to take in bad economic times, and some of the unhappiest times of his life were these five years when he taught school in at least ten different Long Island towns, rooming in the homes of his students, teaching three-month terms to large and heterogeneous classes (some with over eighty students, ranging in age from five to fifteen, for up to nine hours a day), getting very little pay, and having to put up with some very unenlightened people. After the excitement of Brooklyn and New York, these often isolated Long Island towns depressed Whitman, and he recorded his disdain for country people in a series of letters (not discovered until the 1980s) that he wrote to a friend named Abraham Leech: "Never before have I entertained so low an idea of the beauty and perfection of man's nature, never have I seen humanity in so degraded a shape, as here," he wrote from Woodbury in 1840: "Ignorance, vulgarity, rudeness, conceit, and dulness are the reigning gods of this deuced sink of despair."

The little evidence we have of his teaching (mostly from short recollections by a few former students) suggests that Whitman employed what were then progressive techniques—encouraging students to think aloud rather than simply recite, refusing to punish by paddling, involving his students in educational games, and joining his students in baseball and card games.

By 1841, Whitman's second career was at an end. He had interrupted his teaching in 1838 to try his luck at starting his own newspaper, The Long Islander, devoted to covering the towns around Huntington. He bought a press and type and hired his younger brother George as an assistant, but, despite his energetic efforts to edit, publish, write for, and deliver the new paper, it folded within a year, and he reluctantly returned to the classroom. Newspaper work made him happy, but teaching did not, and two years later, he abruptly quit his job as an itinerant schoolteacher. The reasons for his decision continue to interest biographers. One persistent but unsubstantiated rumor has it that Whitman committed sodomy with one of his students while teaching in Southold, though it is not possible to prove that Whitman actually even taught there. The rumor suggests he was run out of town in disgrace, never to return and soon to abandon teaching altogether. But in fact Whitman did travel again to Southold, writing some remarkably unperturbed journalistic pieces about the place in the late 1840s and early 1860s. It seems far more likely that Whitman gave up schoolteaching because he found himself temperamentally unsuited for it. And, besides, he had a new career opening up: he decided now to become a fiction writer. Best of all, to nurture that career, he would need to return to New York City and re-establish himself in the world of journalism.

Mature Journalist

By the mid-1840s, Whitman had a keen awareness of the cultural resources of New York City and probably had more inside knowledge of New York journalism than anyone else in Brooklyn. The Long Island Star recognized his value as a journalist and, once he resettled in Brooklyn, quickly arranged to have him compose a series of editorials, two or three a week, from September 1845 to March 1846. With the death of William Marsh, the editor of the Brooklyn Eagle, Whitman became chief editor of that paper (he served from March 5, 1846 to January 18, 1848). He dedicated himself to journalism in these years and published little of his own poetry and fiction. However, he introduced literary reviewing to the Eagle, and he commented, if often superficially, on writers such as Carlyle and Emerson, who in the next decade would have a significant impact on Leaves of Grass. The editor's role gave Whitman a platform from which to comment on various issues from street lighting to politics, from banking to poetry. But Whitman claimed that what he most valued was not the ability to promote his opinions, but rather something more intimate, the "curious kind of sympathy... that arises in the mind of a newspaper conductor with the public he serves. He gets to love them."

For Whitman, to serve the public was to frame issues in accordance with working class interests—and for Whitman this usually meant white working class interests. He sometimes dreaded slave labour as a "black tide" that could overwhelm white workingmen. He was adamant that slavery should not be allowed into the new western territories because he feared whites would not migrate to an area where their own labour was devalued unfairly by the institution of black slavery. Periodically, Whitman expressed outrage at practices that furthered slavery itself: for example, he was incensed at laws that made possible the importation of slaves by way of Brazil.

Like Lincoln, he consistently opposed slavery and its further extension, even while he knew that the more extreme abolitionists threatened the Union itself. In a famous incident, Whitman lost his position as editor of the Eagle because the publisher, Isaac Van Anden, as an "Old Hunker," sided with conservative pro-slavery Democrats and could no longer abide Whitman's support of free soil and the Wilmot Proviso (a legislative proposal designed to stop the expansion of slavery into the western territories).

New Orleans Sojourn

Fortunately, on February 9, 1846, Whitman met, between acts of a performance at the Broadway Theatre in New York, J. E. McClure, who intended to launch a New Orleans paper, the Crescent, with an associate, A. H. Hayes. In a stunningly short time—reportedly in fifteen minutes—McClure struck a deal with Whitman and provided him with an advance to cover his travel expenses to New Orleans. Whitman's younger brother Jeff, then only fifteen years old, decided to travel with Walt and work as an office boy on the paper. The journey—by train, steamboat, and stagecoach—widened Walt's sense of the country's scope and diversity, as he left the New York City and Long Island area for the first time. Once in New Orleans, Walt did not have the famous New Orleans romance with a beautiful Creole woman, a relationship first imagined by the biographer Henry Bryan Binns and further elaborated by others who were charmed by the city's exoticism and who were eager to identify heterosexual desires in the poet. The published versions of his New Orleans poem called "Once I Pass'd Through a Populous City" seem to recount a romance with a woman, though the original manuscript reveals that he initially wrote with a male lover in mind.

Whatever the nature of his personal attachments in New Orleans, he certainly encountered a city full of colour and excitement. He wandered the French quarter and the old French market, attracted by "the Indian and negro hucksters with their wares" and the "great Creole mulatto woman" who sold him the best coffee he ever tasted. He enjoyed the "splendid and roomy bars" (with "exquisite wines, and the perfect and mild French brandy") that were packed with soldiers who had recently returned from the war with Mexico, and his first encounters with young men who had seen battle, many of them recovering from war wounds, occurred in New Orleans, a precursor of his Civil War experiences. He was entranced by the intoxicating mix of languages—French and Spanish and English—in that cosmopolitan city and began to see the possibilities of a distinctive American culture emerging from the melding of races and backgrounds (his own fondness for using French terms may well have derived from his New Orleans stay).

But the exotic nature of the Southern city was not without its horrors: slaves were auctioned within an easy walk of where the Whitman brothers were lodging at the Tremont House, around the corner from Lafayette Square. Whitman never forgot the experience of seeing humans on the selling block, and he kept a poster of a slave auction hanging in his room for many years as a reminder that such dehumanizing events occurred regularly in the United States. The slave auction was an experience that he would later incorporate in his poem "I Sing the Body Electric."

Walt felt wonderfully healthy in New Orleans, concluding that it agreed with him better than New York, but Jeff was often sick with dysentery, and his illness and homesickness contributed to their growing desire to return home. The final decision, though, was taken out of the hands of the brothers, as the Crescent owners exhibited what Whitman called a "singular sort of coldness" toward their new editor. They probably feared that this northern editor would embarrass them because of his unorthodox ideas, especially about slavery. Whitman's sojourn in New Orleans lasted only three months.

Budding Poet

His trip South produced a few lively sketches of New Orleans life and at least one poem, "Sailing the Mississippi at Midnight," in which the steamboat journey becomes a symbolic journey of life:

Vast and starless, the pall of heaven
Laps on the trailing pall below;
And forward, forward, in solemn darkness,
As if to the sea of the lost we go.

Throughout much of the 1840s Whitman wrote conventional poems like this one, often echoing Bryant, and, at times, Shelley and Keats. Bryant—and the graveyard school of English poetry—probably had the most important impact on his sensibility, as can be seen in his pre-Leaves of Grass poems "Our Future Lot," "Ambition," "The Winding-Up," "The Love that is Hereafter," and "Death of the Nature-Lover." The poetry of these years is artificial in diction and didactic in purpose; Whitman rarely seems inspired or innovative. Instead, tired language usually renders the poems inert. By the end of the decade, however, Whitman had undertaken serious self-education in the art of poetry, conducted in a typically unorthodox way—he clipped essays and reviews about leading British and American writers, and as he studied them he began to be a more aggressive reader and a more resistant respondent. His marginalia on these articles demonstrate that he was learning to write not in the manner of his predecessors but against them.

The mystery about Whitman in the late 1840s is the speed of his transformation from an unoriginal and conventional poet into one who abruptly abandoned conventional rhyme and meter and, in jottings begun at this time, exploited the odd loveliness of homely imagery, finding beauty in the commonplace but expressing it in an uncommon way. What is known as Whitman's earliest notebook (called "albot Wilson" in the Notebooks and Unpublished Prose Manuscripts) may have been written as early as 1847, though much of the writing probably derives from the early 1850s. This extraordinary document contains early articulations of some of Whitman's most compelling ideas. Famous passages on "Dilation," on "True noble expanding American character," and on the "soul enfolding orbs" are memorable prose statements that express the newly expansive sense of self that Whitman was discovering, and we find him here creating the conditions—setting the tone and articulating the ideas—that would allow for the writing of Leaves of Grass.

Racial Politics and the Origins of Leaves of Grass

A pivotal and empowering change came over Whitman at this time of poetic transformation. His politics—and especially his racial attitudes—underwent a profound alteration. As we have noted, Whitman the journalist spoke to the interests of the day and from a particular class perspective when he advanced the interests of white workingmen while seeming, at times, unconcerned about the plight of blacks. Perhaps the New Orleans experience had prompted a change in attitude, a change that was intensified by an increasing number of friendships with radical thinkers and writers who led Whitman to rethink his attitudes toward the issue of race. Whatever the cause, in Whitman's future-oriented poetry blacks become central to his new literary project and central to his understanding of democracy. Notebook passages assert that the poet has the "divine grammar of all tongues, and says indifferently and alike How are you friend? to the President in the midst of his cabinet, and Good day my brother, to Sambo among the hoes of the sugar field."

It appears that Whitman's increasing frustration with the Democratic party's compromising approaches to the slavery crisis led him to continue his political efforts through the more subtle and indirect means of experimental poetry, a poetry that he hoped would be read by masses of average Americans and would transform their way of thinking. In any event, his first notebook lines in the manner of Leaves of Grass focus directly on the fundamental issue dividing the United States. His notebook breaks into free verse for the first time in lines that seek to bind opposed categories, to black and white, to join master and slave:

I am the poet of the body
And I am the poet of the soul
And I am
I go with the slaves of the earth equally with he masters

And I will stand between the masters and the slaves,
Entering into both so that both will understand me alike.

The audacity of that final line remains striking. While most people were lining up on one side or another, Whitman placed himself in that space—sometimes violent, sometimes erotic, always volatile—between master and slave. His extreme political despair led him to replace what he now named the "scum" of corrupt American politics in the 1850s with his own persona—a shaman, a culture-healer, an all-encompassing "I."

The American "I"

That "I" became the main character of Leaves of Grass, the explosive book of twelve untitled poems that he wrote in the early years of the 1850s, and for which he set some of the type, designed the cover, and carefully oversaw all the details. When Whitman wrote "I, now thirty-six years old, in perfect health, begin," he announced a new identity for himself, and his novitiate came at an age quite advanced for a poet. Keats by that age had been dead for ten years; Byron had died at exactly that age; Wordsworth and Coleridge produced Lyrical Ballads while both were in their twenties; Bryant had written "Thanatopsis," his best-known poem, at age sixteen; and most other great Romantic poets Whitman admired had done their most memorable work early in their adult lives. Whitman, in contrast, by the time he had reached his mid-thirties, seemed destined, if he were to achieve fame in any field, to do so as a journalist or perhaps as a writer of fiction, but no one could have guessed that this middle-aged writer of sensationalistic fiction and sentimental verse would suddenly begin to produce work that would eventually lead many to view him as America's greatest and most revolutionary poet.

The mystery that has intrigued biographers and critics over the years has been about what prompted the transformation: did Whitman undergo some sort of spiritual illumination that opened the floodgates of a radical new kind of poetry, or was this poetry the result of an original and carefully calculated strategy to blend journalism, oratory, popular music, and other cultural forces into an innovative

American voice like the one Ralph Waldo Emerson had called for in his essay "The Poet"? "Our log-rolling, our stumps and their politics, our fisheries, our Negroes, and Indians, our boasts, and our repudiations, the wrath of rogues, and the pusillanimity of honest men, the Northern trade, the Southern planting, the Western clearing, Oregon and Texas, are yet unsung," wrote Emerson; "Yet America is a poem in our eyes; its ample geography dazzles the imagination, and it will not wait long for metres." Whitman began writing poetry that seemed, wildly yet systematically, to record every single thing that Emerson called for, and he began his preface to the 1855 Leaves by paraphrasing Emerson: "The United States themselves are essentially the greatest poem." The romantic view of Whitman is that he was suddenly inspired to impulsively write the poems that transformed American poetry; the more pragmatic view holds that Whitman devoted himself in the five years before the first publication of Leaves to a disciplined series of experiments that led to the gradual and intricate structuring of his singular style. Was he truly the intoxicated poet Emerson imagined or was he the architect of a poetic persona that cleverly mimicked Emerson's description?

There is evidence to support both theories. We know very little about the details of Whitman's life in the early 1850s; it is as if he retreated from the public world to receive inspiration, and there are relatively few remaining manuscripts of the poems in the first edition of Leaves, leading many to believe that they emerged in a fury of inspiration. On the other hand, the manuscripts that do remain indicate that Whitman meticulously worked and reworked passages of his poems, heavily revising entire drafts of the poems, and that he issued detailed instructions to the Rome brothers, the printers who were setting his book in type, carefully overseeing every aspect of the production of his book.

Whitman seems, then, to have been both inspired poet and skilled craftsman, at once under the spell of his newly discovered and intoxicating free verse style while also remaining very much in control of it, adjusting and altering and rearranging. For the rest of his life, he would add, delete, fuse, separate, and rearrange poems as he issued six very distinct editions of Leaves of Grass. Emerson once described Whitman's poetry as "a remarkable mixture of the Bhagvat Ghita and the New York Herald," and that odd joining of the scriptural and the vernacular, the transcendent and the mundane, effectively captures the quality of Whitman's work, work that most readers experience as simultaneously magical and commonplace, sublime and prosaic. It was work produced by a poet who was both sage and huckster, who touched the gods with ink-smudged fingers, and who was concerned as much with the sales and reviews of his book as with the state of the human soul.

The First Edition of Leaves of Grass

Whitman paid out of his own pocket for the production of the first edition of his book and had only 795 copies printed, which he bound at various times as his finances permitted. He always recalled the book as appearing, fittingly, on the Fourth of July, as a kind of literary Independence Day. His joy at getting the book published was quickly diminished by the death of his father within a week of the appearance of Leaves. Walter Sr. had been ill for several years, and though he and Walt had never been particularly close, they had only recently traveled together to West Hills, Long Island, to the old Whitman homestead where Walt was born. Now his father's death along with his older brother Jesse's absence as a merchant marine (and later Jesse's growing violence and mental instability) meant that Walt would become the father-substitute for the family, the person his mother and siblings would turn to for help and guidance. He had already had some experience enacting that role even while Walter Sr. was alive; perhaps because of Walter Sr.'s drinking habits and growing general depression, young Walt had taken on a number of adult responsibilities—buying boots for his brothers, for instance, and holding the title to the family house as early as 1847. Now, however, he became the only person his mother and siblings could turn to.

But even given these growing family burdens, he managed to concentrate on his new book, and, just as he oversaw all the details of its composition and printing, so now did he supervise its distribution and try to control its reception. Even though Whitman claimed that the first edition sold out, the book in fact had very poor sales. He sent copies to a number of well-known writers (including John Greenleaf Whittier, who, legend has it, threw his copy in the fire), but only one responded, and that, fittingly, was Emerson, who recognized in Whitman's work the very spirit and tone and style he had called for. "I greet you at the beginning of a great career," Emerson wrote in his private letter to Whitman, noting that Leaves of Grass "meets the demand I am always making of what seemed the sterile and stingy nature, as if too much handiwork, or too much lymph in the temperament, were making our western wits fat and mean." Whitman's was poetry that would literally get the country in shape, Emerson believed, give it shape, and help work off its excess of aristocratic fat.

Whitman's book was an extraordinary accomplishment: after trying for over a decade to address in journalism and fiction the social issues (such as education, temperance, slavery, prostitution, immigration, democratic representation) that challenged thenew nation, Whitman now turned to an unprecedented form, a kind of experimental verse cast in unrhymed long lines with no identifiable meter, the voice an uncanny combination of oratory, journalism, and the Bible—haranguing, mundane, and prophetic—all in the service of identifying a new American democratic attitude, an absorptive and accepting voice that would catalog the diversity of the country and manage to hold it all in a vast, single, unified identity. "Do I contradict myself?" Whitman asked confidently toward the end of the long poem he would come to call "Song of Myself": "Very well then.... I contradict myself;/I am large.... I contain multitudes." This new voice spoke confidently of union at a time of incredible division and tension in the culture, and it spoke with the assurance of one for whom everything, no matter how degraded, could be celebrated as part of itself:

" What is commonest and cheapest and nearest and easiest is Me." His work echoed with the lingo of the American urban working class and reached deep into the various corners of the roiling nineteenth-century culture, reverberating with the nation's stormy politics, its motley music, its new technologies, its fascination with science, and its evolving pride in an American language that was forming as a tongue distinct from British English.

Though it was no secret who the author of Leaves of Grass was, the fact that Whitman did not put his name on the title page was an unconventional and suggestive act (his name would in fact not appear on a title page of Leaves until the 1876 "Author's Edition" of the book, and then only when Whitman signed his name on the title page as each book was sold). The absence of a name indicated, perhaps, that the author of this book believed he spoke not for himself so much as for merica. But opposite the title page was a portrait of Whitman, an engraving made from a daguerreotype that the photographer Gabriel Harrison had made during the summer of 1854. It has become the most famous frontispiece in literary history, showing Walt in workman's clothes, shirt open, hat on and cocked to the side, standing insouciantly and fixing the reader with a challenging stare. It is a full-body pose that indicates Whitman's re-calibration of the role of poet as the democratic spokesperson who no longer speaks only from the intellect and with the formality of tradition and education: the new poet pictured in Whitman's book is a poet who speaks from and with the whole body and who writes outside, in Nature, not in the library. It was what Whitman called "al fresco" poetry, poetry written outside the walls, the bounds, of convention and tradition.

The 1856 Leaves

Within a few months of producing his first edition of Leaves, Whitman was already hard at work on the second edition. While in the first, he had given his long lines room to stretch across the page by printing the book on large paper, in the second edition he sacrificed the spacious pages and produced what he later called his "chunky fat book," his earliest attempt to create a pocket-size edition that would offer the reader what Whitman thought of as the "ideal pleasure"—"to put a book in your pocket and off to the seashore or the forest." On the cover of this edition, published and distributed by Fowler and Wells (though the firm carefully distanced themselves from the book by proclaiming that "the author is still his own publisher"), Whitman emblazoned one of the first "blurbs" in American publishing history: without asking Emerson's permission, he printed in gold on the spine of the book the opening words of Emerson's letter to him: "I greet you at the beginning of a great career," followed by Emerson's name. And, to generate publicity for the volume, he appended to the volume a group of reviews of the first edition—including three he wrote himself along with a few negative reviews—and called the gathering Leaves-Droppings. Whitman was a pioneer of the "any publicity is better than no publicity" strategy. At the back of the book, he printed Emerson's entire letter and wrote a long public letter back—a kind of apologia for his poetry—addressing it to "Master." Although he would later downplay the influence of Emerson on his work, at this time, he later recalled, he had "Emerson-on-the-brain."

With four times as many pages as the first edition, the 1856 Leaves added twenty new poems (including the powerful "Sun-Down Poem," later called "Crossing Brooklyn Ferry") to the original twelve in the 1855 edition. Those original twelve had been untitled in 1855, but Whitman was doing all he could to make the new edition look and feel different: small pages instead of large, a fat book instead of a thin one, and long titles for his poems instead of none at all. So the untitled introductory poem from the first edition that would eventually be named "Song of Myself" was in 1856 called "Poem of Walt Whitman, an American," and the poem that would become "This Compost" appeared here as "Poem of Wonder at the Resurrection of The Wheat." Some titles seemed to challenge the very bounds of titling by incorporating rolling catalogs like the poems themselves: "To a Foil'd European Revolutionaire" appeared as "Liberty Poem for Asia, Africa, Europe, America,

Australia, Cuba, and The Archipelagoes of the Sea." As if to counter some of the early criticism that he was not really writing poetry at all—the review in Life Illustrated, for example, called Whitman's work "lines of rhythmical prose, or a series of utterances (we know not what else to call them)"—Whitman put the word "Poem" in the title of all thirty-two works in the 1856 Leaves. Like them or not, Whitman seemed to be saying, they are poems, and more and more of them were on the way. But, despite his efforts to remake his book, the results were depressingly the same: sales of the thousand copies that were printed were even poorer than for the first edition.

The Bohemian Years

In these years, Whitman was in fact working hard at becoming a poet by forging literary connections: he entered the literary world in a way he never had as a fiction writer or journalist, meeting some of the nation's best-known writers, beginning to socialize with a literary and artistic crowd, and cultivating an image as an artist. Emerson had come to visit Whitman at the end of 1855 (they went back to Emerson's room at the elegant Astor Hotel, where Whitman—dressed as informally as he was in his frontispiece portrait—was denied admission); this was the first of many meetings the two would have over the next twenty-five years, as their relationship turned into one of grudging respect for each other mixed with mutual suspicion. The next year, Henry David Thoreau and Bronson Alcott visited Whitman's home (Alcott described Thoreau and Whitman as each "surveying the other curiously, like two beasts, each wondering what the other would do"). Whitman also came to befriend a number of visual artists, like the sculptor Henry Kirke Brown, the painter Elihu Vedder, and the photographer Gabriel Harrison.

And he came to know a number of women's rights activists and writers, some of whom became ardent readers and supporters of Leaves of Grass. He became particularly close to Abby Price, Paulina Wright Davis, Sarah Tyndale, and Sara Payson Willis (who, under the pseudonym Fanny Fern wrote a popular newspaper column and many popular books, including Fern Leaves from Fanny' s Portfolio, the cover of which Whitman imitated for his first edition of Leaves). These women's radical ideas about sexual equality had a growing impact on Whitman's poetry. He knew a number of abolitionist writers at this time, including Moncure Conway, and Whitman wrote some vitriolic attacks on the fugitive slave law and the moral bankruptcy of American politics, but these pieces (notably "The Eighteenth Presidency!") were never published and remain vestiges of yet another career—stump speaker, political pundit—that Whitman flirted with but never pursued.

Whitman also began in the late 1850s to become a regular at Pfaff's saloon, a favourite hangout for bohemian artists in New York.

It was at Pfaff's, too, that Whitman joined the "Fred Gray Association," a loose confederation of young men who seemed anxious to explore new possibilities of male-male affection. It may have been at Pfaff's that Whitman met Fred Vaughan, an intriguing mystery-figure in Whitman biography. Whitman and Vaughan, a young Irish stage driver, clearly had an intense relationship at this time, perhaps inspiring the sequence of homoerotic love poems Whitman called "Live Oak, with Moss, poems that would become the heart of his Calamus cluster, which appeared in the 1860 edition of Leaves. These poems recor a despair about the failure of the relationship, and the loss of Whitman's bond with Vaughan—who soon married, had four children, and would only sporadically keep in touch with Whitman—was clearly the source of some deep unhappiness for th poet.

1860 Edition of Leaves

Whitman's re-made self-image is evident on the frontispiece of the new edition of Leaves that appeared in 1860. It would be the only time Whitman used this portrait, an engraving based on a painting done by Whitman's artist friend Charles Hine. Whitman's friends called it the "Byronic portrait," and Whitman does look more like the conventional image of a poet—with coiffure and cravat—than he ever did before or after. This is the portrait of an artist who has devoted significant time to his image and one who has also clearly enjoyed his growing notoriety among the arty crowd at Pfaff's.

Ever since the 1856 edition appeared, Whitman had been writing poems at a furious pace; within a year of the 1856 edition's appearance, he wrote nearly seventy new poems. He continued to have them set in type by the Rome brothers and other printer friends, as if he assumed that he would inevitably be publishing them himself, since no commercial publisher had indicated an interest in his book.

But there was another reason Whitman set his poems in type: he always preferred to deal with his poems in printed form instead of in manuscript. He often would revise directly on printed versions of his poetry; for him, poetry was very much a public act, and until the poem was in print he did not truly consider it a poem. Poetic manuscripts were never sacred objects for Whitman, who often simply discarded them; getting the poem set in type was the most important step in allowing it to begin to do its cultural work.

In 1860, while the nation seemed to be moving inexorably toward a major crisis between the slaveholding and free states, Whitman's poetic fortunes took a positive turn. In February, he received a letter from the Boston publishers William Thayer and Charles Eldridge, whose aggressive new publishing house specialized in abolitionist literature; they wanted to become the publishers of the new edition of Leaves of Grass. Whitman, feeling confirmed as an authentic poet now that he had been offered actual royalties, readily agreed, and Thayer and Eldridge invested heavily in the stereotype plates for Whitman's idiosyncratic book—over 450 pages of varied typeface and odd decorative motifs, a visually chaotic volume all carefully tended to by Whitman, who traveled to Boston to oversee the printing.

This was Whitman's first trip to Boston, then considered the literary capital of the nation. Whitman is a major part of the reason that America's literary centre moved from Boston to New York in the second half of the nineteenth century, but in 1860 the superior power of Boston was still evident in its influential publishing houses, its important journals (including the new Atlantic Monthly), and its venerable authors (including Henry Wadsworth Longfellow, whom Whitman met briefly while in town). And, of course, Boston was the city of Emerson, who came to see Whitman shortly after his arrival in the city in March. In one of the most celebrated meetings of major American writers, the Boston Brahmin and the Yankee rowdy strolled together on the Boston Common, while Emerson tried to convince Whitman to remove from his Boston edition the new Enfans d'Adam cluster of poems (after 1860, Whitman dropped the French version of the name and called the cluster Children of Adam), works that portrayed the human body more explicitly and in more direct sexual terms than any previous American poems.

Whitman argued, as he later recalled, "that the sexual passion in itself, while normal and unperverted, is inherently legitimate, creditable, not necessarily an improper theme for poet." "That," insisted Whitman, "is what I felt in my inmost brain and heart, when I only answer'd Emerson's vehement arguments with silence, under the old elms of Boston Common." Emerson's caution notwithstanding, the body—the entire body—would be Whitman's theme, and he would not shy away from any part of it, not discriminate or marginalize or form hierarchies of bodily parts any more than he would of the diverse people making up the American nation. His democratic belief in the importance of all the parts of any whole, was central to his vision: the genitals and the arm-pits were as essential to the fullness of identity as the brain and the soul, just as, in a democracy, the poorest and most despised citizens were as important as the rich and famous. This, at any rate, was the theory of radical union and equality that generated Whitman' s work.

So he ignored Emerson's advice and published the Children of Adam poems in the 1860 edition along with his Calamus cluster; the first cluster celebrated male-female sexual relations, and the second celebrated the love of men for men. The body remained very much Whitman's subject, but it was never separate from the body of the text, and he always set out not just to write about sensual embrace but also to enact the physical embrace of poet and reader. Whitman became a master of sexual politics, but his sexual politics were always intertwined with his textual politics. Leaves of Grass was not a book that set out to shock the reader so much as to merge with the reader and make him or her more aware of the body each reader inhabited, to convince us that the body and soul were conjoined and inseparable, just as Whitman's ideas were embodied in words that ha physical body in the ink and paper that readers held physically in their hands. Ideas, Whitman's poems insist, pass from one person to another not in some ethereal process, but through the bodies of texts, through the muscular operations of tongues and hands and eyes, through the material objects of books.

Whitman was already well along on his radical programme of delineating just what democratic affection would entail. He called his Calamus poems his most political work—"The special meaning of the Calamus cluster," Whitman wrote, "mainly resides in its Political significance"—since in those poems he was articulating a new kind of intense affection between males who, in the developing democratic society and emerging capitalistic system, were being encouraged to become fiercely competitive. Whitman countered this movement with a call for manly love, embrace, and affection. In giving voice to this new camaraderie, Whitman was also inventing a language of homosexuality, and the Calamus poems became very influential poems in the development of gay literature.

In the nineteenth century, however, the Calamus poems did not cause as much sensation as Children of Adam because, even though they portrayed same-sex affection, they were only mildly sensual, evoking handholding, hugging, and kissing, while the Children of Adam poems evoked a more explicit genital sexuality. Emerson and others were apparently unfazed by Calamus and focused their disapprobation on Children of Adam. Only later in the century,when homosexuality began to be formulated in medical and psychological circles as an aberrant personality type, did the Calamus poems begin to be read by some as dangerous and "abnormal" and by others as brave early expressions of gay identity. With the 1860 edition of Leaves, Whitman began the incessant rearrangement of his poems in various clusters and groupings. Whitman settled on cluster arrangements as the most effective way to organize his work, but his notion of particular clusters changed from edition to edition as he added, deleted, and rearranged his poems in patterns that often alter their meaning and recontextualize their significance.

In addition to Calamus and Children of Adam, this edition contained clusters called Chants Democratic and Native American, Messenger Leaves, and another named the same as the book, Leaves of Grass. This edition also contained the first book printings of "Starting from Paumanok" and "Out of the Cradle Endlessly Rocking" (here called "A Word Out of the Sea"), along with over 120 other new poems. He also revised many of his other poems, including "Song of Myself" (here called simply "Walt Whitman"), and throughout the book he numbered his poetic verses, creating a Biblical effect. This was no accident, since Whitman now conceived of his project as involving the construction of what he called a "New Bible," a new covenant that would convert America into a true democracy.

Whitman's time in Boston—the first extended period he had been away from New York since his trip to New Orleans twelve years earlier—was a transforming experience. He was surprised by the way African Americans were treated much more fairly and more as equals than was the case in New York, sharing tables with whites at eating houses, working next to whites in printing offices, and serving on juries. He also met a number of abolitionist writers who would soon become close friends and supporters, including William Douglas O'Connor and John Townsend Trowbridge, both of whom would later write at length about Whitman. When he returned to New York at the end of May, his mood was ebullient. He was now a recognized author; the Boston papers had run feature stories about his visit to the city, and photographers had asked to photograph him (not only did he have a growing notoriety, he was a striking physical specimen at over six feet in height—especially tall for the time—with long, already graying hair and beard). All summer long he read reviews of his work in prominent newspapers and journals. And in November, Whitman's young publishers announced that Whitman's new project, a book of poems he called Banner at Day-Break, would be forthcoming.

The Beginning of the Civil War

But just as suddenly as Whitman's fortunes had turned so unexpectedly good early in 1860, they now turned unexpectedly bad. The deteriorating national situation made any business investment risky, and Thayer and Eldridge compounded the problem by making a number of bad business decisions. At the beginning of 1861, they declared bankruptcy and sold the plates of Leaves to Boston publisher Richard Worthington, who would continue to publish pirated copies of this edition for decades, creating real problems for Whitman every time he tried to market a new edition. Because of the large number of copies that Thayer and Eldridge initially printed, combined with Worthington's ongoing piracy, the 1860 edition became the most commonly available version of Leaves for the next twenty years and diluted the impact (as well as depressing the sales) of Whitman's new editions.

Whitman had dated the title page of his 1860 Leaves "1860-61," as if he anticipated the liminal nature of that moment in American history—the fragile moment, between a year of peace and a year of war. In February 1861 he saw Abraham Lincoln pass through New York on the way to his inauguration, and in April he was walking home from an opera performance when he bought a newspaper and read the headlines about Southern forces firing on Fort Sumter. He remembers a group gathering in the New York streets that night as those with newspapers read the story aloud to the others in the crowd. Even though no one was aware of the full extent of what was to come—Whitman, like many others, thought the struggle would be over in sixty days or so—the nation was in fact slipping into four years of the bloodiest fighting it would ever know. A few days after the firing on Fort Sumter, Whitman recorded in his journal his resolution "to inaugurate for myself a pure perfect sweet, cleanblooded robust body by ignoring all drinks but water and pure milk—and all fat meats late suppers—a great body—a purged, cleansed, spiritualised invigorated body." It was as if he sensed at some level the need to break out of his newfound complacency, to cease his Pfaff's beerhall habits and bohemian ways, and to prepare himself for the challenges that now faced the divided nation. But it would take Whitman some time before he was able to discern the form his war sacrifice would take. Whitman's brother George immediately enlisted in the Union Army and would serve for the duration of the war, fighting in many of the major battles; he eventually was incarcerated as a prisoner-of-war in Danville, Virginia. eorge had a distinguished career as a soldier and left the service as a lieutenant colonel; his descriptions of his war experiences provided Walt with many of his insights into the nature of the war and of soldiers' feelings. Whitman's chronically ill brother Andrew would also enlist but would serve only three months in 1862 before dying, probably of tuberculosis, in 1863. Walt's other brothers—the hot-tempered Jesse (whom Whitman had to have committed to an insane asylum in 1864 after he physically attacked his mother), the recently-married Jeff (on whom fell the burden of caring for the extended family, including his own infant daughter), and the mentally-enfeebled Eddy—did not enlist, and neither did Walt, who was already in his early forties when the war began.

One of the haziest periods of Whitman's life, in fact, is the first year and a half of the war. He stayed in New York and Brooklyn, writing some extended newspaper pieces about the history of Brooklyn for the Brooklyn Daily Standard; these pieces, called "Brooklyniana" and consisting of twenty-five lengthy installments, form a book-length anecdotal history of the city Whitman knew so well but was now about to leave—he would return only occasionally for brief visits. It was during this period that Whitman first encountered casualties of the war that was already lasting far longer than anyone had anticipated. He began visiting wounded soldiers who were moved to New York hospitals, and he wrote about them in a series called "City Photographs" that he published in the New York Leader in 1862.

Whitman had in fact been visiting Broadway Hospital for several years, comforting injured stage drivers and ferryboat workers (serious injuries in the chaotic transportation industry in New York at the time were common). While he was enamoured with the idea of having literary figures as friends, Whitman's true preference for companions had always been and would continue to be working class men, especially those who worked on the omnibuses and the ferries ("all my ferry friends," as he called them), where he enjoyed the endless rhythms of movement, the open road, the back-and-forth journeys, with good companions. He reveled in the energy and pleasure of travel instead of worrying about destinations: "I cross'd and recross'd, merely for pleasure," he wrote of his trips on the ferry. He remembered fondly the "immense qualities, largely animal" of the colorful omnibus drivers, whom he said he enjoyed "for comradeship, and sometimes affection" as he would ride "the whole length of Broadway," listening to the stories of the driver and conductor, or "declaiming some stormy passage" from one of his favourite Shakespeare plays.

So his hospital visits began with a kind of obligation of friendship to the injured transportation workers, and, as the Civil War began taking its toll, wounded soldiers joined the transportation workers on Whitman's frequent rounds. These soldiers came from all over the country, and their reminiscences of home taught Whitman about the breadth and diversity of the growing nation. He developed an idiosyncratic style of informal personal nursing, writing down stories the patients told him, giving them small gifts, writing letters for them, holding them, comforting them, and kissing them. His purpose, he wrote, was "just to help cheer and change a little the monotony of their sickness and confinement," though he found that their effect on him was every bit as rewarding as his on them, for the wounded and maimed young men aroused in him "friendly interest and sympathy," and he said some of "the most agreeable evenings of my life" were spent in hospitals. By 1861, his New York hospital visits had prepared him for the draining ordeal he was about to face when he went to Washington, D.C., where he would nurse thousands of injured soldiers in the makeshift hospitals there. Whitman once said that, had he not become a writer, he would have become a doctor, and at Broadway Hospital he developed close friendships with many of the physicians, even occasionally assisting them in surgery. His fascination with the body, so evident in his poetry, was intricately bound to his attraction to medicine and to the hospitals, where he learned to face bodily disfigurations and gained the ability to see beyond wounds and illness to the human personalities that persisted through the pain and humiliation. It was a skill he would need in abundance over the next three years as he began yet another career.

To the Battlefield

With the nation now locked in an extended war, all of Whitman's deepest concerns and beliefs were under attack. Leaves of Grass had been built on a faith in union, wholeness, the ability of a self and a nation to contain contradictions and absorb diversity; now the United States had come apart, and Whitman's very project was now in danger of becoming an anachronism as the Southern states sought to divide the country in two. Leaves had been built, too, on a belief in the power of affection to overcome division and competition; his Calamus vision was of a "continent indissoluble" with "inseparable cities" all joined by "the life-long love of comrades." But now the young men of America were killing each other in bloody battles; fathers were killing sons, sons fathers, brothers brothers. Whitman's prospects for his "new Bible" that would bind a nation, build an affectionate democracy, and guide a citizenry to celebrate its unified diversity, were shattered in the fratricidal conflict that engulfed America.

Like many Americans, Whitman and his family daily

checked the lists of wounded in the newspapers, and one day in December 1862 the family was jolted by the appearance of the name of " G. W. Whitmore" on the casualty roster from Fredericksburg. Fearful that the name was a garbled version of George Washington Whitman's, Walt immediately headed to Virginia to seek out his brother. Changing trains in Philadelphia, Whitman's pocket was picked on the crowded platform, and, penniless, he continued his journey to Washington, where, fortunately, he ran into William Douglas O'Connor, the writer and abolitionist he had met in Boston, who loaned him money. Futilely searching for George in the nearly forty Washington hospitals, he finally decided to take a government boat and army-controlled train to the battlefield at Fredericksburg to see if George was still there.

After finding George's unit and discovering that his brother had received only a superficial facial wound, Whitman's relief turned to horror as he encountered a sight he would never forget: outside of a mansion converted into a field hospital, he came upon "a heap of amputated feet, legs, arms, hands, andc., a full load for a one-horse cart." They were, he wrote in his journal, "human fragments, cut, bloody, black and blue, swelled and sickening." Nearby were "several dead bodies... each cover'd with its brown woolen blanket."

The sight would continue to haunt this poet who had so confidently celebrated the physical body, who had claimed that the soul existed only in the body, that the arms and legs were extensions of the soul, the legs moving the soul through the world and the hands allowing the soul to express itself. Now a generation of young American males, the very males on which he had staked the future of democracy, were literally being disarmed, amputated, killed. It was this amputation, this fragmenting of the Union—in both a literal and figurative sense—that Whitman would address for the next few years, as he devoted himself to becoming the arms and legs of the wounded and maimed soldiers in the Civil War hospitals. By running errands for them, writing letters for them, encircling them in his arms, Whitman tried, the best he could, to make them whole again.

This extraordinary hospital service, which took a tremendous toll on Whitman's own health as he spent countless long nights in the poorly ventilated wards, began spontaneously during his mission to George. He had fully anticipated that he would return to New York after determining that George was safe, but, after telegraphing his mother and the rest of the family that he had found George, he decided to stay with his brother for a few days. During this time he got to know the young soldiers, both Union and Confederate (he talked to a number of Southern prisoners of war). He assisted in the burial of the dead still lying on the bloody battlefield, where on December 13 there had been 18,000 Northern and Southern troops killed or wounded (and where, the next day, Robert E. Lee, sickened by the carnage, declined to attack General Ambrose Burnside's Union troops, even though they were in a vulnerable position). Although Whitman had already written some of the poems that he would eventually publish in his Civil War book Drum-Taps (notably the "recruitment" poems like "Beat! Beat! Drums!" or "First O Songs for Prelude" that evoked the frightening yet exhilarating energy of cities arming for battle), it was only now, encountering the horrifying aftereffects of a real battle, that the powerful Civil War poems began to emerge. In the journal he kept while at George's camp, Whitman noted a "sight at daybreak—in a camp in front of the hospital tent on a stretcher, each with a blanket spread over him—I lift up one and look at the young man's face, calm and yellow,—'tis strange! (Young man: I think this face of yours the face of my dead Christ!)" As would be the case with many of the poems in Drum-Taps, this journal sketch gradually was transformed into a poem:

A sight in camp in the daybreak gray and dim,
As from my tent I emerge so early sleepless.
As slow I walk in the cool fresh air the path near
by the hospital tent,
Three forms I see on stretchers lying, brought out
there untended lying,
Over each the blanket spread, ample brownish woolen
blanket,

Gray and heavy blanket, folding, covering all.
Then to the third—a face nor child nor old, very calm, beautiful yellow-white ivory;
Young man I think I know you—I think this face is the face of the Christ himself,
Dead and divine and brother of all, and here he lies again.

The journal entry and poem offer a glimpse into how Whitman began restructuring his poetic project after the Civil War began. He was still writing a "new Bible" here, re-experiencing the Crucifixion in Fredericksburg. But this crucifixion does not redeem sinners and create an atonement with God so much as it posits divinity in everyone and mourns senseless loss: this one young man's death amidst the thousands is as significant as any in history. And, for Whitman, the massive slaughter of young soldier-Christs would create for all those who survived the war an obligation to construct a nation worthy of their great sacrifice. The America that Whitman would write of after the Civil War would be a more chastened, less innocent nation, a nation that had gone through its baptism in blood and one that would from now on be tested against the stern measure of this bloodshed.

During the days he spent with George's unit, Whitman often went into the makeshift hospital outside of which he had seen the pile of amputated limbs. "I do not see that I do much good to these wounded and dying," he wrote; "but I cannot leave them." As if to underscore his own attempts to hold the Union together, to reconcile rather than punish, to help love triumph over revenge, Whitman found himself particularly attracted to a nineteen-year-old Confederate soldier from Mississippi, who had had a leg amputated.

Whitman visited him regularly in the battlefield hospital and then continued to visit him when the soldier was transferred to a Washington hospital. "Our affection is an affair quite romantic," he wrote. It wouldn't be the last intimacy he would experience with a Confederate soldier; at the end of the war, Whitman would enter the longest affectional relationship of his life with a former Confederate soldier named Peter Doyle. Something surprising—and perhaps unexpected even to Whitman—was happening to the Calamus emotions that he had described in 1860; the intimate expressions of manly friendship now became generalized, perhaps sublimated, in the poet's many close relationships with injured soldiers over the next three years. Extant letters from these soldiers clearly indicate the intensity of the love that these young men felt for Whitman, and Whitman's letters to them demonstrate that the affection was reciprocated. The language of this correspondence is difficult to categorize—it is partly that of lovers, partly that of friends, partly that of son to father and father to son (many of the letters to Whitman are addressed to "Dear Father"), and partly that of calm, wise, old counselor to confused, scared, and half-literate young men.

To Washington, D.C.

We cannot be certain when Whitman made his decision to stay in Washington, D.C. Like virtually all of the abrupt changes in his life, this one came with no planning, no advance notice, no preparation. He had gone to New Orleans on a similar spur-of-the-moment decision, just as he had suddenly quit teaching, just as he had packed up and gone to Boston, and just as he would years later decide overnight to settle in Camden, New Jersey. He was a profoundly unsettled person, who seemed able to shuck expected obligations and even relationships without much regret: he existed, as he said, on a kind of "Open Road": "The long brown path before me leading wherever I choose.... I will scatter myself among men and women as I go":

Allons! We must not stop here,
However sweet these laid-up stores, however
convenient this dwelling we cannot remain here,
However shelter'd this port and however calm
these waters we must not anchor here,
However welcome the hospitality that surrounds us
we are permitted to receive it but a little
while.

One day Whitman simply left Brooklyn and New York and his family home to find his brother,and he never really came back. Perhaps the decision was made while he was in the field hospital, nursing the wounded and developing his relationship with the young Mississippi soldier; it was then that he wrote to his mother and told her he might seek employment for awhile in Washington, and it was then that he wrote to Emerson to ask for letters of recommendation to the Secretary of State and the Secretary of the Treasury, who were both acquaintances of Emerson.

But perhaps his decision was conclusively made on his trip back from Fredericksburg to Washington, right after a somber New Year's Day 1863, when Whitman—quickly earning the trust and respect of the doctors at the battlefield—was put in charge of a trainload of casualties who had to be transferred to hospitals in the capital. While the wounded were being moved from a train to a steamboat for the trip up the Potomac, Whitman wandered among them, writing down their messages to their families, promising to send them, comforting the soldiers with his calm and concern. Perhaps by the time he got to Washington, determined to stay a few days in order to visit wounded soldiers from Brooklyn, he already knew at some level that he would have to remain there for the duration of the war.

His Boston connections were serving him well now; not only did he get letters of introduction from Emerson, but he got a room in the boarding house of William Douglas O'Connor and, through the efforts of Charles Eldridge—the publisher of the 1860 Leaves who was now assistant to the Army Paymaster—he got a part-time job as a copyist in the Paymaster's office. O'Connor and his wife Nellie provided Whitman his meals, and the poet began receiving contributions from his brother Jeff and others in Brooklyn who heard of his work in the hospitals. Whitman used what funds he had to buy small gifts for the wounded soldiers—candy and tobacco and flavored syrup and books—and he soon became a familiar figure in the hospitals. Prematurely gray and looking a decade or two older than his forty-three years, Whitman must have seemed to the soldiers—many of whom were still in their teens—some sort of tattered Saint Nick, handing out treats and bringing good cheer. Many referred to Whitman as "Old Man," and his presence was for some of the young men avuncular, for some paternal, and, for almost all, magical. Though he admired the Christian Commission, an agency organized by several churches that recruited volunteers to help in the hospitals, Whitman acted independently.

He had nothing but contempt for the United States Sanitary commission, the governmental body charged with nursing the soldiers and repairing them so they could return to battle: to Whitman, these agents kept their distance from the soldiers and worked primarily for pay. Whitman's mission was different, as eccentric as his poetry: he was, in the act of nursing the wounded, trying to define and demonstrate a new kind of affection, a democratic camaraderie. He always insisted that he gained more from the soldiers than they received from him; he considered those years of hospital service "the greatest privilege and satisfaction... and, of course, the most profound lesson of my life."

Washington Years

To better support his hospital work, Whitman began seeking more remunerative employment and pounded the pavement in Washington, trying to exploit every connection he had in order to find a good job. The nation's capital was in a chaotic—even surreal—state in 1863, with unpaved, muddy streets and many half-built governmental edifices, including the Capitol building itself, with its vast new dome rising above the city, but still in only skeletal form. President Lincoln insisted that construction of the capital's buildings proceed at full pace, so, while the nation was tearing itself apart in civil war, the nation's capital was continuing to erect a unified and elegant governmental centre, designed by the French architect Pierre L'Enfant. It was as if the capital had become a metaphor of the nation itself, half-built and in a struggle to determine whether it would end in fulfillment or destruction.

Some of the newly constructed buildings almost immediately became hospitals, and when Whitman described the Civil War as turning the nation into a ward of casualties—

America, "though only in her early youth," Whitman wrote, was "already to hospital brought"—he no doubt had in mind the way the emerging governmental centre of the country was being transformed into a vast hospital. The U. S. Patent Office became a hospital in 1863, and Whitman noted the irony of the "rows of sick, badly wounded and dying soldiers" surrounding the "glass cases" displaying American inventions—guns and machines and other signs of progress. The wrecked bodies dispersed among the displays were what "progress" had brought, the result of new inventions that had created modern warfare. Washington was a noisy city during these years: the noise in the city was of construction; the noise just outside the city was of destruction, and the two activities conjoined in the dozens of makeshift Washington hospitals that held the shattered bodies of America's young men.

It is not possible to know how many soldiers Whitman actually nursed during his years in Washington, but the number was certainly in the tens of thousands (Whitman estimated he visited "from eighty thousand to a hundred thousand of the wounded and sick"). Walking the wards was for him like walking America: every bed contained a representative of a different region, a different city or town, a different way of life. He loved the varied accents and the diverse physiognomies. "While I was with wounded and sick in thousands of cases from the New England States, and from New York, New Jersey, and Pennsylvania, and from Michigan, Wisconsin, Ohio, Indiana, Illinois, and all the Western States, I was with more or less from all the States, North and South, without exception."

His trip to New Orleans had taken him across a good part of the nation, but it was in the hospital wards that he really traveled the United States and crossed boundaries otherwise not easily crossed: "I was with many rebel officers and men among our wounded, and gave them always what I had, and tried to cheer them the same as any... Among the black soldiers, wounded or sick, and in the contraband camps, I also took my way whenever in their neighborhood, and did what I could for them." And with all those he met, he both sought and offered love: "What an attachment grows up between us, started from hospital cots, where pale young faces lie and wounded or sick bodies," he wrote; "The doctors tell me I supply the patients with a medicine which all their drugs and bottles and powders are helpless to yield." He had become a physician after all, dispensing the medicine of hope and affection, the same medicine he hoped would heal a country, suture its wounds, repair its fracture. And he sought to dispense this medicine not only to soldiers on his hospital visits but to all Americans through his books.

Drum-Taps and the End of the War

During all the time of his hospital service, Whitman was writing poems, a new kind of poem for him, poems about the war experience, but almost never about battles—rather about the aftereffects of warfare: the moonlight illuminating the dead on the battlefields, the churches turned into hospitals, the experience of dressing wounds, the encounter with a dead enemy in a coffin, the trauma of battle nightmares for soldiers who had returned home. He gathered these poems along with the few he had written just before the war (the ones that Thayer and Eldridge has originally planned to publish as Banner at Day-Break) and worked on combining them in a book called Drum-Taps, the title evoking both the beating of the drums that accompanied soldiers into battle as well as the beating out of "Taps," the death march sounded at the burial of soldiers (originally played on the drums instead of the trumpet).

After the burst of creativity in the mid-and late-1850s that resulted in the vastly expanded 1860 Leaves, Whitman had not written many poems until he got to Washington, where the daily encounters with soldiers opened a fresh vein of creativity, resulting in a poetry more modest in ambition and more muted in its claims, a poetry in whic death was no longer something indistinguishable from life ("Has any one supposed it lucky to be born?," Whitman had written in "Song of Myself"; "I hasten to inform him or her it is just as lucky to die, and I know it") but rather now revealed itself as something horrifying, grotesque, and omnipresent. The poems were so different from any that had appeared in Leaves, in fact, that Whitman originally assumed they could not be joined in the same book with those earlier poems. It would be a long, slow process that would eventually allow the absorption of Drum-Taps into Leaves of Grass.

As the war entered its final year, Whitman was facing physical and emotional exhaustion. 1864 began with one of his closest soldier-friends, Lewis Brown (with whom he had imagined living after the war was over), having his leg amputated; Whitman watched the operation through a window at Armory Square Hospital. In February and March, he traveled to the Virginia battlefront to nurse soldiers in field hospitals, then in April he stood for three hours watching General Burnside's troops march through Washington until he could pick out his brother George. He marched with him and gave him news from home. It would be the last time Whitman would see his brother before George was captured by Confederate troops after a battle in the fall. During the early summer, Whitman began to complain of a sore throat, dizziness, and a "bad feeling" in his head. Physician friends urged him to check into one of the hospitals he had been visiting, and they finally convinced him to go back to New York for a rest. Whitman took his manuscript of Drum-Taps with him to Brooklyn, hoping to publish it himself while he was there. Soon after he left Washington, the capital was attacked by the Confederates and many thought it was about to be captured; Whitman missed the most terrifying months of the war in the District of Columbia.

In Brooklyn, Whitman could not stop doing what had now become both a routine and a reason for his existence: he visited wounded soldiers in New York-area hospitals. But he also re-established contacts with old friends from the Pfaff's beerhall days, and he explored some new beer saloons with them. He wrote some more articles for the New York Times and other papers, and he took care of pressing family matters, including the commitment of his increasingly unstable brother Jesse to the Kings County Lunatic Asylum (where he would die six years later). The year ended with the arrival at the Whitman family home of George's personal items, including his war diary, which Whitman presumably read at this time. Though Whitman did not then know it, George had been sent to the Libby Prison in Richmond, Virginia, and would also serve time in military prisons in Salisbury, North Carolina, and finally in Danville, Virginia. In the hope of effecting George's release, Whitman began a campaign, in both newspaper articles and in letters to government officials, to support a general exchange of prisoners between the Confederacy and the Union, something Union generals were generally against because they believed such an exchange would benefit the South by returning troops to an army in desperate need of more men.

By the beginning of 1865, Whitman was very anxious to return to Washington, which he now considered to be his home. Friends there had been working on getting him a better government position, and O'Connor helped arrange a clerkship in the Indian Bureau of the Department of the Interior. Whitman carried his Drum-Taps manuscript back to Washington, hoping that his increased income might allow him to publish the book. He moved to a new apartment, run by what he called a "secesh" landlady, and he began work in the Indian Bureau; his desk was in the U.S. Patent Office Building, which he had been visiting when it was used as a temporary hospital. As a clerk there, he met delegations of various Indian tribes from the West, and, just as he had come to know the geographical range of America through his hospital visits, so now he came to experience Native Americans.

He had included Indians in his poems of America, cataloguing "the red aborigines" in "Starting from Paumanok," for example, celebrating the way they "charg the water and the land with names" (thus Whitman always preferred the name "Paumanok" to "Long Island" and often argued that aboriginal names for American places were always superior to names imported from Europe). The impact of Whitman's experiences at the Indian Bureau is apparent in such later poems as "Osceola" and "Yonnondio," memorializing what had come to seem to him the inevitable loss of native cultures.

George Whitman was released from Danville prison in February and returned to the Whitman home in Brooklyn in March. Whitman got a furlough from the Indian Bureau so that he could go see George, and, while in Brooklyn, he arranged with a New York printer for the publication of *Drum-Taps*. He signed a contract on April 1, and then, eight days later, while he was still in Brooklyn, the Civil War ended, with General Lee surrendering at Appomattox; five days after that, President Lincoln was assassinated at Ford's Theatre in Washington. It is ironic that Whitman, who spent most of the final two years of the war in the capital, was not there for its most traumatic and memorable events: he was back in New York during the main Confederate assault on Washington, and he was in New York again when the capital celebrated the end of the war and then mourned the loss of the president.

But the fact that Whitman was at his mother's home in Brooklyn led to one of his greatest poems, because he heard the news about Lincoln that April morning when the lilac bushes were blooming in his mother's dooryard, where he went to console himself and where he inhaled the scent of the lilacs, which became for him viscerally bound to the memory of Lincoln's death. He began writing his powerful elegy to Lincoln, "When Lilacs Last in the Dooryard Bloom'd," after *Drum-Taps* had already been delivered to the printer.

He was able quickly to add to *Drum-Taps*, before the book was set in type, a brief poem about Lincoln's death, "Hush'd Be the Camps To-day," but his "Lilacs" elegy and his uncharacteristically rhymed and metered elegy for Lincoln, "O Captain! My Captain!," were written after the book was in press. Whitman therefore compiled a *Sequel to Drum-Taps* and had it printed up when he went back to Washington. In October he returned to Brooklyn to oversee the collating and binding of *Sequel* with *Drum-Taps*. He subtitled *Sequel* "'When Lilacs Last in the Dooryard Bloom'd and Other Pieces," and the very title registered the fragmentation that now characterized his poetry and his nation, very much shattered and in pieces (in "Lilacs," he described the "debris and debris" of the war's casualties and of the nation's current condition). He dated the Sequel 1865-66, offering another significantly hyphenated moment. Just as his 1860-61 Leaves marked the division between a nation at peace and a nation rent by war, so now did the sequel mark the reunification, a country moving from a year of war to the difficult first year of its reunified peace, from the horror of disintegration to the challenge of reconstruction.

In joining Drum-Taps and Sequel, Whitman created a book whose physical form echoed the challenges the postwar nation was facing as it entered the stormy period of Reconstruction. Whitman, too, was entering a period of poetic reconstruction, searching for ways to absorb the personal and national trauma of the Civil War into Leaves of Grass. As soon as the war ended, Whitman began to realise that the nation's hopes and history had to be reunified and that his original goals for Leaves of Grass—to project an optimistic democratic future for America—should not be abandoned but rather had to be integrated with the trauma of the Civil War. He faced the difficult task now of re-opening Leaves of Grass to find a way to absorb into his growing book the horror of the nation's fratricidal war.

Peter Doyle

Whitman's life was undergoing many changes in the weeks and months following the end of the war. One major event happened unexpectedly: on a stormy night, while riding the streetcar home after dinner at John and Ursula Burroughs' apartment, Whitman began talking with the conductor, a twenty-one-year-old Irish immigrant and former Confederate soldier named Peter Doyle. Doyle later recalled that Whitman was the only passenger, and "we were familiar at once—I put my hand on his knee—we understood." "From that time on," Doyle recalled, "we were the biggest sort of friends." It would be a friendship that would last for the rest of Whitman's life, and it was the most intense and romantic friendship the poet would have. Like Whitman, Doyle came from a large family, and Walt got to know Doyle's widowed mother and his siblings well; they came to be a second family for him.

Whitman continued visiting soldiers in Washington hospitals during the first years following the war, as the number of hospitals gradually decreased and only the most difficult cases remained, but he now focused his attention increasingly on this single young former artilleryman from the South. Like so many of Whitman's closest friends, Doyle had only a rudimentary education and was from the working class. These young men were reflections of Whitman's own youthful self, and he saw his poetry as speaking for them, putting into words what they could not, becoming the vocalization of the common man, without aristocratic airs, without elite schooling, without the weary formalities of tradition.

For Whitman, then, Doyle represented America's future: healthy, witty, handsome, good-humored, hard-working, enamored of ood times, he gave Whitman's life some energy and hope during an otherwise bleak time. They rode the streetcars together, drank at the Union Hotel bar, took long walks outside the city, and quoted poetry to each other (Whitman recited Shakespeare, Doyle limericks). As Whitman's health continued to deteriorate in the late 1860s and early 1870s, the young former soldier nursed the aging former nurse and offered comfort to the poet just as Walt had to so many sick soldiers. And just as Whitman had picked up the germs of many of his poems from the stories soldiers had told him, so now he picked up from Doyle—who had been at Ford's Theatre the night John Wilkes Booth shot the president—the narrative of the assassination of Lincoln that he would use for his Lincoln lectures that he would deliver regularly in his later years.

Only in 1870 did the Doyle-Whitman relationship encounter severe problems. In some of the most intriguing and often-discussed entries in all of Whitman's notebooks, the poet records a cryptic resolution: "To give up absolutely and for good, from the present hour, this feverish, fluctuating, useless undignified pursuit of 16.4—too long, persevered in,—so humiliating." Critics eventually broke Whitman's numeric/ alphabetic code and realized that Whitman was writing about his relationship with Doyle. Whitman goes on to urge himself to "Depress the adhesive nature/ It is in excess—making life a torment/ Ah this diseased, feverish disproportionate adhesiveness/ Remember Fred Vaughan." Vaughan, the close friend who probably inspired Whitman's Calamus poems, shared many traits with Doyle, and Whitman came to be jealous of both men when they did not return his love with the fervor he demanded. Soon after Whitman had met Doyle, he revised his Calamus sequence and removed the darker poems that expressed despair at being abandoned. But in 1870, those same dark emotions reappeared, though somehow this time Whitman and his partner managed to work their way through the trouble. They never lived together, though Walt dreamed of doing so, and, while their relationship would never regain the intensity it had in the mid-1860s, Doyle and Whitman continued to correspond and Doyle visited Whitman regularly for the next two decades after the poet moved to Camden, New Jersey.

The Good Gray Poet

Just when Whitman was feeling secure in his government employment, all hell broke loose. In May, 1865, a new Secretary of the Interior, James Harlan of Iowa, was sworn in and immediately set out to clean up his department, issuing a directive to abolish non-essential positions and to dismiss any employee whose "moral character" was questionable. Harlan was a formidable figure—a former U. S. Senator, Methodist minister, and president of Iowa Wesleyan College—and, when he saw Whitman's working copy of the 1860 Leaves of Grass (which the poet kept in his desk so that he could revise his poems during slow times at the office)—he was appalled. On June 20, Whitman (along with a number of other Interior Department employees) received a dismissal notice.

Whitman quickly turned to his fiery friend O'Connor, who at that time worked in the Treasury Department. O'Connor, at some risk to his own career, took immediate action: he contacted the Assistant Attorney General, J. Hubley Ashton, who in turn talked with Harlan, only to find that not only was Harlan dead set against rescinding the dismissal order, he was ready to prevent Whitman from getting work in any other governmental agency. Ashton talked Harlan out of interfering with Whitman's appointment outside of Interior, and then he convinced Attorney General James Speed to hire Whitman in his office. Whitman became a clerk in the Attorney General's Office the next day, liked the work better (he aided in the preparation of requests for pardons from Confederates and later copied documents for delivery to the President and Cabinet members), and held the job until 1874, when he forfeited it because of ill health.

The whole flap over Whitman's firing seemed to be over in a day, but O'Connor, a highly regarded editor, novelist, and journalist in addition to a governmental servant, could not control his rage at Harlan and began to write a diatribe against the moralistic Secretary of the Interior and his "commission of an outrage"—the unceremonious dumping of Walt Whitman, "the Kosmical man—... the ADAMUS of the nineteenth century—not an individual, but MANKIND." O'Connor went on for nearly fifty pages, excoriating Harlan and sanctifying Whitman, offering a ringing endorsement of the poet's work and his life, emphasizing his hospital work and his love of country, and locating any indecency in Harlan's "horrible inanity of prudery," not in the poetry itself.

Whitman offered O'Connor advice and suggestions on the piece, which O'Connor titled "The Good Gray Poet," creating an epithet that would attach itself to Whitman from then on. The pamphlet was published at the beginning of 1866 and had a major impact on the changing public perception of Whitman: though O'Connor did not downplay Whitman' frankness about the body, in his hands the transformation had begun from outrageous, immoral, indiscriminate, and radical poet of sex to saint-like, impoverished, aging poet of strong American values.

Reconstructing Leaves of Grass

In August and September of 1866, he took a leave from his job to go to New York and arrange for the printing of a new edition of Leaves. While there, he experienced the quickly changing and vastly expanding New York City—he wandered Central Park, took boat rides, and rekindled friendships with his stage-driver and ferry-boat-worker friends, and he oversaw the typesetting of Leaves, which finally appeared near the end of the year, even though the title page dated the book 1867.

The 1867 Leaves of Grass is the most carelessly printed and the most chaotic of all the editions. Whitman had problems with the typesetters, whose work was filled with errors. He bound the book in five distinct formats, some with only the new edition of Leaves of Grass, some with Leaves plus Drum-Taps, some with Leaves, Drum-Taps, and Sequel, some with all of these along with another new cluster called Songs Before Parting, and some with only Leaves and Songs Before Parting. He was obviously confused about what form his book should take. He always believed that the history of Leaves paralleled the history of himself, and that both histories embodied the history of America in the nineteenth century, so we can read the 1867 edition as Whitman's first tentative attempt to absorb the Civil War into his book.

By literally sewing the printed pages of Drum-Taps and Sequel into the back of some of the issues, he creates a jarring textual effect, as pagination and font fracture while he adds his poems of war and division to his poems of absorption and nondiscrimination. The Union has been preserved, but this stripped and undecorated volume—the only edition of Leaves to contain no portrait of the poet—manifests a kind of forced reconciliation, a recognition that everything now has to be reconfigured. Leaves of Grass, like the nation, was now entering a long period of reconstruction.

Whitman would keep rearranging, pruning, and adding to Leaves in order to try to solve the structural problems so evident in the 1867 edition. By 1870, Leaves took a radically new shape when the fifth edition appeared (known as the 1871-72 edition because of the varying dates on the title page, but actually first printed in 1870). This complex edition, which, like the 1867, appeared in several versions, reveals Whitman's attempt to fully absorb the Civil War and its aftermath into his book, as the Drum-Taps poems are given their own "cluster" but also are scattered into other parts of Leaves, as the war experience bleeds out into the rest of the poems in sometimes subtle small additions and changes. This edition contains some revealing clusters of poems that appear here and then disappear in the much better known 1881 arrangement; in the 1871-72 edition, "Marches now the War is Over" and "Songs of Insurrection" are two clusters that capture the charged historical moment of Reconstruction that this edition responds to.

In the development from the 1867 Leaves to the better integrated 1871-1872 Leaves, Whitman was aided by the intervening efforts of the English writer William Michael Rossetti who edited Poems by Walt Whitman, the first British edition of Whitman's work. Rossetti's arrangement of the poems helped Whitman see new possibilities in his work, specifically how Drum-Taps could be integrated into the larger project of Leaves of Grass. Rossetti believed, however, that Whitman's work had to be expurgated for the sensibilities of British readers, and, as the English edition progressed, Whitman took various positions on Rossetti's suggestions for censoring, once seeming to grant permission (through his friend Moncure Conway) to substitute words for "father-stuff" and "onanist," but later telling Rossetti that "I cannot and will not consent, of my own volition, to countenance an expurgated edition of my pieces."

Rossetti's diplomatic approach was to alter no words in Whitman's poems (though he often changed titles). Instead, if a poem might offend too many readers or provoke censors, he omitted it altogether. Rossetti regarded Whitman as one the great poets of the English language and hoped that this selection of poems would augur a complete printing in England. Poems by Walt Whitman, reprinting approximately half of the 1867 Leaves of Grass, was critical for Whitman since it made him English friends who later would help sustain him financially and who would advance his reputation on both sides of the Atlantic.

Democratic Vistas and Other New Projects

In 1870 Whitman published Democratic Vistas and

Passage to India (both works carried the date 1871 on their title pages). Passage to India, a volume of seventy-five poems with one-third of them new, was intended as a follow-up volume to Leaves of Grass, one that would inaugurate a new emphasis in Whitman's poetry on the "Unseen soul" and would thus complement his earlier songs of the "Body and existence." (Poor health eventually made Whitman curtail the plan.) The title poem moves from the material to the spiritual. Much of "Passage to India" celebrates the highly publicized work of engineers, especially the suggestive global linking accomplished by the transcontinental railroad, the Suez Canal, and the Atlantic cable.

(Whitman's enthusiasm for engineering accomplishments was magnified because of his pride in his brother Jeff who had moved west in 1867 to become chief engineer charged with building and overseeing waterworks for St. Louis—a "great work–a noble position," Walt exclaimed). For Whitman, modern material accomplishments were most important as means to better understand the "aged fierce enigmas" at the heart of spiritual questions. "Passage to India" is grand in conception and has had many admirers, but the poem's rhetorical excesses–apparent even in its heavy reliance on exclamation marks–reveal a poet not so much at odds with his subject matter as flagging in inspiration.

Whitman's Stroke and Move to Camden

Whitman's steady routine of life–mixing work as a Washington clerk with his ongoing literary projects–was fundamentally altered when a series of blows turned 1873 into one of the worst years in his life. On January 23, he suffered a stroke; in February his sister-in-law Mattie died of cancer; in May his beloved mother began to fail. Whitman—partially paralyzed, with weakness in his left leg and arm—managed to travel to Camden, New Jersey, arriving three days before his mother's death. He returned to Washington at the beginning of June, hoping to resume his job. But by the middle of the month he was back in Camden to stay, moving into a working-class neighborhood with his brother George and his wife Lou. *Acts of Memory:* Throughout the Camden years, despite his physical decline, the poet published steadily. Not long after his stroke, for example, he expanded and reworked journalism and notebook entries in composing Memoranda During the War. The book was published at the end of Reconstruction when a rise in immigration and racial conflict strained national cohesion, and, to Whitman's mind, lent urgency to his argument that affectionate bonds between men constituted the vital core of American democracy. The prose in this volume is taut, concise, detailed, and unflinching. Although the Civil War received more press coverage than any previous war, Whitman worried that its true import would be lost, that what he called "the real war" would never be remembered. He lamented the lack of attention to the common soldiers and to the fortitude and love he had seen in his many visits with soldiers in the hospitals.

Harry Stafford: In addition to his literary friends, Whitman continued to maintain key emotional ties with working-class men, often substantially younger men. Whitman's relationship with Doyle gradually dwindled as the two men saw less and less of one another. Harry Stafford displaced Doyle as his boy, his "darling son." Stafford, an emotionally unstable young man of eighteen when Whitman first met him in 1876, did odd jobs at the Camden New Republic. The Stafford family regarded Whitman as a type of mentor and were pleased with the poet's interest in the young man. Stafford's mother was especially solicitous of Whitman as he strove to nurse himself back to health after his stroke through the restorative powers of the natural scene at the Stafford's farm near Timber Creek, approximately ten miles from Camden.

The nature of Whitman's relationship with Stafford remains mysterious. We know that the poet and Harry wrestled together (leaving John Burroughs dismayed at the way they "cut up like two boys"); that a friendship ring given by Whitman to Stafford went back and forth numerous times as the relationship developed; and that they shared a room together when traveling. Whitman and Stafford also discussed attractive women (as the poet had with Peter Doyle). After Stafford married in 1884, the two men maintained a friendly relationship.

The 1881-1882 edition

Whitman's work, repeatedly endorsed by English readers and by other European admirers, especially in France and Germany, received a further boost in 1881 when a mainstream Boston publisher, James R. Osgood and Co., decided to issue Leaves of Grass under its imprint. As was the case over twenty years earlier when Thayer and Eldridge offered him respectable Boston publication, Whitman could now anticipate the benefits of high visibility, good distribution, and institutional validation (a paradoxical idea, of course, for a renegade poet). Once again, however, things soon went awry. Oliver Stevens, the Boston district attorney, wrote to Osgood on March 1, 1882: "We are of the opinion that this book is such a book as brings it within the provisions of the Public Statutes respecting obscene literature and suggest the propriety of withdrawing the same from circulation and suppressing the editions thereof." The New England Society for the Suppression of Vice encouraged this proceeding, but numerous reviews had also predicted trouble for the book.

Osgood attempted to strike a compromise, and Whitman, too, thinking that the changes might involve only ten lines "and half a dozen words or phrases," worked to find a way around the ban. But Whitman's position stiffened once he realized how extensive the changes would have to be. The offending passages appeared in "Song of Myself," "From Pent-Up Aching Rivers," "I Sing the Body Electric," "A Woman Waits for Me," "Spontaneous Me," "Native Moments," "The Dalliance of the Eagles," "By Blue Ontario's Shore," "To a Common Prostitute," "Unfolded Out of the Folds," "The Sleepers," and "Faces." For most poems, particular passages or words were found offensive, but the district attorney insisted that "A Woman Waits for Me" and "To a Common Prostitute" had to be removed altogether. Intriguingly, the "Calamus" section and other poems treating male-male love raised no concern, perhaps because the male-male poems infrequently venture beyond hand-holding and hugging while the male-female poems are frank about copulation. Whitman wrote to Osgood: "The list whole and several is rejected by me, and will not be thought of under any circumstances." Osgood ceased selling Leaves and gave the plates to Whitman, who took them to Philadelphia publisher Rees Welsh. Rees Welsh printed around 6,000 copies of the book, and sales, initially at least, were brisk. Within the Rees Welsh company, David McKay in particular was supportive of Whitman; soon McKay began publishing Whitman through his own firm. The suppression controversy had another benefit as well: it helped restore an important friendship with O'Connor, who came to Whitman's defence once again after a period of estrangement.

In the year Leaves was banned in Boston, Whitman wrote "Memorandum at a Venture," which argues that the "current prurient, conventional treatment of sex is the main formidable obstacle" to the advancement of women in politics, business, and social life. Whitman's depictions of women have received a fair amount of criticism (D. H. Lawrence, for one, claimed that Whitman reduced women to wombs). Leaves of Grass clearly emphasized motherhood, but Whitman valued other roles for women as well. In fact, the women he most celebrated were those who challenged traditional ways, including Margaret Fuller, Frances Wright, George Sand, Delia Bacon, and others. Some nineteenth-century women criticized Whitman: Elizabeth Cady Stanton, for example, was understandably troubled by the skewed understanding of women's sexuality suggested by "A Woman Waits for Me," even as she endorsed the freedom and assertiveness Whitman insisted on when he said, in the same poem, that women must "know how to swim, row, ride, wrestle, shoot, run, strike, retreat, advance, resist, defend themselves."

Most women of his day looked beyond his occasional lapses. Many wrote him letters of appreciation for the liberating value of his poetry. In addition, notable writers ranging from Kate Chopin to Charlotte Perkins Gilman to Edith Wharton admired his work both because of what he said about women and because his vision of comradeship–ideally based on mutuality and equality, whatever the reality of his own relationships–lent itself readily to a critique of hierarchical relations between men and women.

Life Stories

Specimen Days was issued as a prose counterpart to the 1881-1882 Leaves of Grass. Whitman described it as the "most wayward, spontaneous, fragmentary book ever printed," and, as an autobiography, the book is anomalous. Whitman sheds little light on what remains a central mystery: the development of the first edition of Leaves of Grass. After a brief section on family background, Whitman moves rapidly past his "long foreground" to focus instead on the war (relying heavily on material used in Memoranda). Aware that no other major writer could match his direct and extensive connection to the war, he continues to argue that the hospitals were central to the war just as the war was definitional for American experience.

Following this section, Whitman shifts to nature reflections evoked by the Stafford farm setting at Timber Creek where Whitma underwent a self-imposed, idiosyncratic, but effective regimen of physical therapy (including wrestling with saplings and taking mud baths) to restore his body from the ravages of stroke. He also describes his 1879 trip to attend the quarter-centennial celebration of the Kansas settlement and to visit his brother Jeff in St.

Louis. Whitman journeyed as far as Denver and the Rockies, finding in the landscape a grandeur that matched his earlier imaginings of it and a ruggedness that justified his approach to American poetry. Consistently in Specimen Days, Whitman kept his standing in the national pantheon in mind. In sections such as "My Tribute to Four Poets" and the accounts of the deaths of Emerson, Longfellow, and Carlyle, Whitman seeks to establish a newly magnanimous position in relation to his key predecessors. Showing a generosity rarely displayed in his criticism before, he now praises fellow poets he once derided as "jinglers, and snivellers, and fops."

Specimen Days has only recently begun to get much critical attention, and it is now being read as an eccentric and experimental work, a prose counterpart to Whitman's radically new poetry.

Mickle Street

In the 1880s, as Whitman was compiling authoritative versions of his writings and overseeing various accounts of his life, he was also putting his domestic arrangements in better order. He had been living with his brother George's family, but when George retired and moved the family to a farm outside of town, Walt refused to leave Camden. With money saved from royalties from the 1881-1882 edition of Leaves combined with a loan from publisher George W. Childs, the poet bought "a little old shanty of my own." In March 1884 he moved into the only home he ever owned. Lacking a furnace and in need of repairs, the two-story frame house at 328 Mickle Street suited Whitman well, he said. His personal room quickly took on a distinctive aura: many visitors noted how the poet resided in a sea of chaotic papers.

The Annexes

After the suppression controversy, Whitman retained the structure of Leaves of Grass, relegating the poetry written after 1881 to appendices—or, as the poet called them, annexes—to the main book. Typically, new material appeared in separate publications first, as, for example, was the case with November Boughs, a volume containing sixty-four new poems gathered under the title "Sands at Seventy" and various prose works previously published in periodicals. These prose writings are effective, especially "Father Taylor," "Robert Burns as Poet and Person," and "Slang in America." Good-Bye My Fancy was published initially as a miscellany of prose and verse. Whitman later printed thirty-one poems from the book in "Good-Bye my Fancy... 2d Annex" to Leaves of Grass. Whitman lacked the poetic power of his early years, but he was still capable of writing engaging poems such as "Osceola," "A Twilight Song," and "To the Sun-Set Breeze."

Final Illness and Death

Whitman seemed to endure his final months through sheer force of will. He was in fact very sick, beset by an array of ailments. For some time, he had been making preparations for the end. He had a large mausoleum built in Camden's Harleigh Cemetery, on a plot given to him in 1885, shortly after the cemetery was opened. The large tomb was paid for in part by Whitman with money donated to him so that he could buy a house in the country and in part by Thomas Harned, one of his literary executors. (Eventually, several family members–Hannah, George, Louisa, Edward, and his parents—were reinterred in the same tomb, on which the inscription reads simply "Walt Whitman.") On December 24, 1891, the poet composed his last will and testament. In an earlier will of 1873 he had bequeathed his silver watch to Peter Doyle, but now, with Doyle largely absent from his life, he made changes, giving his gold watch to Traubel and a silver one to Harry Stafford.

Whitman was nursed in his final illness by Frederick Warren Fritzinger, a former sailor. Whitman liked Warry's touch, which blended masculine strength and feminine tenderness. The poet's last words–a request to be moved in bed, "Shift, Warry"–were addressed to Fritzinger. The poet died on March 26, 1892, his hand resting in that of Traubel. The cause of death was miliary tuberculosis, with other contributing factors. The autopsy revealed that one lung had completely collapsed and the other was working only at one-eighth capacity; his heart was "surrounded by a large number of small abscesses and about two and half quarts of water." Daniel Longaker, Whitman's physician in the final year, noted that the autopsy showed Whitman to be free of alcoholism or syphilis. He emphatically rejected the "slanderous accusations that debauchery and excesses of various kinds caused or contributed to his break-down."

Talking Back to Whitman

In "Poets to Come" Whitman claimed: "I am a man who, sauntering along without fully stopping, turns a casual look upon you and then averts his face,/Leaving it to you to prove and define it,/Expecting the main things from you." That casual look has had an uncanny impact as countlesswriters have sought to complete Whitman's project and thereby to better know themselves. The responses have been varied, ranging from indictments to accolades. Poetic responses to Whitman sometimes fall into his cadences and in other ways mimic his style, but many poets have understood, with William Carlos Williams, that the only way to write like Whitman is to write unlike Whitman. To an unusual degree, however, his legacy has not been limited to the genre in which he made his fame. Beyond poetry, Whitman has had an extensive and unpredictable impact on fiction, film, architecture, music, painting, dance, and other arts.

Whitman has enjoyed great international renown. Perhaps William Faulkner can match Whitman's impact on South America, but no U.S. writer, including Faulkner, has had a comparable influence in as many parts of the world. Leaves of Grass has been translated in complete editions in Spain, France, Germany, Italy, China, and Japan, and partial translations have appeared in all major languages but Arabic. Whitman's importance stems not only from his literary qualities but also from his standing as a prophet of liberty and revolution: he has served as a major icon for socialists and communists. On the other hand, he has also been invoked on occasion by writers and politicians on the far right, including the National Socialists in Germany. In general, Whitman's influence internationally has been most felt in liberal circles as a writer who articulated the beauty, power, and always incompletely fulfilled promise of democracy.

"My book and the war are one," Whitman once said. He might have saidas well that his book and the U.S. are one. Whitman has been of crucial importance to minority writers who have talked back to him–extending, refining, rewriting, battling, endorsing, and sometimes rejecting the work of a writer who strove so insistently to define national identity and t imagine an inclusive society. Recent critics sometimes decry Whitman's shortcomings and occasional failure to live up to his own finest ideals. But minority writers from Langston Hughes to June Jordan and Yusef Komunyakaa have, with rare exceptions, warmed to an outlook extraordinary for its sympathy, generosity, and capaciousness. Whitman's absorption by people from all walks of life justifies his bold claim of 1855 that "the proof of a poet is that his country absorbs him as affectionately as he has absorbed it." Over a century after his death, Whitman is a vital presence in American cultural memory. Television shows depict him. Musicians allude to him. Schools and bridges are named after him. Truck stops, apartment complexes, parks, think tanks, summer camps, corporate centers, and shopping malls bear his name. Look for him, just as he said you should, under your bootsoles.

Chapter 3

Chronology

Born on May 31, 1819, Walt Whitman was the second son of Walter Whitman, a housebuilder, and Louisa Van Velsor. The family, which consisted of nine children, lived in Brooklyn and Long Island in the 1820s and 1830s. At the age of twelve Whitman began to learn the printer's trade, and fell in love with the written word. Largely self-taught, he read voraciously, becoming acquainted with the works of Homer, Dante, Shakespeare, and the Bible. Whitman worked as a printer in New York City until a devastating fire in the printing district demolished the industry. In 1836, at the age of 17, he began his career as teacher in the one-room school houses of Long Island. He continued to teach until 1841, when he turned to journalism as a full-time career. He founded a weekly newspaper, Long-Islander, and later edited a number of Brooklyn and New York papers.

In 1848, Whitman left the Brooklyn Daily Eagle to become editor of the New Orleans Crescent. It was in New Orleans that he experienced at first hand the viciousness of slavery in the slave markets of that city. On his return to Brooklyn in the fall of 1848, he founded a "free soil" newspaper, the Brooklyn Freeman, and continued to develop the unique style of poetry that later so astonished Ralph Waldo Emerson. In 1855, Whitman took out a copyright on the first edition of Leaves of Grass, which consisted of twelve untitled poems and a preface. He published the volume himself, and sent a copy to Emerson in July of 1855. Whitman released a second edition of the book in 1856, containing thirty-three poems, a letter from Emerson praising the first edition, and a long open letter by Whitman in response. During his subsequent career, Whitman continued to refine the volume, publishing several more editions of the book. At the outbreak of the Civil War, Whitman vowed to live a "purged" and "cleansed" life. He wrote freelance journalism and visited the wounded at New York-area hospitals. He then traveled to Washington, D.C. in December 1862 to care for his brother who had been wounded in the war. Overcome by the suffering of the many wounded in Washington, Whitman decided to stay and work in the hospitals. Whitman stayed in the city for eleven years. He took a job as a clerk for the Department of the Interior, which ended when the Secretary of the Interior, James Harlan, discovered that Whitman was the author of Leaves of Grass, which Harlan found offensive. Harlan fired the poet.

Whitman struggled to support himself through most of his life. In Washington he lived on a clerk's salary and modest royalties, and spent any excess money, including gifts from friends, to buy supplies for the patients he nursed. He had also been sending money to his widowed mother and an invalid brother. From time to time writers both in the states and in England sent him "purses" of money so that he could get by.

In the early 1870s, Whitman settled in Camden, where he had come to visit his dying mother at his brother's house. However, after suffering a stroke, Whitman found it impossible to return to Washington. He stayed with his brother until the 1882 publication of Leaves of Grass gave Whitman enough money to buy a home in Camden. In the simple two-story clapboard house, Whitman spent his declining years working on additions and revisions to a new edition of the book and preparing his final volume of poems and prose, Good-Bye, My Fancy. After his death on March 26, 1892, Whitman was buried in a tomb he designed and had built on a lot in Harleigh Cemetery.

1819 31 May, Walter Whitman born at West Hills, Huntington Township, New York, the second child of Walter Whitman, house builder, and Louisa Van Velsor, both descendants of early settlers on Long Island. Seven other Whitman children survive infancy: Jesse, Mary Elizabeth, Hannah Louisa; Andrew Jackson; George Washington; Thomas Jefferson; and Edward.

1823 27 May, Whitman family moves to Brooklyn expecting housing boom.

1825 4 July, Marquis de Lafayette visits Brooklyn and, according to Whitman's recollection, embraces him.

1825–30 Attends public school in Brooklyn. Family frequently relocates within city.

1830–31 Quits school; works as an office boy for lawyer, doctor.

1831–32 Learns printing trade as apprentice for Long Island Patriot.

1832–35 Summer 1832, works at Worthington's printing house. Fall 1832 to May 1835, works as compositor on Long Island Star. 1833, Whitman family moves back to Long Island.

1835–36 Works as a printer in New York but is unemployed after a great fire in printing district, 12 August 1836.

1836–38 Teaches school on Long Island at East Norwich, Hempstead, Babylon, Long Swamp, and Smithtown.

1838–39 Edits weekly newspaper, Long Islander, Huntington; works on Long Island Democrat, Jamaica.

1840–41 Fall 1840, campaigns for Martin Van Buren; teaches school on Long Island at Trimming Square, Woodbury, Dix Hills, and Whitestone.

1841 May, moves to New York City; works as a compositor for The New World. July, addresses Democratic Party rally in City Hall Park. August, publishes "Death in the School-Room " in Democratic Review.

1842 November, Franklin Evans; or The Inebriate published as an extra to The New World.

1842–45 Works briefly for the Aurora, Evening Tattler,

Statesman, Democrat and Mirror and contributes to other papers in New York City.

1845–46 August 1845, returns to Brooklyn; works for Brooklyn Evening Star until March 1846.

1846–48 March 1846 to January 1848, edits Brooklyn Daily Eagle. Attends opera regularly.

1848 January, quits from Daily Eagle. February, goes to New Orleans with brother Jeff to edit Daily Crescent. May, resigns position and returns to Brooklyn via Mississippi and Great Lakes.

1848–49 9 September 1948, first issue of Brooklyn Weekly Freeman, a "free-soil" newspaper founded and edited by Whitman; office burns after first issue. Spring Freeman becomes a daily; Whitman edits until 11 September 1849. July, examined by phrenologist Lorenzo Fowler.

1849–54 Operates job-printing office, bookstore, and house building business; does freelance journalism. 31 March 1851, addresses Brooklyn Art Union; writes "Pictures" in 1853.

1855 15 May, takes out copyright on the first edition of Leaves of Grass, containing twelve poems and a preface. Leaves is printed by the Rome brothers in Brooklyn during first week of July. Father dies on 11 July. Ralph Waldo Emerson writes to poet on 21 July: "I greet you at the beginning of a great career."

1855–56 November 1855 to August 1856 writes for Life Illustrated; writes a political tract, "The Eighteenth Presidency!" Between August and September 1856, phrenologists Fowler and Wells publish second edition of Leaves of Grass, containing thirty-two poems, Emerson's letter, and an open letter by Whitman in reply to Emerson. November, visited by Henry David Thoreau and Bronson Alcott in Brooklyn.

1857–60 Spring 1857 to Summer 1859, edits Brooklyn Daily Times; unemployed during the winter of

1859–1860; frequents Pfaff's restaurant, a centre of New York's literary bohemia.

1860 March, goes to Boston to oversee third edition of Leaves of Grass, published by Thayer and Eldridge. Urged by Emerson to "expurgate" the "Children of Adam" poems.

1861–62 12 April 1861, the Civil War begins; Whitman's brother George enlists. Writes freelance journalism; visits the sick and injured at New York Hospital. December 1862, goes to Virginia where he learns that George has been wounded at Fredricksburg; remains in camp two weeks.

1863–64 Moves to Washington, D.C.; visits military hospitals and supports himself as part-time clerk in Army Paymaster's Office. Becomes friends with William D. O'Connor and John Burroughs. December 1863, brother Andrew dies of tuberculosis aggravated by alcoholism. June 1864, returns to Brooklyn for six months on sick leave. 5 December 1864, has brother Jesse committed to King's County Lunatic Asylum.

1865 Returns to Washington after 24 January appointment to clerkship in Indian Bureau of Department of the Interior. 4 March, attends Lincoln's second inauguration. 14 April, Lincoln assassinated. May, begins printing Drum-Taps, but suspends printing to add a sequel commemorating Lincoln. 30 June, discharged from position by Secretary James Harlan, supposedly because of authorship of obscene poetry. Is transferred to a clerkship in Attorney General's Office. Summer, writes "When Lilacs Last in the Dooryard Bloom'd" and "O Captain! My Captain!" October, publishes Drum-Taps and Sequel. Begins relationship with Peter Doyle, an eighteen-year old Confederate horse-car conductor, in Washington.

1866 O'Connor publishes The Good Gray Poet (New

York: Bunce and Huntington), a defence co-written by Whitman, in response to the poet's firing by Harlan.

1867 John Burroughs supports Whitman in Notes on Walt Whitman as Poet and Person (New York: American News Company). 6 July, William Michael Rossetti publishes an appreciation of "Walt Whitman's Poems" in the London Chronicle. Fourth edition of Leaves of Grass printed in New York; publishes "Democracy," first part of Democratic Vistas, in December in the Galaxy.

1868 Poems of Walt Whitman, selected and edited by Rossetti, published in London (John Camden Hotten, publisher). "Personalism," second part of Democratic Vistas, published in the May Galaxy.

1869 Develops substantial following in England; Anne Gilchrist and, about this time, Edward Carpenter read Rossetti edition and are attracted to Whitman.

1870 Suffers depression; prints fifth edition of Leaves of Grass, and Democratic Vistas and Passage to India, all in Washington D.C., and dated 1871. May, Anne Gilchrist publishes "An Englishwoman's Estimate of Walt Whitman" in The Radical, Boston.

1871 Algernon Charles Swinburne greets Whitman in Songs Before Sunrise; Alfred, Lord Tennyson and John Addington Symonds send affectionate letters. Anne Gilchrist writes a marriage proposal; Whitman politely declines. Rudolph Schmidt translates Democratic Vistas into Danish. 7 September, Whitman reads After All, Not to Create Only at American Institute Exhibition in New York City (published in Boston by Roberts Brothers).

1872 1 June, Thérèse Bentzon publishes critical article on Whitman in Revue des Deux Mondes. 26 June,

	reads "As A Strong Bird on Pinions Free" at Dartmouth College commencement (published in Washington, D.C.). Succumbs to heat prostration; quarrels with O'Connor; writes will.
1873	23 January, suffers paralytic stroke. Mother dies on 23 May. "Song of the Universal" read at Tufts College commencement by proxy. June, Whitman leaves Washington and moves in with his brother George in Camden, New Jersey.
1874	12 July, receives adulatory letter from Carpenter. Midsummer, discharged from his position in Washington. Publishes "Song of the Redwood-Tree" and "Prayer of Columbus" in Harper's Magazine.
1876	Publishes "Author's" or "Centennial" edition of Leaves of Grass and Two Rivulets, a matched set of volumes, and Memoranda During the War; and "Walt Whitman's Actual American Position" in West Jersey Press, an unsigned article that leads to an international controversy about America's neglect of Whitman. Befriends Harry Stafford, a printers' employee; frequently visits the Stafford family farm at Timber Creek. September, Anne Gilchrist visits the United States with her children, rents a house, and hopes to marry Whitman.
1877	28 January, lectures on Thomas Paine in Philadelphia. Painted by George W. Waters in New York. May, Edward Carpenter visits Whitman in Camden; Dr. Richard Maurice Bucke visits Whitman and becomes a close friend. Whitman visits Burroughs in Esopus, New York, with Harry Stafford.
1878	Too sick to give planned lecture on "The Death of Abraham Lincoln" in spring. June, visits J.H. Johnston and John Burroughs in New York.
1879	14 April, gives first Lincoln lecture in New York. Anne Gilchrist returns to England. September,

travels west as far as Colorado; falls ill, and stays with brother Jeff in St. Louis.

1880 April, gives Lincoln lecture in Philadelphia. January, returns to Camden. June to October, travels in Canada and visits Bucke in London, Ontario.

1881 15 April, gives Lincoln lecture in Boston. August to October, visits Boston to supervise a new edition of Leaves of Grass published by James R. Osgood containing the final arrangement of 293 poems. Visits Emerson in Concord.

1882 January, Oscar Wilde visits Whitman in Camden. April, Osgood withdraws edition of Leaves of Grass on complaint of Boston District Attorney. Rees Welsh reprints Osgood edition in Philadelphia and issues Specimen Days and Collect. Publicity of Boston "suppression" of Whitman causes unprecedented boom in sales of Leaves of Grass. Becomes friends with Pearsall Smith, wealthy Philadelphia glass merchant and prominent Quaker.

1883 McKay publishes Bucke's Walt Whitman a biography written with contributions from Whitman.

1884 March, buys house at 328 Mickle Street, Camden, New Jersey, with royalties from McKay edition of Leaves of Grass. June, Carpenter visits a second time. Becomes friends with Horace Traubel, Thomas Harned, Talcott Williams, Thomas Donaldson, and Robert Ingersoll.

1885 July, has heat stroke. Friends, headed by Donaldson, present him with horse and buggy.

1886 Gives Lincoln lecture in Elkton, Maryland; Camden; Philadelphia; and Haddonfield, New Jersey. Pall Mall Gazette promotes fund which presents Whitman with eighty pounds. Boston supporters send $800 for purchase of summer cottage on Timber Creek.

1887 14 April, Lincoln lecture in New York City at Madison Square Theater attracts many notables and nets $600, followed by reception at Westminster Hotel. Sculptured by Sidney Morse; painted by Herbert Gilchrist, J.W. Alexander, and Thomas Eakins.

1888 June, suffers another paralytic stroke followed by severe illness. Makes a new will naming Richard Maurice Bucke, Thomas B. Harned, and Horace Traubel as literary executors. Publishes November Boughs.

1889 Seventieth birthday party commemorated in Camden's Compliment to Walt Whitman (ed. Horace Traubel. Philadelphia: David McKay).

1890 April, delivers Lincoln lecture for the last time, Philadelphia. 19 August, writes to John Addington Symonds; declares Symond's homosexual interpretation of "Calamus" poems "damnable" and claims to have fathered six illegitimate children. October, Whitman contracts to have $4,000 tomb built for himself in Harleigh Cemetery, Camden, New Jersey.

1891 Publishes Good-bye My Fancy and Deathbed edition of Leaves of Grass (both published by McKay, dated 1892). Prepares Complete Prose Works. Last birthday dinner at Mickle Street. December, catches pneumonia.

1892 26 March, dies at Mickle Street; 30 March, buried in Harleigh Cemetery, Camden, New Jersey.

Chapter 4

Historical Context

Historical Context

The history of American poetry, at least since Walt Whitman, has shifted like the swinging of a pendulum, going first to the side of form-free expression and inevitably swinging to the opposite side, which appreciates formal structure as being necessary to the imitation of life, and then swinging back again with the next generation. Before Whitman, American poetry had no character that was uniquely its own, and instead used forms that were inherited from Europe. Even the most innovative early-American poets, including Walt Whitman and Edgar Allan Poe were more known for their ideas and for working within existing techniques than they were for improvising with form; Whitman's contemporary, Emily Dickinson, wrote in the 1860s in a form that owed little to tradition, but she wrote in the same form consistently.

Walt Whitman's collection of poems Leaves of Grass, first published in 1855 and revised in subsequent editions throughout his lifetime, is as lively in its structure as it is in its insights. He touched upon themes that had not been covered in poetry before (including an unheard of degree of sensuality and homosexuality that shocked readers and made him lose his government job), and he matched his original content with a style that continually adjusted itself, line by line. He seldom used a regular, repeating rhyme scheme, but then it would not be unusual for a Whitman poem to break into a stretch of rhyming pattern and then break out; he repeated when he found it necessary for emphasis (as in the lines "Lisped to me the low and delicious word death/And again death, death, death, death."); he alternated stanzas that had over twenty lines with stanzas that had two and poems that ran for twelve pages with poems that consisted of just a few lines. In short, Whitman defined American poetry by throwing out all of the old rules and assumptions and using whatever techniques he felt necessary for describing what life in this country was like.

The key to Whitman's genius was that, free-form as his poetry was, he did in fact apply technique, without which it would be difficult to distinguish his artistry from common rumblings. The question that faced poets who followed him concerned how much freedom could be allowed and how much technique could be left out to still have something defined as poetry. To capture a democratic society such as the United States, which has no strict social order, it would not be appropriate to use a strict traditional poetic structure: such poetry tries to show form and tradition to be myths. In the twentieth century we have seen a great parade of artistic movements whose work does not look like traditional poetry because it is defying tradition and trying to create new ways of expression.

At the end of the 1800s and early in the 1900s, society became disillusioned with hoping that rational, orderly thought could truly understand the world, and the forms and techniques that artists had at their disposal were seen as meaningless. The general term that is used to cover this artistic stance is Modernism, although this term is not very meaningful in general discussions because it covers a wide span of artistic practices across a number of years. Some examples of Modernism are Absurdism, which purposely offends audiences' sense of character development and motive in order to provoke thought, and Imagist poetry, which focuses on conveying a specific image to the audience but does not provide the image with meaning or significance. We can see the influence of Modernism's belief in freedom of artistic style in the form of "l(a". But this poem also uses its radically unique form to address the poet's personal emotion. To the extent that it is more concerned with the message than with its own uniqueness, it can be seen as a response to the way Modernism stresses style for style's sake. In this sense the poem fits into the next phase of artistic development, Postmodernism. During the 1930s when the country was in the middle of the Great Depression, Americans found the mad-artistic-genius syndrome of the previous cycle to be too self-indulgent, and poets started to once again write about what they believed in. Compassion and making a better world could not be expressed by poetry that had purely private meanings, but reusing the same old forms in the same old ways would lead to an approval of old social orders that Americans did not believe in anymore. Postmodernism merges the artistic freedom that Modernists took to an extreme with a greater concern for the artist's function in society.

By the 1950s, when this poem was published, there was no real dominant school of poetry, but the freedom that the Modern age stressed had led to a number of styles and sensibilities operating at once. Confessionalist poets drew from personal experience, and in order to convey their experiences to a wide audience, they used traditional techniques of rhyme, rhythm, and symbolism — but certainly not as rigidly as those techniques had been used before Whitman. Beat poets, on the other hand, emphasized spontaneous expression, and therefore sacrificed consciousness of poetic style in an attempt to capture life's uncertainty. In this environment, cummings offended many as belonging to the "other side" — both too original and too deliberate. Although cummings's style owes some to the writers who came before him, his greatness was that he created new ways to be unique and still be meaningful.

Compare and Contrast

1950s: Millions of Americans watched the televised Army-McCarthy Hearings, during which Senator Joseph McCarthy, whose investigation of Communism in public figures had ruined careers and bullied people into testifying against friends, was condemned by the Senate for misconduct.

1973: The Senate Watergate Hearings were broadcast to

the country, with high-ranking government officials testifying to their part in burglary and wiretapping charges; this lead to a Senate vote the next year to impeach President Nixon.

1988: The televised Iran-Contra hearings found that members of President Reagan's administration had sold weapons illegally to Iran in order to illegally give money to the Nicaraguan Contras.

Today: With the greater number of television stations made available by cable television, political hearings seldom capture the entire nation's attention by being broadcast on one of the larger networks.

1958: The first integrated circuit was invented.

1969: CompuServe, the first commercial online service, was started.

Today: More than 40 percent of U.S. households own personal computers, and the number is still growing.

1958: The federal deficit was $2,790,000,000.

1968: The federal deficit was $25,161,000,000.

1978: The federal deficit was $59,161,000,000.

1988: The federal deficit was $155,151,000,000.

Today: After reaching a high of nearly 300 billion dollars, the deficit is being reduced.

Chapter 5

Life of Walt Whitman

When Walt Whitman published his first edition of Leaves of Grass on or around the fourth day of July in 1855, he believed he was embarking on a personal literary journey of national significance. Setting out to define the American experience, Whitman consciously hoped to answer Ralph Waldo Emerson's 1843 essay, "The Poet," which called for a truly original national poet, one who would sing of the new country in a new voice. The undertaking required unlimited optimism, especially considering the fact that Whitman had published only a small handful of poems prior to 1855; however, Whitman felt confident that the time was ripe and that the people would embrace him. This optimism and confidence resulted largely from his awareness of the tremendous changes in the American literary world that had taken place during his lifetime.

At the time of Whitman's birth in 1819, the Constitution and the democratic ideas upon which this country was founded were only a generation old; America was a land of seemingly unlimited space, resources, and possibilities, yet a land with no cultural roots to call its own. In 1820, a year after Whitman's birth, Sydney Smith of Britain's Edinburgh Review was prompted to ask, "In the four quarters of the globe, who reads an American book?" But the period between Smith's remark and the publication of Whitman's first edition of Leaves of Grass in 1855 was one of remarkable and unprecedented change in America, particularly in the world of books.

By 1855, America could boast one of the world's largest

and most advanced publishing industries, producing distinctly "American" books by authors such as Poe, Hawthorne, Melville, Stowe, Fuller, Thoreau, and Emerson. The amazing growth of American literature and of the supporting publishing industry was the result of a self-conscious effort by authors and publishers to establish for America a literary culture of its own. The resulting increase in, or rather the sudden appearance of, authorship in this country was made possibly only through American ingenuity, innovation, and technology in pulbishing. In short, the advent of modern pulbishing practices during this period brought books to the peopl in heretofore unimaginable numbers, spawning as a result one of the greatest periods in the history of American literature.

Working as a printer, editor, jounalist, and publisher during the years of the publishing industry's phenomenal growth, Whitman became keenly aware that the tools necessary for his emergence as the new, democratic poet were at his disposal. He believed he could bring poetry to the common people, and with the publication of his 1855 Leaves of Grass, he assumed for himself the role of the American Poet, referring to himself as "one of the roughs," a common man. Whitman carefully continued to cultivate his literary personality throughout his career, especially through the relatively new field of photography. As he revised and enlarged Leaves of Grass (8 editions and numerous printings would appear between 1855 and 1891), Whitman's goal as the self-styled national poet became more clearly defined.

Leaves of Grass is essentially a poem in process, with each succeeding edition representing a unique period in the poet's life as well as the nation's. This is perhaps best illustrated by Whitman's Civil War poetry. Originally published in 1865 as a separate volume entitled Drum Taps, these poems were later integrated into Leaves of Grass, growing in importance in the book as the war's historical significance became clearer in Whitman's mind. He would eventually claim that Leaves of Grass "revolves around that four year's war, which, as I was in the midst of it, becomes, in "Drum-Taps," pivotal to the rest entire." Today, more than a century after the publication of the final edition of Leaves of Grass, Whitman's place in American literary history often seems as nebulous and enigmatic as the ideas upon which America was founded. Numerous poets since Whitman have consciously either placed themselves in the wake of his tradition or reacted violently against him, and the aesthetic value of Whitman's poetry continues to be a controversial subject.

The intention of this exhibit is not to make a critical appraisal of Whitman's work; instead, it is hoped that the materials assembled here will help explain the phenomenon which was Walt Whitman. While the subject matter and themes present in Whitman's poetry reflect the historical attitudes and concerns of his day, the books themselves are also artifacts of a fascination and extremely dynamic period of American publishing history.

Chapter 6

Analysis

Whitman's poetry is democratic in both its subject matter and its language. As the great lists that make up a large part of Whitman's poetry show, anything—and anyone—is fair game for a poem. Whitman is concerned with cataloguing the new America he sees growing around him. Just as America is far different politically and practically from its European counterparts, so too must American poetry distinguish itself from previous models. Thus we see Whitman breaking new ground in both subject matter and diction.

In a way, though, Whitman is not so unique. His preference for the quotidian links him with both Dante, who was the first to write poetry in a vernacular language, and with Wordsworth, who famously stated that poetry should aim to speak in the "language of ordinary men." Unlike Wordsworth, however, Whitman does not romanticize the proletariat or the peasant. Instead he takes as his model himself. The stated mission of his poetry was, in his words, to make "n attempt to put a Person, a human being (myself, in the latter half of the 19th century, in America) freely, fully, and truly on record." A truly democratic poetry, for Whitman, is one that, using a common language, is able to cross the gap between the self and another individual, to effect a sympathetic exchange of experiences.

This leads to a distinct blurring of the boundaries between the self and the world and between public and private. Whitman prefers spaces and situations—like journeys, the out-of-doors, cities—that allow for ambiguity in these respects. Thus we see poems like "Song of the Open Road" and

"Crossing Brooklyn Ferry," where the poet claims to be able to enter into the heads of others. Exploration becomes not just a trope but a mode of existence.

For Whitman, spiritual communion depends on physical contact, or at least proximity. The body is the vessel that enables the soul to experience the world. Therefore the body is something to be worshipped and given a certain primacy. Eroticism, particularly homoeroticism, figures significantly in Whitman's poetry. This is something that got him in no small amount of trouble during his lifetime. The erotic interchange of his poetry, though, is meant to symbolize the intense but always incomplete connection between individuals. Having sex is the closest two people can come to being one merged individual, but the boundaries of the body always prevent a complete union. The affection Whitman shows for the bodies of others, both men and women, comes out of his appreciation for the linkage between the body and the soul and the communion that can come through physical contact. He also has great respect for the reproductive and generative powers of the body, which mirror the intellect's generation of poetry.

The Civil War diminished Whitman's faith in democratic sympathy. While the cause of the war nominally furthered brotherhood and equality, the war itself was a quagmire of killing. Reconstruction, which began to fail almost immediately after it was begun, further disappointed Whitman. His later poetry, which displays a marked insecurity about the place of poetry and the place of emotion in general (see in particular "When Lilacs Last in the Dooryard Bloom'd"), is darker and more isolated.

Whitman's style remains consistent throughout, however. The poetic structures he employs are unconventional but reflect his democratic ideals. Lists are a way for him to bring together a wide variety of items without imposing a hierarchy on them. Perception, rather than analysis, is the basis for this kind of poetry, which uses few metaphors or other kinds of symbolic language. Anecdotes are another favored device. By transmitting a story, often one he has gotten from another individual, Whitman hopes to give his readers a sympathetic experience, which will allow them to incorporate the anecdote into their own history. The kind of language Whitman uses sometimes supports and sometimes seems to contradict his philosophy. He often uses obscure, foreign, or invented words. This, however, is not meant to be intellectually elitist but is instead meant to signify Whitman's status as a unique individual. Democracy does not necessarily mean sameness. The difficulty of some of his language also mirrors the necessary imperfection of connections between individuals: no matter how hard we try, we can never completely understand each other. Whitman largely avoids rhyme schemes and other traditional poetic devices. He does, however, use meter in masterful and innovative ways, often to mimic natural speech. In these ways, he is able to demonstrate that he has mastered traditional poetry but is no longer subservient to it, just as democracy has ended the subservience of the individual.

Chapter 7

Summary of Selected Works of Walt Whitman

"Starting from Paumanok"

Summary and Form

"Starting from Paumanok" first appeared in the 1860 edition of Leaves of Grass and was modified several times. The final version is that of the 1881 edition. This poem is Whitman's literary manifesto, an elaborate and often confounding statement of his poetic project. Whitman intends to quite literally start from Paumanok (a Native American name for Long Island, New York), the place of his birth. He will journey forth geographically as well as philosophically, and his travels will qualify him to "strike up for a New World": to lose himself in the maelstrom of American life and become the first truly American poet.

"Starting from Paumanok" delineates poetic materials as well as principles. Whitman dictates not only how but what he will write, in his lengthy lists of place-names, people, machines, and actions. The lists contained in this poem are a good example of Whitman's ability to encode meaning in form. By listing without analyzing, by refusing to subject his materials to linguistic devices such as metaphor, Whitman creates a more democratic form of poetry, in which not even the almighty poet himself has pride of place. The voice of the poet submerges and surfaces at odd intervals, losing itself in a list at one moment only to trumpet forth a series of proclamations the next. This suggests a loss of control, but also freedom. Whitman wants to catalogue, not master.

Commentary

Whitman makes several major statements about the purpose of poetry in this piece. The first comes at the beginning of the sixth section, when he proclaims that he "will make the poems of materials, for I think they are to be the most spiritual poems,/And I will make the poems of my body and of mortality,/For I think I shall then supply myself with the poems of my soul and of immortality." Here Whitman questions several traditional assumptions about poetry. Transcendence, universality of emotion, and immortality have long been considered the basis of poetry: good verse, previous generations of poets have proclaimed, situates itself outside its time and place, and through the common ground of human experience ensures immortality for itself and its author. Whitman wants to stand this premise on end. Only by capturing his specific moment and— importantly—a sense of his physical self can he write poetry that achieves a maximum intellectual and spiritual content.

In part there is a very practical reason for Whitman to take this stance: as the open frontiers, factories, steamboats, and printing presses that show up in this poem suggest, Whitman was living and writing during a period of great change. The world was modernizing, and the assumption that a common ground existed between generations had to be challenged. Perhaps too much had changed already, and this suggests that perhaps too much would change in the future for the kind of transcendental, anti-material poems favored in the past to survive. By focusing on the material world Whitman can at least re-create enough of his surroundings to enable a future reader to read the poem sympathetically. In other words, Whitman's poems ensure their survival by encapsulating their own context.

At the same time, though, Whitman makes statements that seem to contradict this principle of specificity and materiality. As he writes in the twelfth section, he "will not make poems with reference to parts,/But I will make poems, songs, thoughts, with reference to ensemble,/And I will not sing with reference to a day, but with reference to all days,/And I will not make a poem nor the least part of a poem but has reference to the soul,/Because having look'd at the objects of the universe, I find there is no one nor any particle of one but has reference to the soul." Again this has to do with Whitman's sense of the modern world. True to his democratic principles of inclusivity, he feels that "modern" does not necessarily equate with "superior." While the world may seem to be a very different place than it was in Shakespeare's time, Whitman understands that he is too submerged in it to be able to evaluate it clearly.

Thus it is not for him to pick and choose which things are truly significant, and it is not for him to try to make claims for his specific place and time. Instead, he must try to capture himself as accurately as possible in the moment of perceiving: without judging, he must write down what he sees in its entirety, because everything has some relevance, no matter how hidden it may be. Therefore he cannot choose, say, the Fourth of July to epitomize an American day: he must try to depict all of his days.

The final section of "Starting from Paumanok" seems to leave all of Whitman's abstract, universalizing aspirations behind. Instead the poet exhorts a "camerado" (a comrade—Whitman loves to invent or bastardize words) to join with him so the two of them, hand in hand, can journey forth. The desire for intimacy spelled out in so many of Whitman's poems is at odds with his more worldly or materialist writings. Again this can be read as a response to modernity: the rapidly changing world often leads to geographical and social dislocation and therefore isolation.

At the same time, Whitman also wants to point out the erotic energy of his poetry. The furious torrents of words force one to try to make connections between them, just as one tries to make connections with other human beings. The sense of movement and urgency in the final "haste on with me" suggests a new way of relating that is technological and physical rather than emotional or spiritual.

"Song of Myself"

Summary and Form

This most famous of Whitman's works was one of the original twelve pieces in the 1855 first edition of Leaves of Grass. Like most of the other poems, it too was revised extensively, reaching its final permutation in 1881. "Song of Myself" is a sprawling combination of biography, sermon, and poetic meditation. It is not nearly as heavy-handed in its pronouncements as "Starting at Paumanok"; rather, Whitman uses symbols and sly commentary to get at important issues. "Song of Myself" is composed more of vignettes than lists: Whitman uses small, precisely drawn scenes to do his work here.

This poem did not take on the title "Song of Myself" until the 1881 edition. Previous to that it had been titled "Poem of Walt Whitman, an American" and, in the 1860, 1867, and 1871 editions, simply "Walt Whitman." The poem's shifting title suggests something of what Whitman was about in this piece. As Walt Whitman, the specific individual, melts away into the abstract "Myself," the poem explores the possibilities for communion between individuals. Starting from the premise that "what I assume you shall assume" Whitman tries to prove that he both encompasses and is indistinguishable from the universe.

Commentary

Whitman's grand poem is, in its way, an American epic. Beginning in medias res—in the middle of the poet's life—it loosely follows a quest pattern. "Missing me one place search another," he tells his reader, "I stop somewhere waiting for you." In its catalogues of American life and its constant search for the boundaries of the self "Song of Myself" has much in common with classical epic. This epic sense of purpose, though, is coupled with an almost Keatsian valorization of repose and passive perception. Since for Whitman the birthplace of poetry is in the self, the best way to learn about poetry is to relax and watch the workings of one's own mind.

While "Song of Myself" is crammed with significant detail, there are three key episodes that must be examined. The first of these is found in the sixth section of the poem. A child asks the narrator "What is the grass?" and the narrator is forced to explore his own use of symbolism and his inability to break things down to essential principles. The bunches of grass in the child's hands become a symbol of the regeneration in nature. But they also signify a common material that links disparate people all over the United States together: grass, the ultimate symbol of democracy, grows everywhere. In the wake of the Civil War the grass reminds Whitman of graves: grass feeds on the bodies of the dead. Everyone must die eventually, and so the natural roots of democracy are therefore in mortality, whether due to natural causes or to the bloodshed of internecine warfare. While Whitman normally revels in this kind of symbolic indeterminacy, here it troubles him a bit. "I wish I could translate the hints," he says, suggesting that the boundary between encompassing everything and saying nothing is easily crossed.

The second episode is more optimistic. The famous "twenty-ninth bather" can be found in the eleventh section of the poem. In this section a woman watches twenty-eight young men bathing in the ocean. She fantasizes about joining them unseen, and describes their semi-nude bodies in some detail. The invisible twenty-ninth bather offers a model of being much like that of Emerson's "transparent eyeball": to truly experience the world one must be fully in it and of it, yet distinct enough from it to have some perspective, and invisible so as not to interfere with it unduly. This paradoxical set of conditions describes perfectly the poetic stance Whitman tries to assume. The lavish eroticism of this section reinforces this idea: sexual contact allows two people to become one yet not one—it offers a moment of transcendence. As the female spectator introduced in the beginning of the section fades away, and Whitman's voice takes over, the eroticism becomes homoeroticism. Again this is not so much the expression of a sexual preference as it is the longing for communion with every living being and a connection that makes use of both the body and the soul (although Whitman is certainly using the homoerotic sincerely, and in other ways too, particularly for shock value).

Having worked through some of the conditions of perception and creation, Whitman arrives, in the third key episode, at a moment where speech becomes necessary. In the twenty-fifth section he notes that "Speech is the twin of my vision, it is unequal to measure itself,/It provokes me forever, it says sarcastically,/Walt you contain enough, why don't you let it out then?" Having already established that he can have a sympathetic experience when he encounters others ("I do not ask the wounded person how he feels, I myself become the wounded person"), he must find a way to re-transmit that experience without falsifying or diminishing it. Resisting easy answers, he later vows he "will never translate self at all." Instead he takes a philosophically more rigorous stance: "What is known I strip away." Again Whitman's position is similar to that of Emerson, who says of himself, "I am the unsettler." Whitman, however, is a poet, and he must reassemble after unsettling: he must "let it out then." Having catalogued a continent and encompassed its multitudes, he finally decides: "I too am not a bit tamed, I too am untranslatable,/I sound my barbaric yawp over the roofs of the world." "Song of Myself" thus ends with a sound—a yawp—that could be described as either pre-or post-linguistic. Lacking any of the normal communicative properties of language, Whitman's yawp is the release of the "kosmos" within him, a sound at the borderline between saying everything and saying nothing. More than anything, the yawp is an invitation to the next Walt Whitman, to read into the yawp, to have a sympathetic experience, to absorb it as part of a new multitude.

"Crossing Brooklyn Ferry"

Summary and Form

This poem first appeared in the 1856 edition and received its final modifications for the 1881 edition. While "Crossing Brooklyn Ferry," like most of Whitman's poems, contains little in the way of a describable formal structure, it features a great deal of random internal patternings created by the repetition of words and phrases. This sense of repetition and revisiting reinforces the thematic content of the poem, which looks at the possibility of continuity within humanity based on common experiences.

Commentary

This poem seeks to determine the relationship of human beings to one another across time and space. Whitman wonders what he means (not as a poet but as another anonymous individual) to the crowds of strangers he sees every day. He assumes that they see the same things he does, and that they react in the same way, and that this brings them together in a very real sense. This is different than the "what I assume you shall assume" credo of "Song of Myself." Here Whitman's sense of shared spaces and shared experiences is akin to that of the Romantics, namely Wordsworth and Coleridge. This poem can be profitably compared to Wordsworth's "Tintern Abbey" and Coleridge's "This Lime-tree Bower." In both of those poems someone important to the poet—Wordsworth's sister, Coleridge's friend—is taken to a place that has been important to the poet. Wordsworth accompanies his sister, and is able to take delight in seeing her repeat his experience. Coleridge is not able to go with his friend, however, and he sits at home, wondering if his friend's experience will have any meaning for either of them. While Wordsworth is more concerned with the idea of the power of place, Coleridge, like Whitman, is more interested in the relevance of shared experience, and its ability to potentially transcend barriers of space and mortality.

In the end Whitman seems to give more credence to shared experience than Coleridge does. Reminding himself that others have seen, and fifty years from now will still be seeing, the islands of New York City, he realizes that others have also shared his range of emotional and spiritual experience. This makes him significant as an individual but also part of a larger whole. Curiously this leads Whitman to turn to the physical as a locus for identity: "I too had receiv'd identity by my body,/That I was I knew was of my body, and what I should be I knew I should be of my body." The body is both a vehicle for individual specificity and a means by which to partake of common experience: it is where the self and the world come together.

In his description of the New York waterfront Whitman does not differentiate between the natural and the man-made. Steamships and buildings are described in the same terms as seagulls and waves. This seems to be Whitman's nod to historical specificity, which can disrupt continuity of experience. Fifty years before Whitman's ferry crossing, the steamships and the skyline were not there, and he knows this. It is these minor changes that enable him to be specific, and that allow perspective on human existence.

"Out of the Cradle Endlessly Rocking"

Summary and Form

This poem was written in 1859 and incorporated into the 1860 edition of Leaves of Grass. It describes a young boy's awakening as a poet, mentored by nature and his own maturing consciousness. The poem is loose in its form, except for the sections that purport to be a transcript of the bird's call, which are musical in their repetition of words and phrases. The opening of the poem is marked by an abundance of repeated prepositions describing movement—out, over, down, up, from—which appear regularly later in the poem and which convey the sense of a struggle, in this case the poet's struggle to come to consciousness.

Unlike most of Whitman's poems, "Out of the Cradle" has a fairly distinct plot line. A young boy watches a pair of birds nesting on the beach near his home, and marvels at their relationship to one another. One day the female bird fails to return. The male stays near the nest, calling for his lost mate. The male's cries touch something in the boy, and he seems to be able to translate what the bird is saying. Brought to tears by the bird's pathos, he asks nature to give him the one word "superior to all." In the rustle of the ocean at his feet, he discerns the word "death," which continues, along with the bird's song, to have a presence in his poetry.

Commentary

This is another poem that links Whitman to the Romantics. The "birth of the poet" genre was of particular importance to Wordsworth, whose massive Prelude details his artistic coming-of-age in detail. Like Wordsworth, Whitman claims to take his inspiration from nature. Where Wordsworth is inspired by a wordless feeling of awe, though, Whitman finds an opportunity to anthropomorphize, and nature gives him very specific answers to his questions about overarching concepts. Nature is a tabula rasa onto which the poet can project himself. He conquers it, inscribes it. While it may become a part of him that is always present, the fact that it does so seems to be by his permission.

The epiphany surrounding the word "death" seems appropriate, for in other poems of Whitman's we have seen death described as the ultimate tool for democracy and sympathy. Here death is shown to be the one lesson a child must learn, whether from nature or from an elder. Only the realization of death can lead to emotional and artistic maturity. Death, for one as interested as Whitman in the place of the individual in the universe, is a means for achieving perspective: while your thoughts may seem profound and unique in the moment, you are a mere speck in existence. Thus the contemplation of death allows for one to move beyond oneself, to consider the whole. Perhaps this is why the old crone disrupts the end of the poem: she symbolizes an alternative possibility, the means by which someone else may have come to the same realization as Whitman. In the end the bird, although functionally important in Whitman's development, is insignificant in the face of the abstract sea: death, which is the concept he introduces, remains as the important factor.

Thus although "Out of the Cradle" can be described as a poem about the birth of the poet, it can also be read as a poem about the death of the self. In the end, on the larger scale, these two phenomena are one and the same.

As I Ebb'd with the Ocean of Life"

Summary and Form

Following "Out of the Cradle Endlessly Rocking," this poem is another newcomer to the 1860 edition of Leaves of Grass. If "Out of the Cradle" describes the birth and adolescence of a poet, then "As I Ebb'd" poem is one of mid-life crisis. This is Whitman's "Dejection Ode," the place where he faces up to the fact that his poetry might not be doing what he wants it to be doing.

The occasion of the poem is a walk along the beach, during which the narrator is "seeking types" and trying to create poetry. Suddenly he is struck by massive doubt, and sees his poetry as a manifestation of ego that approaches neither the universal nor his fundamental self. He sees the shore as a place of wrecks and corpses strewn on the sand, and realizes that he himself will be no more than debris someday.

Commentary

The centre of this poem is Whitman's assertion that "I have not once had the least idea who or what I am,/But that before all my arrogant poems the real Me stands yet untouch'd, untold, altogether unreached.../...I have not really understood any thing, not a single object, and...no man ever can." By trying to write poetry he has opened himself up to attack, both by external forces—cruel nature, his fellow man—and by internal doubts. The imagery of this poem reflects the ruin that he feels awaits him: scum, scales, and corpses litter the beach.

What is truly remarkable about the poem, though, is that Whitman, like Coleridge before him, is able to turn the dejection and the imagery of ruin into poetry. While he may end in ruin, and his poetry may be nothing but garbage on the beach, here he is writing poetry about the junk on the beach before him. It is a part of the world too. While he may be failing in his attempts to understand himself and the world, Whitman is nonetheless creating something that may last, even if just as refuse. The attack on his own ego in this poem is a direct result of the kind of perspective gained at the end of "Out of the Cradle." Faced with death and decay Whitman must admit his own relative smallness in the face of the universe. While this has left him with some hope at the end of the earlier poem, here he explores its darker consequences. Since he must admit that death will rob him of the chance even to fully know himself, he cannot see any way to possibly comment on the whole of the universe. He is left in the position of merely asking later generations to heed his wreck.

By Blue Ontario's Shore"

Summary and Form

This is another one of the 1856 poems that received its final modifications for the 1881 edition of Leaves of Grass. One of Whitman's more dramatic poems, at times "By Blue Ontario's Shore" seems to be almost a soliloquy or dramatic monologue as the speaker reaches ever-greater rhetorical heights in service of his mission. And what is this mission? The poem recounts an encounter with a "Phantom" on the shores of Lake Ontario, who demands that he "hant... the poem that comes from the soul of America." The narrator is as daunted as he is inspired, and the poem is an effort to define the conditions necessary for truly American poetry. "By Blue Ontario's Shore" is significant for the rhetorical set-pieces it contains: compare certain sections of this poem to contemporary oratory, like Lincoln's Gettysburg Address or the speeches of the abolitionists.

Whitman, in this poem, is taking his place in a larger American tradition that includes not only public figures like Lincoln and Frederick Douglass, but also America's most significant intellectuals, particularly Emerson, whose own writing is characterized by rhetorical flights which are tempered with logic and intellectual argument. Since he is writing poetry, and not engaged in scholarly argument or political debate, Whitman, unlike these others, is not bound by his purpose. Instead, he takes the opportunity to create a fusion of poetry and rhetoric that is in places some of his most interesting poetry.

Commentary

In the Phantom's call for an American poem and the narrator's subsequent exploration of the conditions for such poetry Whitman picks up on an argument made by Emerson in his essay "The American Scholar." Like Emerson, Whitman is interested in the relationship of a new American literature to previous literatures. How can American literature show that it is worthy of consideration alongside the best of British and classical writings, while at the same time declaring its independence of earlier models? The answer, for Whitman, lies in the subject matter at hand, which is both fresh and original and reflective of the country's unique political system. Situated at a time when the Civil War loomed on the horizon and in a place that saw a great deal of the fighting during the War of 1812, this poem's narrator is put in mind of America's particular place in the world.

The narrator is careful to define precisely what a poet should be. In the tenth section of the poem he describes the American poet as one who is an "arbiter" and an "equalizer," who "bestows on every object or quality its fit proportion." The poet is independent and objective: "he judges not as the judge judges but as the sun falling around a helpless thing." While this may sound like Whitman is arguing for the poet to maintain an aristocracy or meritocracy (like Shelley's poet as "unacknowledged legislator of the world"), in fact the poet's mission is rooted in more democratic, and more specifically American, principles. For, as he proclaims, "nothing out of its place is good, nothing in its place is bad."

In a country where anything is possible if one only has the drive and the personal qualities to make it happen, everything should be in its place, for "this America is only you and me." This means that the possibilities for a fresh new American poetry are endless. Like the political compact behind democracy, the American poetic compact is with the individual, and not with any larger social movement or aesthetic. Clearly this justifies Whitman's own poetic work: "The whole theory of the universe is directed unerringly to one single individual—namely to You."

Whitman wishes to place some other conditions on the American poet, however. The twelfth section of "By Blue Ontario's Shore," in particular, sounds like a series of interview questions for the prospective American bard. Whitman is concerned not only with American poetry's fidelity to the individual but with its ability to compete in the arena of world literature. He charges the American poet with "the work of surpassing all [previous poets] have done." To do this the poet must avoid those things that have "been better told or done before." Above all the poet must create poetry of which no one can say that we have "imported this or the spirit of it in some ship." In other words, the poet must surpass but also leave behind previous models. One way to do this is by creating a new foundational epic, by adorning the individual, and the "days of the present," rather than glorifying the past. "Bards for own land only invoke," to take the raw materials of the new continent and make them into poetry.

"When Lilacs Last in the Dooryard Bloom'd"

Summary and Form

This 1865 poem is part of a series of pieces written after Lincoln's assassination. While it does not display all the conventions of the form, this is nevertheless considered to be a pastoral elegy: a poem of mourning that makes use of elaborate conventions drawn from the natural world and rustic human society. Virgil is the most prominent classical practitioner of the form; Milton's "Lycidas" and Shelley's "Adonais" are the two best-known examples in the English tradition. One of the most important features of the pastoral elegy is the depiction of the deceased and the poet who mourns him as shepherds. While the association is not specifically made in this poem, it must surely have been in Whitman's mind as he wrote: Lincoln, in many ways, was the "shepherd" of the American people during wartime, and his loss left the North in the position of a flock without a leader. As in traditional pastoral elegies, nature mourns Lincoln's death in this poem, although it does so in some rather unconventional ways. The poem also makes reference to the problems of modern times in its brief, shadowy depictions of Civil War battles. The natural order is contrasted with the human one, and Whitman goes so far as to suggest that those who have died violent deaths in war are actually the lucky ones, since they are now beyond suffering. Above all this is a public poem of private mourning. In it Whitman tries to determine the best way to mourn a public figure, and the best way to mourn in a modern world. In his resignation at the end of the poem, and in his use of disconnected motifs, he suggests that the kind of ceremonial poetry a pastoral elegy represents may no longer have a place in society; instead, symbolic, intensely personal forms must take over.

Commentary

"When Lilacs Last in the Dooryard Bloom'd" is composed of three separate yet simultaneous poems. One follows the progress of Lincoln's coffin on its way to the president's burial. The second stays with the poet and his sprig of lilac, meant to be laid on the coffin in tribute, as he ruminates on death and mourning. The third uses the symbols of a bird and a star to develop an idea of a nature sympathetic to yet separate from humanity. The progression of the coffin is followed by a sad irony. Mourners, dressed in black and holding offerings of flowers, turn out in the streets to see Lincoln's corpse pass by. The Civil War is raging, though, and many of these people have surely lost loved ones of their own.

Yet their losses are subsumed in a greater national tragedy, which in its publicness and in the fact that this poem is being written as part of the mourning process, is set up to be a far greater loss than that of their own family members. In this way the poem implicitly asks the question, "What is the worth of a man? Are some men worth more than others?" The poet's eventual inability to mourn, and the depictions of anonymous death on the battlefields, suggest that something is wrong here. The poet vacillates on the nature of symbolic mourning. At times he seems to see his offering of the lilac blossom as being symbolically given to all the dead; at other moments he sees it as futile, merely a broken twig.

He wonders how best to do honour to the dead, asking how he would decorate the tomb. He suggests that he would fill it with portraits of everyday life and everyday men. This is a far cry from the classical statuary and elaborate floral arrangements usually associated with tombs. The language in the poem follows a similar shift. In the first stanzas the language is formal and at times even archaic, filled with exhortations and rhetorical devices. By the end much of the ceremoniousness has been stripped away; the poet offers only "lilac and star and bird twined with the chant of soul." Eventually the poet simply leaves behind the sprig of lilac, and "cease from song," still unsure of just how to mourn properly. The final image of the poem is of "the fragrant pines and the cedars dusk and dim." All has been worked through save nature, which remains separate and beyond. The death-song of the bird expresses an understanding and a beauty that Whitman, even while he incorporates it into his poem, cannot quite master for himself. Unlike the pastoral elegies of old, which use a temporary rift with nature to comment on modernity, this one shows a profound and permanent disconnection between the human and natural worlds. "When Lilacs Last in the Dooryard Bloom'd" mourns for Lincoln in a way that is all the more profound for seeing the president's death as only a smaller, albeit highly symbolic, tragedy in the midst of a world of confusion and sadness.

"The Sleepers"

Summary and Form

"The Sleepers" is one of the poems from the 1855 first edition of Leaves of Grass. This is a simple poem, dedicated to exploring an idea of democratic empathy. Structurally this poem is composed of lists and anecdotes loosely arranged. The non-hierarchical nature of the poem reinforces the idea of democracy on which it is based: a list works through juxtaposition and random assemblage, not analysis or evaluation.

Commentary

This poem explores one of the major principles behind Whitman's poetry, that of empathy. Whitman makes the assertion here that he can identify so completely with another human being as to dream the same dreams they do. Through sleep, which acts as a leveler or democratizing force (much as death does in other places in Whitman's poetry), all consciousnesses become equally accessible and equally worthwhile. It is important to notice that while Whitman advocates a democratic equality here he does not wish to destroy the great diversity of persons and experiences: we are not all the same.

The type of empathy Whitman claims to be able to achieve extends so far as to allow him to incorporate others' anecdotes and past experiences into his own narrative. That things can be vicariously experienced is a powerful concept, for it enables the kind of democratic communion Whitman describes here. Furthermore, it makes possible a kind of understanding between old and young, whites and Indians, masters and slaves. This potential for sympathy can drive democracy still further. There is something highly erotic about this communion of souls, which comes through very strongly at certain points in this poem. Whitman focuses on a male lover here, and while certainly biographical evidence can account for this it should also be noted as a symbol of ultimate sympathy and communication. For Whitman, who believes that the body is an indispensable part of the soul, sex represents not just physical eroticism but also the highest form of emotional and intellectual discourse. Such intense communion is not endlessly sustainable, though, and thus Whitman differentiates between this state of poetry-making and the mundane daytime world. Unconsciousness—sleep—stands in for a kind of democratic utopia that is achievable only at ideal moments. In its highest form this is a state of possibility and flux that washes away the misunderstandings of the everyday and replaces them with, to quote Keats, "sleep and poetry."

I Sing the Body Electric"

Summary and Form

This is another of the poems from the original 1855 edition of Leaves of Grass. Whitman here explores the physical body at length. In other poems he has established the interconnectedness of the body and the soul; here he celebrates the primacy of the body and its importance in forging connections between people. This is yet another poem of lists, which again imply a democratizing force at work. Whitman's egalitarianism is a particularly important aspect of this poem, for it allows him to argue against the kind of valorization of the body implicit in slavery. The lists alternate with anecdotal and propositional sections, which allow Whitman to work out some of the issues surrounding the body. This makes "Body Electric" one of his more highly structured poems. Just as various organs and features come together in the greater structure of the human body, so too do the various bits and pieces of Whitman's poetry come together in a greater whole.

Commentary

Whitman prizes the body most for its generative qualities. This is most evident in the fifth and sixth sections of the poem, where he examines first the female and then the male body, praising both for their "sacred" status. The woman is much more strongly associated with reproduction: she is "the gates of the body, and... the gates of the soul." The man is more a figure of "action and power," although he too is associated with propagation. The small anecdote of the "common farmer" is an interesting case. The farmer is seen through the eyes of his children, who "love him." While the love of the children is not presented erotically, it shades into the erotic gaze of the poet, who longs to "sit by him... that and he might touch each other." The ability of this simple man to build a sort of family dynasty seems to be what attracts the poet.

Women are of course generative in the same literal sense in this poem. The eighth stanza opens with the image of " woman's body at auction": obviously a slave auction. Strangely the poet, in the previous stanza, has spoken of helping an auctioneer sell a male slave. The auctioneer "does not half know his business" and the poet helps him by cataloguing the wonders of the man's body. Both the male and the female slave are touted as the parents of multitudes. This makes them attractive as property: they can become essentially breeding stock for their masters. This kind of extreme valuation of the body would seem to be the extreme case of the kind of body-centrism Whitman advocates. In fact, though, it is the opposite. For Whitman, the body has primacy in its ability to generate experience, which can be compared metaphorically to the generation of children. The body can connect both erotically and spiritually with the bodies of others. In all this, the role of the body as the conduit between the soul and the world remains crucial. The slave auctions show a kind of debased, misguided worship of the physical. The final stanza of the poem gives a catalogue of body parts, both the poet's and others'. The parts listed have functions, of course, but they also provide the raw materials for poetry: "these are not the parts and poems of the body only, but of the soul." The body becomes sacred through its linkage with the soul; while it is only the soul's helper or accomplice, it nevertheless does not deserve second-rate status, for it enables not only spirituality but also poetry.

"Song of the Open Road"

Summary and Form

This poem was one of the twenty new poems in the 1856 edition of Leaves of Grass. Like "Crossing Brooklyn Ferry," which appeared at the same time, it celebrates a communion and a democracy based on place. Here Whitman sets up the out-of-doors as a utopian, democratic space, in which all men can come together. This poem shows more structure than many of Whitman's works. From the cry of "Allons!" that opens many of the stanzas, to the lists and repeated phrases (the "efflux of the soul," the "fluid and repeating character") this poem truly does have the character of a song: musical and rhythmic, while at the same time completely unconventional.

Commentary

In this poem Whitman celebrates the out-of-doors, and the road in particular, as a space where men can come together in a meaningful way, where status and social markers matter less. A road is something everyone uses, whether they are rich or poor, and it forces all levels of people to associate with one another. The road, furthermore, signifies mobility: one can take the road to somewhere new, and in America that means somewhere one can start over. For Whitman, too, the road is a space for gathering the material for poetry. As he travels along it, he sees a variety of people and places, and hears a plethora of stories. He argues against staying in one place for too long, although the hospitality may be a lure, for only the tests of the open road will do. By contrast, indoor spaces are fixed and so stultifying as to be almost toxic. "You must not stay sleeping and dallying there in the house," he commands. Indoors is a place of "secret silent loathing and despair," where death always lurks and people's bones are almost visible as signs of their mortality and innate debasement. True companionship is not possible in this indoor world, for people, bound by "customs," live too close together and knowledge of one another is a liability rather than a linkage of love.

This is a call to arms, an exhortation to those who are strong enough to join Whitman on the road. While for him the journey is the source of poetry, he sees it as something larger, as a way of life. The poetry is secondary. As he says, "I and mine do not convince by arguments, similes, rhymes,/We convince by our presence." What is at stake is therefore more fundamental and more universal than literature. The road is a symbol of a democratic and vital society that just happens to make for good poetry.

Chapter 8

Major Works

Walt Whitman (1819-1892), American poet, essayist, and journalist wrote numerous influential poems including "Song of Myself";

I celebrate myself, and sing myself,
And what I assume you shall assume,
For every atom belonging to me as good belongs to you...
I too am not a bit tamed, I too am untranslatable,
I harbor for good or bad, I permit to speak at every hazard,
Nature without check with original energy
and "I Sing the Body Electric";
I have perceiv'd that to be with those I like is enough,
To stop in company with the rest at evening is enough,
To be surrounded by beautiful, curious, breathing, laughing flesh is enough,

To pass among them, or touch any one, or rest my arm ever so lightly round his or her neck for a moment—what is this, then?

I do not ask any more delight—I swim in it, as in a sea.

There is something in staying close to men and women, and looking on them, and in the contact and odor of them, that pleases the soul well; All things please the soul—but these please the soul well.

First appearing in 1855 when he was thirty-six years of age, Leaves of Grass was Whitman's self-published collection of twelve poems that he would revise and add to many times during his life. Though at first it stirred little interest in the literary world, Ralph Waldo Emerson wrote of it as "the most extraordinary piece of wit and wisdom that America has yet produced". Whitman was an iconoclast, breaking new ground in abandoning rhyme and meter over the use of free verse, in opposition to the structured rigidity of the European poets of the time. Expressing his philosophy on such issues as democracy, war, politics, race, and slavery, some of his poems are patriotic; some of them celebrations of nature and homosexual love with vivid descriptions of the human form. He was quite confident that what he was doing was important though he caused much controversy; some of his works were banned for a time and he had many critics including D.H.

Lawrence and Oliver Wendell Holmes, but he also gained many admirers in North America and Europe including Lord Alfred Tennyson, Henry David Thoreau, Dante Gabriel Rossetti, Oscar Wilde, Pablo Neruda, William Carlos William, Arthur Rimbaud, Allan Ginsberg, Langston Hughes, June Jordan, and Jack Kerouac. Today Leaves of Grass has been translated to dozens of languages and is read widely the world over. Whitman would become an icon for socialists, communists, and homosexuals, though ultimately remains one of the most important literary figures to contribute to the Western Canon, even into the 21st century. Walt Whitman was born on 31 May, 1819 in West Hills, a village near Hempstead in Long Island, New York, in the newly formed United States, the son of Louisa van Velsor and Walter Whitman, farmer and carpenter. Walt had nine siblings and was very close to his mother and would remain so for the rest of his life whether living with her or through correspondence.

When the family moved to Brooklyn or "Mannahatta" as he would later call it, young Walt attended public school and loved taking the ferry, which became a theme in many of his later works as did his visits to his grandparents' farm on Long Island and its shores.

Others will see the islands large and small;
Fifty years hence, others will see them as they cross,
the sun half an hour high.

A hundred years hence, or ever so many hundred years hence, others will see them, will enjoy the sunset, the pouring-in of the flood-tide, the falling-back to the sea of the ebb-tide.

It avails not, time nor place—distance avails not, I am with you, you men and women of a generation, or ever so many generations hence, Just as you feel when you look on the river and sky, so I felt, Just as any of you is one of a living crowd, I was one of a crowd—"Crossing Brooklyn Ferry"

Largely self-taught, Whitman attended lectures and visited museums and libraries where he studied theatre, history and geography as well as the works of Sir Walter Scott, Thomas Carlyle, James Fenimore Cooper, William Shakespeare, Dante Alighieri, Johann Wolfgang von Goethe, Homer, and Emerson.

By the age of fourteen and living alone, (the rest of the family had moved back to West Hills) Whitman was working at his first job of many in the publishing industry at the newspaper Patriot, learning the trade and getting some of his articles printed. He then turned to teaching at Long Island schools after fires in New York City destroyed a number of publishing companies. He did not especially enjoy it and longed for the big city's sophisticated vibrancy and intellectual stimulation.

A million people—manners free and superb—open voices—hospitality—the most courageous and friendly young men; The free city! no slaves! no owners of slaves!

The beautiful city! the city of hurried and sparkling waters! the city of spires and masts!

The city nested in bays! my city!
The city of such women, I am mad to be with them!
I will return after death to be with them!
The city of such young men, I swear I cannot live happy, without I often go talk, walk, eat, drink, sleep, with them!—"Mannahatta"

It was a time of great change and opportunity in America and Whitman was soon back in New York attending the opera and writing. He was editor of his own paper The Long Islander between 1838 and 1839. He had been writing poems all along and perhaps from years of successful journalism he next decided to try his hand at fiction. His first short story published was "Death in the School Room". Between 1840 and 1845 he had numerous articles and stories published in newspapers and magazines including American Review and the Sunday Times on various topics such as the public school system and politics.

In 1846 Whitman became the editor for the Brooklyn Eagle, a position he held for three years. The same year he and his brother Jeff traveled to New Orleans, where Whitman came face to face with the inhumane treatment of slaves. He wrote a number of poems inspired by his travels to the south which marked a definite period of evolution in his philosophy and vision as poet.

A woman's Body at auction!
She too is not only herself—she is the teeming mother of mothers;
She is the bearer of them that shall grow and be mates to the mothers.—"I Sing the Body Electric"
Vast and starless, the pall of heaven
Laps on the trailing pall below;
And forward, forward, in solemn darkness,

As if to the sea of the lost we go.—"Sailing the Mississippi at Midnight" Times were changing but not without conflict. During the American Civil War (1861-1865) Whitman's own brother George was injured. Rushing to his bedside, Whitman soon became a nurse, compassionately assisting in the care and treatment of the multitudes of sick and wounded in Washington D.C. hospitals. He also helped them write letters home;

Open the envelope quickly,
O this is not our son's writing, yet his name is sign'd,
O a strange hand writes for our dear son, O stricken mother's soul! All swims before her eyes, flashes with black, she catches the main words only, Sentences broken, gunshot wound in the breast, cavalry skirmish, taken to hospital,

At present low, but will soon be better.—"Come Up from the Fields, Father" I sit by the restless all the dark night, some are so young, Some suffer so much, I recall the experience sweet and sad, (Many a soldier's loving arms about this neck have cross'd and rested, Many a soldier's kiss dwells on these bearded lips.)—"The Wound Dresser"

Profoundly affected by so much suffering and death, Whitman wrote many poems during this time included in Drum Taps. Louisa May Alcott had also been a devoted nurse and wrote her Hospital Sketches, while Whitman wrote Memoranda During the War, and a tribute to president Abraham Lincoln upon the news of his death; O Captain! my Captain! our fearful trip is done, The ship has weather'd every rack, the prize we sought is won,

The port is near, the bells I hear, the people all exulting,
While follow eyes the steady keel, the vessel grim and daring;
But O heart! heart! heart!
O the bleeding drops of red,
Where on the deck my Captain lies,
Fallen cold and dead.—"Oh Captain! My Captain!"

Whitman spent most of his free time and money caring for the sick; he was earning modest royalties from his writings and also earned a small income as a clerk in the Indian Bureau of the Department of the Interior. It is claimed that he was fired when the Secretary of the Interior, James Harlan, found out he was the author of Leaves of Grass. He then obtained a position as clerk in the Attorney General's office in Washington. Whitman's Democratic Vistas and Passage to India, celebrating achievements in engineering, were published in 1870. After suffering a stroke in 1873, he moved to Camden, New Jersey, living with his brother George and his family for a while before buying his own "little old shanty" on Mickle Street.

During the following years Whitman traveled to the West, though suffered increasing problems due to the stroke and failing health. He continued to socialize with his many friends and acquaintances in America and Europe, and set to the massive task of revising and expanding previous works and writing new ones including; Specimen Days and Collect; November Boughs, a collection of his journalistic essays, and Good-bye My Fancy.

Walt Whitman died on 26 March, 1892 in Camden, New Jersey and lies buried in the tomb he designed himself in Harleigh Cemetery, alongside many of his other family members. It is simply inscribed "WALT WHITMAN". There is now a famous portrait of him c1873, in profile, with flowing beard, wearing a hat and holding a butterfly made of cardboard inscribed under its wings with a poem by John Mason Neale.

Come, said my soul,
Such verses for my Body let us write, (for we are one,)
That should I after return,
Or, long, long hence, in other spheres,
There to some group of mates the chants resuming,
(Tallying Earth's soil, trees, winds, tumultuous waves,)
Ever with pleas'd smile I may keep on,

Ever and ever yet the verses owning—as, first, I here and now Signing for Soul and Body, set to them my name,—Walt Whitman, Preface to Leaves of Grass At the last, tenderly, From the walls of the powerful fortress'd house, From the clasp of the knitted locks, from the keep of the well-closed doors,

Let me be wafted.
Let me glide noiselessly forth;
With the key of softness unlock the locks—with a whisper,
Set ope the doors soul,- "The Last Invocation

1839: "Fame's Vanity." Long Island Democrat 23 October 1839: "My Departure." Long Island Democrat 27 November 1839: 2.

1840: "Young Grimes." Long Island Democrat 1 January 1840: "The Inca's Daughter." Long Island Democrat 5 May 1840: "The Love That is Hereafter." Long Island Democrat 19 May 1840: "We All Shall Rest At Last." Long Island Democrat 14 July 1840: "The Spanish Lady." Long Island Democrat 4 August 1840: 2.

"The End of All." Long Island Democrat 22 September 1840: "The Columbian's Song." Long Island Democrat 27 October 1840: 1841

"The Winding-Up." Long Island Democrat 22 June 1841:

"Each Has His Grief." The New World 3 (20 November 1841): [321]. Revised from "We All Shall

Rest at Last" in the Long Island Democrat, 14 July 1840. "The Punishment of Pride." The New World 3 (18 December 1841): 394.

1842: "Ambition." Brother Jonathan 1 (29 January 1842): An earlier version of this poem entitled "Fame's Vanity" appeared in the Long Island Democrat, 27 November 1839.

"No Turning Back." Sunday Times 14 August 1842: .

"A Sketch." The New World (10 December 1842): 374.

1843

"Death of the Nature-Lover." Brother Jonathan 4 (11 March 1843): 290. An earlier version of this poem entitled "My Departure" appeared in the Long Island Democrat, 23 October 1839.

1844: "Tale of a Shirt: A Very Pathetic Ballad." Sunday Times and Noah's Weekly Messenger 31 March 1844:

1846: "The Play-Ground." Brooklyn Daily Eagle 1 June 1846: "Ode: To be Sung on Fort Greene." The Brooklyn Daily Eagle 2 July 1846: .

1848: "The Mississippi at Midnight." New Olreans Daily Crescent 6 March 1848: . Revised as "Sailing the Mississippi at Midnight," Specimen Days and Collect (1882–83).

1850: "Song for Certain Congressmen." New York Evening Post 2 March 1850: . Revised as "Dough-Face Song" in Specimen Days and Collect (1882–83).

"Blood-Money." New York Daily Tribune, Supplement. 22 March 1850: 1. Reprinted in the New York Evening Post (30 April 1850) and in Specimen Days. "Resurgemus." New York Daily Tribune 21 June 1850: 3. Partially reprinted in "Art and Artists" in Brooklyn Daily Advertiser (3 April 1851); revised as ["Suddenly out of its stale and drowsy lair"] in Leaves of Grass; reprinted as "Poem of the Dead Young Men of Europe, the 72nd and 73rd Years of These States," in Leaves of Grass; and as "Europe, The 72nd and 73rd Years of These States," in Leaves of Grass (1881–82).

1859: "A Child's Reminiscence." New-York Saturday Press 24 December 1859: 1. This poem later appeared as "A Word Out of the Sea," Leaves of Grass; as "Out of the Cradle Endlessly Rocking," in "Sea-Shore Memories," Passage to India; and finally in "Sea Drift," Leaves of Grass (1881–82).

1860: "You and Me and To-Day." New-York Saturday Press 14 January 1860: 2. This poem later appeared as "Chants Democratic 7," Leaves of Grass and as "With Antecedents," Leaves of Grass. "Poemet [Of him I love day and night]." New-York Saturday Press 28 January 1860: 2. This poem later appeared as "Calamus No. 17," Leaves of Grass; as "Of Him I Love Day and Night," Leaves of Grass; and, with slight changes in the text, in "Passage to India," Leaves of Grass (1871-72).

"Poemet [That shadow, my likeness]." New-York Saturday Press 4 February 1860: 2. This poem later appeared as "Calamus No. 40," Leaves of Grass; as "That Shadow My Likeness," Leaves of Grass; and, with slight changes in the text, in Leaves of Grass (1881–82).

"Leaves." New-York Saturday Press 11 February 1860: 2. The three poems printed under the title of "Leaves" were numbered "1," "2," and "3" but not otherwise individually titled for their publication in the Saturday Press. They later appeared separately as (in order of appearance):

"Calamus No. 21," Leaves of Grass; Reprinted as "That Music Always Round Me," Leaves of Grass and in "Whispers of Heavenly Death," Leaves of Grass (1871-72).

"Calamus No. 37," Leaves of Grass; Reprinted as "A Leaf for Hand in Hand," Leaves of Grass.

"Enfans d'Adam No. 15," Leaves of Grass; Reprinted as "As Adam Early in the Morning," Leaves of Grass.

"Bardic Symbols." Atlantic Monthly 5 (April 1860): 445-447. Revised as "Leaves of Grass. 1" in Leaves of

Grass and reprinted as "Elemental Drifts," Leaves of Grass. The final version of the poem, "As I Ebb'd With the Ocean of Life," was published in Leaves of Grass (1881–82).

"The Errand-Bearers." The New-York Times 27 June 1860: 2. Revised as "A Broadway Pageant (Reception Japanese Embassy, June 16, 1860)" in Drum-Taps and reprinted in Leaves of Grass (1881–82).

1861: "Beat! Beat! Drums!" Harper's Weekly 5 (28 September 1861): 623. Although dated 28 September 1861, the issue of Harper's Weekly featuring Whitman's "Beat! Beat! Drums!" actually appeared one week earlier, on 21 September 1861. (See Sculley Bradley and Harold W. Blodgett, ed., Leaves of Grass: A Norton Critical Edition [New York: W. W. Norton, 1973] and Ted Genoways, Walt Whitman and the Civil War: America's Poet During the Lost Years of 1860–1862 [Berkeley: University of California Press, forthcoming].) The poem appeared on the same day in the weekly newspaper the New York Leader, also dated 28 September 1861. The poem was reprinted in the Brooklyn Daily Eagle on 23 September 1861 and the Boston Daily Evening Transcript on 24 September 1861. The Brooklyn Daily Eagle printing includes the attribution, "From Harper's Weekly." In the following weeks, the poem appeared in numerous other newspapers throughout the United States. Whitman included the poem, with slight revision, in Drum-Taps.

"Little Bells Last Night." New York Leader 12 October 1861: . Revised as "I Heard You Solemn Sweet Pipes of the Organ" in Sequel to Drum-Taps (1865–66).

"Old Ireland." New York Leader 2 November 1861: . Reprinted with some revisions in Drum-Taps.

1865: "O Captain! My Captain!" New-York Saturday Press 4 November 1865: 218. This poem was reprinted in Sequel to Drum-Taps; with revision in Passage to

India (1871, 1876); and finally in "Drum-Taps," Leaves of Grass (1881–82).

1867: "A Carol of Harvest, for 1867." Galaxy 4 (September 1867): 605-609. Reprinted in Tinsley's Magazine in October 1867. Whitman revised the poem for Passage to India. After some further revision, the poem appeared as "The Return of the Heroes" in Leaves of Grass (1881–82).

1868: "Whispers of Heavenly Death." The Broadway, A London Magazine 10 (October 1868): 21-22. "Whispers of Heavenly Death" was the title given to a collection of five numbered poems first published in Broadway. When reprinted as part of a larger cluster in Passage to India, the poems were retitled "Whispers of Heavenly Death," "Darest Thou Now O Soul," "A Noiseless Patient Spider," "The Last Invocation," and "Pensive and Faltering."

1869: "Proud Music of the Sea-Storm." Atlantic Monthly 23 (February 1869): 199-203. This poem was slightly revised and reprinted as "Proud Music of the Storm" in Passage to India, Two Rivulets, and in Leaves of Grass (1881–82).

"The Singer in the Prison." Saturday Evening Visitor 25 December 1869: . Reprinted in Passage to India.

1870: "Brother of All, With Generous Hand." Galaxy 9 (January 1870): 75-76. Reprinted in Passage to India, in the group "Passage to India" of Leaves of Grass and Two Rivulets, and, after some revision, under the new title "Outlines for a Tomb" in Leaves of Grass (1881–82).

"Warble for Lilac-Time." Galaxy 9 (May 1870): 686. Whitman revised the poem for reprinting in Passage to India, in the New York Daily Grahpic (12 May 1873), in the group "Passage to India" of Leaves of Grass and Two Rivulets, and in its present form in Leaves of Grass (1881–82).

1871: "O Star of France!" Galaxy 11 (June 1871): 817. Collected in As a Strong Bird on Pinions Free and

Other Poems, reprinted in Two Rivulets, and, after some revision, in Leaves of Grass (1881–82).

"After All, Not to Create Only." New York Commercial Advertiser 7 September 1871: . This poem was published on the same day in the New York Evening Post, p. 2. It was reprinted in several newspapers and as a pamphlet, After All, Not to Create Only; as "Song of the Exposition" in Two Rivulets; and with some revisions in Leaves of Grass (1881–82).

"After All, Not to Create Only." New York Evening Post 7 September 1871: . This poem was printed on the same day in the New York Commercial Advertiser 7 September 1871: . It was reprinted in several newspapers and as a pamphlet, After All, Not to Create Only; as "Song of the Exposition" in Two Rivulets; and with some revisions in Leaves of Grass (1881–82).

1872: "The Mystic Trumpeter." Kansas Magazine 1 (February 1872): 113-114. Reprinted in the Washington Daily Morning Chronicle, 7 February 1872; in translation by Csukássy Józset, Fõvárosi Lapok (Budapest), 19 January 1873, p. [61]; and in As a Strong Bird on Pinions Free.

"Virginia—The West." Kansas Magazine 1 (March 1872): 219. Reprinted in As A Strong Bird on Pinions Free.

"As a Strong Bird on Pinions Free." New York Herald 26 June 1872: 3. This poem was later published with seven other poems in a pamphlet, As a Strong Bird on Pinions Free. It was later included as a supplement bound with Two Rivulets. Later, Whitman changed the title to "Thou Mother with Thy Equal Brood," added a new opening stanza, and additional revisions, and incorporated the poem into Leaves of Grass (1881-82).

1873: "Nay, Tell Me Not To-day the Publish'd Shame." New York Daily Graphic 5 March 1873: 2. Reprinted in Conservator 7 (October 1896): 121-122; Leaves of Grass. "With All the Gifts, America." New York Daily Graphic 6 March 1873: 2. Reprinted in Two Rivulets. "The Singing Thrush." New York Daily Graphic 15 March 1873: 2. Reprinted as "Wandering at Morn" in Two Rivulets.

"Spain." New York Daily Graphic 24 March 1873: 2. Reprinted as "Spain, 1873-74" in Two Rivulets.

"Sea Captains, Young or Old." New York Daily Graphic 4 April 1873: 2. Reprinted as "Song for All Seas, All Ships" in Two Rivulets.

1874: "Song of the Redwood-Tree." Harper's Monthly Magazine 48 (February 1874): 366-367. Reprinted in the "Centennial Songs" section of Two Rivulets.

"Prayer of Columbus." Harper's Monthly Magazine 48 (March 1874): 524-525. Reprinted in the "Two Rivulets" section of Two Rivulets.

"A Kiss to the Bride." New York Daily Graphic 21 May 1874: 608. Reprinted in Leaves of Grass.

"Song of the Universal." New York Daily Graphic 17 June 1874: 818. This poem was printed on the same day in the New York Evening Post, 17 June 1874. Reprinted in New York World, 19 June 1874; Camden New Republic, 20 June 1874; and in Two Rivulets.

"The Song of the Universal." The New York Evening Post 17 June 1874: . This poem was printed on the same day in the New York Daily Graphic, 17 June 1874. Reprinted in New York World, 19 June 1874; Camden New Republic, 20 June 1874; and in Two Rivulets.

"An Old Man's Thought of School." New York Daily Graphic 3 November 1874: 11. Reprinted in Two Rivulets.

1876: "Or From that Sea of Time." New York Daily Tribune 19 February 1876: 4. This poem appeared in the Daily Tribune as part of a prepublication review of Two Rivulets and Leaves of Grass. It was reprinted in the "Two Rivulets" section of Two Rivulets.

"Eidólons." New York Daily Tribune 19 February 1876: 4. This poem appeared in the Daily Tribune as part of a prepublication review of Two Rivulets and Leaves of Grass. It was reprinted in the "Two Rivulets" section of Two Rivulets.

"Out from Behind This Mask." New York Daily Tribune 19 February 1876: 4. This poem appeared in the Daily Tribune as part of a prepublication review of Two Rivulets and Leaves of Grass. It was reprinted as "Out from Behind This Mask: To confront My Portrait, illustrating 'the Wound-Dresser,' in Leaves of Grass" in the "Two Rivulets" section of Two Rivulets.

"To a Locomotive in Winter." New York Daily Tribune 19 February 1876: 4. This poem appeared in the Daily Tribune as part of a prepublication review of Two Rivulets and Leaves of Grass. It was reprinted in the "Two Rivulets" section of Two Rivulets.

"Come, said my Soul." New York Daily Tribune 19 February 1876: 4. This poem appeared in the Daily Tribune as part of a prepublication review of Two Rivulets and Leaves of Grass. According to the Comprehensive Reader's Edition of Leaves of Grass, it appeared first in the New York Daily Graphic on 25 December 1874, though at this time we have not been able to verify this information. The poem was reprinted on the title page of Leaves of Grass.

"After an Interval." New York Daily Tribune 19 February 1876: 4. This poem appeared in the Daily Tribune as part of a prepublication review of Two Rivulets and Leaves of Grass. It was reprinted in Leaves of Grass.

"When the Full-Grown Poet Came." New York Daily Tribune 19 February 1876: 4. This poem appeared in the Daily Tribune as part of a prepublication review of Two Rivulets and Leaves of Grass. It was reprinted in Leaves of Grass.

"The Beauty of the Ship." New York Daily Tribune

19 February 1876: 4. This poem appeared in the Daily Tribune as part of a prepublication review of Two Rivulets and Leaves of Grass. It was reprinted in Leaves of Grass.

"A Song by the Potomac." New York Daily Tribune 19 February 1876: 4. This poem appeared in the Daily Tribune as part of a prepublication review of Two Rivulets and Leaves of Grass. It appeared previously under the title "By Broad Potomac's Shore" in As a Strong Bird on Pinions Free and was reprinted in Two Rivulets and Leaves of Grass (1881–82).

"Ship of Democracy." New York Daily Tribune 19 February 1876: 4. This poem appeared in the Daily Tribune as part of a prepublication review of Two Rivulets and Leaves of Grass. This appearance is the first instance of the poem under the title "Ship of Democracy," but it appeared earlier as section three of the poem "As a Strong Bird on Pinions Free" in the volume As a Strong Bird on Pinions Free.

"A Death-Sonnet for Custer." New York Daily Tribune (10 July 1876): 5. Reprinted as "From Far Dakotas Cañon," Leaves of Grass (1881–82).

1879: "What Best I See in Thee." The Philadelphia Press 17 December 1879: 8. Reprinted in Leaves of Grass (1881–82).

1880: The Dalliance of the Eagles." Cope's Tobacco Plant (November 1880): 552. Revised slightly for inclusion in "By the Roadside," Leaves of Grass (1881–82).

1881: "Patrolling Barnegat." Harper's Monthly Magazine 62 (April 1881): 701. Reprinted in the American (May 1881) and Leaves of Grass (1881–82).

"A Summer Invocation." The American 2 (14 June 1881): 120. Reprinted as "Thou Orb Aloft Full-Dazzling" in Leaves of Grass (1881–82).

"The Sobbing of the Bells." The Boston Weekly Globe (27 September 1881): . Reprinted as "The Sobbing of the Bells. (Midnight, Sept. 19-20, 1881)" in Leaves of Grass (1881–82).

1884: "With Husky-Haughty Lips, O Sea!" Harper's Monthly Magazine 68 (March 1884): 607. Reprinted in the "Sands at Seventy" annex to Leaves of Grass.

"Red Jacket (From Aloft)." The Philadelphia Press 10 October 1884. Reprinted in the "Sands at Seventy" annex to Leaves of Grass.

"If I Should Need to Name, O Western World" Philadelphia Press 26 October 1884: 5. Reprinted as "Election Day, November, 1884" in the "Sands at Seventy" annex to Leaves of Grass.

"The Dead Tenor." Critic 5 (8 November 1884): 222. Reprinted in the "Sands at Seventy" annex to Leaves of Grass.

1885: "Of That Blithe Throat of Thine." Harper's Monthly Magazine 70 (January 1885): 264. Reprinted in the "Sands at Seventy" annex to Leaves of Grass.

"Ah, Not This Granite Dead and Cold." The Philadelphia Press 22 February 1885. Reprinted as "Washington's Monument, February, 1885" in the "Sands at Seventy" annex to Leaves of Grass.

"As One by One Withdraw the Lofty Actors." Harper's Weekly 4 (16 May 1885): 310. Reprinted as "Grant" in Critic 7 (15 August 1885): 80; and revised as "Death of General Grant" in the "Sands at Seventy" annex to Leaves of Grass.

"The Voice of the Rain." Outing 6 (August 1885): 570. Reprinted in the "Sands at Seventy" annex to Leaves of Grass.

"Fancies at Navesink." The Nineteenth Century 18 (August 1885): 234-237. The eight poems, "The Pilot in the mist," "Had I the choice," "You Tides with ceaseless sell," " Last of Ebb, and Daylight waning," "[And yet not you alone]," "Proudly the Flood comes in," "By that long scan of Waves," and "Then last of all," were reprinted in "Sands at Seventy," Leaves of Grass. In the Nineteenth Century printing, "And Yet Not You Alone" appears at the top of page 236 without a title.

1886: "The Man-of-War Bird." The Athenaeum 2527 (April 1876): 463. Reprinted as "Thou Who Hast Slept All Night Upon the Storm" in Progress (Philadelphia), 16 November 1878 and as "To the Man-of-War-Bird" in Leaves of Grass (1881–82).

1887: "Shakespeare Bacon's Cipher." The Cosmopolitan 4 (October 1887): 142. Reprinted in Good-Bye My Fancy under the title "Shakspere-Bacon's Cipher."

"November Boughs." Lippincott's Magazine 40 (November 1887): 722-723. "November Boughs" was the title given to a collection of four poems first published in Lippincott's Magazine and reprinted in the "Sands at Seventy" annex to Leaves of Grass: "You Lingering Sparse Leaves of Me," "Going Somewhere," "After the Supper and Talk," and "Not Meagre, Latent Boughs Alone."

"Yonnondio." Critic 11. (26 November 1887): 267 Reprinted in the "Sands at Seventy" annex to Leaves of Grass. "As the Greeks Signal Flame." New York Herald 15 December 1887: 3. Reprinted in the Boston Daily Advertiser (17 December 1887); Munyon's Illustrated World (January 1888); and then in the "Sands at Seventy" annex to Leaves of Grass.

"Twilight." Century Illustrated Monthly Magazine 37 (December 1887): 264. Reprinted in the "Sands at Seventy" annex to Leaves of Grass.

1888: "To Those Who've Fail'd." New York Herald 27 January 1888: 6. Reprinted in the "Sands at Seventy" annex to Leaves of Grass.

"Halcyon Days." New York Herald 29 January 1888: 12. Reprinted in the "Sands at Seventy Annex" to Leaves of Grass.

"After the Dazzle of Day." New York Herald 3 February 1888: 4. Reprinted in the "Sands at Seventy" annex to Leaves of Grass.

"America." New York Herald 11 February 1888: 4. Reprinted in the "Sands at Seventy" annex to Leaves of Grass.

"Abraham Lincoln (Born Feb. 12, 1809)." New York Herald 12 February 1888: 12. Reprinted in the "Sands at Seventy" annex to Leaves of Grass.

"True Conquerors." New York Herald 15 February 1888: 6. Reprinted in the "Sands at Seventy" annex to Leaves of Grass.

"Soon Shall the Winter's Foil Be Here." New York Herald 21 February 1888: 6. Reprinted in the "Sands at Seventy" annex to Leaves of Grass.

"The Dismantled Ship." New York Herald 23 February 1888: 4. Reprinted in the "Sands at Seventy" annex to Leaves of Grass.

"Old Salt Kossabone." New York Herald. 25 February 1888: 6. Reprinted in the "Sands at Seventy" annex to Leaves of Grass.

"Mannahatta." New York Herald 27 February 1888: 4. Reprinted in the "Sands at Seventy" annex to Leaves of Grass.

"Paumanok." New York Herald 29 February 1888: 6. Reprinted in the "Sands at Seventy" annex to Leaves of Grass. "From Montauk Point." New York Herald 1 March 1888: 6. Reprinted in the "Sands at Seventy" annex to Leaves of Grass.

"My Canary Bird." New York Herald 2 March 1888: 6. Reprinted in the "Sands at Seventy" annex to Leaves of Grass.

"A Prairie Sunset." New York Herald 9 March 1888: 6. Reprinted in the "Sands at Seventy" annex to Leaves of Grass.

"The Dead Emperor." New York Herald 10 March 1888: 6. Reprinted in the "Sands at Seventy" annex to Leaves of Grass.

"The First Dandelion." New York Herald 12 March 1888: 4. Reprinted in the "Sands at Seventy" annex to Leaves of Grass.

"The Wallabout Martyrs." New York Herald 16 March 1888: 4. Reprinted in the "Sands at Seventy" annex to Leaves of Grass.

"The Bravest Soldiers." New York Herald 18 March 1888: 14. Reprinted in the "Sands at Seventy" annex to Leaves of Grass.
"Orange Buds by Mail from Florida." New York Herald 19 March 1888: 4. Reprinted in the "Sands at Seventy" annex to Leaves of Grass.
"Continuities." New York Herald 20 March 1888: 6. Reprinted in the "Sands at Seventy" annex to Leaves of Grass.
"Broadway." New York Herald 10 April 1888: 6. Reprinted in the "Sands at Seventy" annex to Leaves of Grass.
"Life." New York Herald 15 April 1888: 16. Reprinted in the "Sands at Seventy" annex to Leaves of Grass.
"The Final Lilt of Songs." New York Herald 16 April 1888: 4. Reprinted as "To Get the Final Lilt of Songs" in the "Sands at Seventy" annex to Leaves of Grass.
"To-day and Thee." New York Herald 23 April 1888: 6. Reprinted in the "Sands at Seventy" annex to Leaves of Grass.
"Queries to My Seventieth Year." New York Herald 2 May 1888: 6. Reprinted in the "Sands at Seventy" annex to Leaves of Grass.
"The United States to Old World Critics." New York Herald 8 May 1888: 6. Reprinted in the "Sands at Seventy" annex to Leaves of Grass.
"Out of May's Shows Selected." New York Herald 10 May 1888: 6. Reprinted in the "Sands at Seventy" annex to Leaves of Grass.
"As I Sit Writing Here." New York Herald 14 May 1888: 4. Reprinted in the "Sands at Seventy" annex to Leaves of Grass.
"A Carol Closing Sixty-Nine." New York Herald 21 May 1888: 4. Reprinted in the "Sands at Seventy" annex to Leaves of Grass.
"Life and Death." New York Herald 23 May 1888: 6. Reprinted in the "Sands at Seventy" annex to Leaves of Grass.

"The Calming Thought of All." New York Herald 27 May 1888: 12. Reprinted in the "Sands at Seventy" annex to Leaves of Grass.

"Twenty Years." The Magazine of Art August 1888: [348].

"[Over and through the burial chant]." New York Herald 12 August 1888: 7. Reprinted as "Interpolation Sounds" in Good-Bye My Fancy.

"Old Age's Lambent Peaks." Century Illustrated Monthly Magazine 38 (September 1888): 735. Reprinted in the "Sands at Seventy" annex to Leaves of Grass.

1889: "To the Year 1889." Critic 14 (5 January 1889): 7. Reprinted under the new title "To the Pending Year" in Good-Bye My Fancy.

"A Voice from Death." New York World 7 June 1889. Reprinted in Good-Bye My Fancy.

"Bravo, Paris Exposition!" Harper's Weekly 33 28 September 1889: 774. Reprinted in Good-Bye My Fancy. "My 71st Year." Century Illustrated Monthly Magazine 39 (November 1889): 31. Reprinted in Good-Bye My Fancy.

1890: "Old Age's Ship and Crafty Death's." Century Illustrated Monthly Magazine 40 (February 1890). 553. Reprinted in Good-Bye My Fancy.

"A Twilight Song." Century Illustrated Monthly Magazine 40 (May 1890): 27 Published with the subtitle "For unknown buried soldiers, North and South." Revised and reprinted in Good-Bye My Fancy.

"For Queen Victoria's Birthday." Philadelphia Public Ledger 24 May 1890: 9. This poem was reprinted in the Critic, 16 (24 May 1890), 262 and in four London periodicals. It was included without the note in Good-Bye My Fancy.

"To the Sunset Breeze." Lippincott's Magazine 46 (December 1890): 861. Reprinted in Good-Bye My Fancy.

1891: "The Pallid Wreath." Critic 18 (10 January 1891): 18. Reprinted in Good-Bye My Fancy.

"Old-Age Echoes." Lippincott's Magazine 47 (March 1891): 376. "Old Age Echoes" was the title given to a collection of four poems first published in Lippincott's Magazine and reprinted in Good-Bye My Fancy: "Sounds of the Winter," "The Unexpress'd," "Sail Out for Good, Eidólon Yacht," and "After the Argument."

"The Commonplace." Munyon's Magazine 7.2 (March 1891). Reprinted in Good-bye My Fancy.

"Ship Ahoy!" Youth's Companion (12 March 1891): 152. Reprinted in Good-bye My Fancy.

"Old Chants." Truth (19 March 1891). Reprinted in Good-Bye My Fancy.

1892: "Death's Valley." Harper's Monthly Magazine 84 (April 1892): 707-709. Reprinted in Leaves of Grass.

"A Thought of Columbus." Once A Week (2 July 1892): 4.

Chapter 9

Complete Text of Selected Works of Waltman

Leaves of Grass

Come, said my soul,
Such verses for my Body let us write,
That should I after return,
Or, long, long hence, in other spheres,
There to some group of mates the chants resuming,
(Tallying Earth's soil, trees, winds, tumultuous waves,)
Ever with pleas'd smile I may keep on,
Ever and ever yet the verses owning—as, first, I here and now
Signing for Soul and Body, set to them my name,
Walt Whitman

O Captain! my Captain!

O Captain! my Captain! our fearful trip is done;
The ship has weather'd every rack, the prize we sought is won;
The port is near, the bells I hear, the people all exulting,
While follow eyes the steady keel, the vessel grim and daring:
But O heart! heart! heart!
O the bleeding drops of red,
Where on the deck my Captain lies,
Fallen cold and dead.
O Captain! my Captain! rise up and hear the bells;
Rise up‹for you the flag is flung‹for you the bugle trills;
For you bouquets and ribbon'd wreaths‹for you the

shores a-crowding; For you they call, the swaying mass, their eager faces turning;

Here Captain! dear father!
This arm beneath your head;
It is some dream that on the deck,
You've fallen cold and dead.

My Captain does not answer, his lips are pale and still;
My father does not feel my arm, he has no pulse nor will;
The ship is anchor'd safe and sound, its voyage closed and done; From fearful trip, the victor ship, comes in with object won;

Exult, O shores, and ring, O bells!
But I, with mournful tread,
Walk the deck my Captain lies,
Fallen cold and dead.

O Me! O life!

O ME! O life!... of the questions of these recurring;

Of the endless trains of the faithless‹of cities fill'd with the foolish; Of myself forever reproaching myself, (for who more foolish than I, and who more faithless?) Of eyes that vainly crave the light‹of the objects mean‹of the struggle ever renew'd; Of the poor results of all‹of the plodding and sordid crowds I see around me; Of the empty and useless years of the rest‹with the rest me intertwined; The question, O me! so sad, recurring‹What good amid these, O me, O life?

Answer

That you are here‹that life exists, and identity;
That the powerful play goes on, and you will contribute a verse.

I Celebrate Myself, and Sing Myself

I celebrate myself, and sing myself,
And what I assume you shall assume,
For every atom belonging to me as good belongs to you.
I loaf and invite my soul,

I lean and loaf at my ease observing a spear of summer grass. My tongue, every atom of my blood, formed from this

soil, this air, Born here of parents born here from parents the same, and their parents the same,
I, now thirty-seven years old in perfect health begin,
Hoping to cease not till death.
Creeds and schools in abeyance,
Retiring back awhile sufficed at what they are, but never forgotten,
I harbor for good or bad, I permit to speak at every hazard,
Nature without check with original energy.

Houses and Rooms are Full of Perfumes, the Shelves are Crowded with Perfumes,

Houses and rooms are full of perfumes, the shelves are crowded with perfumes,
I breathe the fragrance myself and know it and like it,
The distillation would intoxicate me also, but I shall not let it.
The atmosphere is not a perfume, it has no taste of the distillation, it is odorless,
It is for my mouth forever, I am in love with it,
I will go to the bank by the wood and become undisguised and naked,
I am mad for it to be in contact with me.
The smoke of my own breath,
Echoes, ripples, buzzed whispers, love root, silk thread, crotch and vine,
My respiration and inspiration, the beating of my heart, the passing of blood and air through my lungs,
The sniff of green leaves and dry leaves, and of the shore and dark-colored sea rocks, and of hay in the barn,
The sound of the belched words of my voice loosed to the eddies of the wind,
A few light kisses, a few embraces, a reaching around of arms,
The play of shine and shade on the trees as the supple boughs wag,
The delight alone or in the rush of the streets, or along the fields and hillsides,

The feeling of health, the full-noon trill, the song of me rising from bed and meeting the sun.

Have you reckoned a thousand acres much? have you reckoned the earth much?

Have you practiced so long to learn to read?

Have you felt so proud to get at the meaning of poems?

Stop this day and night with me and you shall possess the origin of all poems,

You shall posses the good of the earth and sun (there are millions of suns left),

You shall no longer take things at second or third hand, nor look through the eyes of the dead, nor feed on the specters in books,

You shall not look through my eyes either, nor take things from me,

You shall listen to all sides and filter them from yourself.

I have Heard what the Talkers were Talking, the Talk of the Beginning and the End

I have heard what the talkers were talking, the talk of the beginning and the end,

But I do not talk of the beginning or the end.

There was never any more inception than there is now,

Nor any more youth or age than there is now,

And will never be any more perfection than there is now,

Nor any more heaven or hell than there is now.

Urge and urge and urge,

Always the procreant urge of the world.

Out of the dimness opposite equals advance, always substance and increase, always sex,

Always a knit of identity, always distinction, always a breed of life.

To elaborate is no avail, learned and unlearned feel that it is so.

Sure as the most certain sure, plumb in the uprights, well entreatied, braced in the beams,

Stout as a horse, affectionate, haughty, electrical, I and this mystery here we stand. Clear and sweet is my soul, and clear and sweet is all that is not my soul. Lack one lacks both, and the unseen is proved by the seen,

That that becomes unseen and receives proof in its turn.

Showing the best and dividing it from the worst age vexes age,

Knowing the perfect fitness and equanimity of things, while they discuss I am silent, and go bathe and admire myself.

Welcome is every organ and attribute of me, and of any man hearty and clean,

Not an inch nor a particle of an inch is vile, and none shall be less familiar than the rest.

I am satisfied — I see, dance, laugh, sing;

As the hugging and loving bedfellow sleeps at my side through the night, and withdraws at the peep of the day with stealthy tread,

Leaving me baskets covered with white towels swelling the house with their plenty,

Shall I postpone my acceptation and realization and scream at my eyes,

That they turn from gazing after and down the road,

And forthwith cipher and show me to a cent,

Exactly the value of one and exactly the value of two, and which is ahead?

Trippers and Askers Surround Me,

Trippers and askers surround me, People I meet, the effect upon me of my early life or the ward and city I live in, or the nation, The latest dates, discoveries, inventions, societies, authors old and new, My dinner, dress, associates, looks, compliments, dues, The real or fancied indifference of some man or woman I love, The sickness of one of my folks or of myself, or ill-doing or loss or lack of money, or depressions or exaltations, Battles, the horrors of fratricidal war, the fever of doubtful news, the fitful events; These come to me days and nights and go from me again, But they are not the Me myself. Apart from the pulling and hauling stands what I am,

Stands amused, complacent, compassionating, idle, unitary, Looks down, is erect, or bends an arm on an impalpable certain rest, Looking with side-curved head curious what will come next, Both in and out of the game and watching and wondering at it. Backward I see in my own days where I sweated through fog with linguists and contenders, I have no mockings or arguments, I witness and wait.

I Believe in you my soul, the other I am Must not Abase Itself to you,

I believe in you my soul, the other I am must not abase itself to you, And you must not be abased to the other. Loaf with me on the grass, loose the stop from your throat, Not words, not music or rhyme I want, not custom or lecture, not even the best, Only the lull I like, the hum of your valved voice. I mind how once we lay such a transparent summer morning, How you settled your head athwart my hips, and gently turned over upon me, And parted the shirt from my bosom bone, and plunged your tongue to my bare-stripped heart, And reached till you felt my beard, and reached till you held my feet. Swiftly arose and spread around me the peace and knowledge that pass all the argument of the earth, And I know that the hand of God is the promise of my own, And I know that the spirit of God is the brother of my own,

And that all the men ever born are also my brothers,
And the women my sisters and lovers,
And that a kelson of the creation is love,
And limitless are leaves stiff or drooping in the fields,
And brown ants in the little wells beneath them,
And mossy scabs of the worm fence, heaped stones, elder, mullein and pokeweed.

A Child Said What is the Grass? Fetching it to me with Full hands,

Song of Myself, by Walt Whitman: A child said What is the grass? fetching it to me with full hands, How could I answer the child? I do not know what it is any more than he. I guess it must be the flag of my disposition, out of hopeful green stuff woven. Or I guess it is the handkerchief of the Lord,

A scented gift and remembrancer designedly dropped,

Bearing the owner's name someway in the corners, that we may see and remark, and say Whose? Or I guess the grass is itself a child, the produced babe of the vegetation.

Or I guess it is a uniform hieroglyphic, And it means, Sprouting alike in broad zones and narrow zones, Growing among black folks as among white, Canuck, Tuckahoe, Congressman, Cuff, I give them the same, I receive them the same.

And now it seems to me the beautiful uncut hair of graves.

Tenderly will I use you curling grass,

It may be you transpire from the breasts of you men,

It may be if I had known them I would have loved them,

It may be you are from old people, or from offspring taken soon out of their mothers' laps, And here you are the mothers' laps. This grass is very dark to be from the white heads of old mothers,

Darker than the colorless beards of old men,

Dark to come from under the faint red roof of mouths.

O I perceive after all so many uttering tongues,

And I perceive they do not come from the roofs of mouths for nothing. I wish I could translate the hints about the dead young men and women, And the hints about old men and mothers, and the offspring taken soon out of their laps. What do you think has become of the young and old men? And what do you think has become of the women and children? They are alive and well somewhere, The smallest sprout shows there is really no death, And if ever there was it led forward life, and does not wait at the end to arrest it, And ceased the moment life appeared. All goes onward and outward, nothing collapses, And to die is different from what anyone supposed, and luckier.

Has Anyone Supposed it Lucky to be Born?

Has anyone supposed it lucky to be born?

I hasten to inform him or her it is just as lucky to die, and I know it. I pass death with the dying and birth with the new-washed babe, and am not contained between my hat and boots, And peruse manifold objects, no two alike and everyone good, The earth good and the stars good, and their adjuncts all good.

I am not an earth nor an adjunct of the earth, I am the mate and companion of people, all just as immortal and fathomless as myself, (They do not know how immortal, but I know.) Every kind for itself and its own, for me mine male and female, For me those that have been boys and that love women, For me the man that is proud and feels how it stings to be slighted, For me the sweetheart and the old maid, for me mothers and the mothers of mothers, For me lips that have smiled, eyes that have shed tears, For me children and the begetters of children. Undrape! you are not guilty to me, nor stale nor discarded, I see through the broadcloth and gingham whether or no, And am around, tenacious, acquisitive, tireless, and cannot be shaken away.

The Little One Sleeps in its Cradle,

The little one sleeps in its cradle, I lift the gauze and look a long time, and silently brush away flies with my hand.

The youngster and the red-faced girl turn aside up the bushy hill,

I peeringly view them from the top.

The suicide sprawls on the bloody floor of the bedroom,

I witness the corpse with its dabbled hair, I note where the pistol has fallen. The blab of the pave, tires of carts, sluff of boot soles, talk of the promenaders,

The heavy omnibus, the driver with his interrogating thumb, the clank of the shod horses on the granite floor,

The snow sleighs, clinking, shouted jokes, pelts of snowballs, The hurrahs for popular favorites, the fury of roused mobs, The flap of the curtained litter, a sick man inside borne to the hospital, The meeting of enemies, the sudden oath, the blows and fall, The excited crowd, the policeman with his star quickly working his passage to the centre of the crowd, The impassive stones that receive and return so many echoes,

What groans of overfed or half-starved who fall sunstruck or in fits,

What exclamations of women taken suddenly who hurry home and give birth to babes,

What living and buried speech is always vibrating here, what howls restrained by decorum,

Arrests of criminals, slights, adulterous offers made, acceptances, rejections with convex lips,

I mind them or the show or resonance of them — I come and I depart.

The big Doors of the Country Barn Stand Open and Ready,

The dried grass of the harvest time loads the slow-drawn wagon, The clear light plays on the brown gray and green intertinged, The armfuls are packed to the sagging mow. I am there, I help, I came stretched atop of the load, I felt its soft jolts, one leg reclined on the other, I jump from the crossbeams and seize the clover and timothy, And roll head over heels and tangle my hair full of wisps.

Alone far in the Wilds and Mountains I hunt,

Alone far in the wilds and mountains I hunt,
Wandering amazed at my own lightness and glee,
In the late afternoon choosing a safe spot to pass the night,
Kindling a fire and broiling the fresh-killed game,

Falling asleep on the gathered leaves with my dog and gun by my side. The Yankee clipper is under her sky sails, she cuts the sparkle and scud, My eyes settle the land, I bend at her prow or shout joyously from the deck. The boatmen and clam-diggers arose early and stopped for me, I tucked my trouser ends in my boots and went and had a good time; You should have been with us that day round the chowder kettle.

I saw the marriage of the trapper in the open air in the far west, the bride was the red girl, Her father and his friends sat near cross-legged and dumbly smoking, they had moccasins to their feet and large thick blankets hanging from their shoulders, On a bank lounged the trapper, he was dressed mostly in skins, his luxuriant beard and curls protected his neck, he held his bride by the hand,

She had long eyelashes, her head was bare, her coarse straight locks descended up her voluptuous limbs and reached to her feet. The runaway slave came to my house and stopped outside, I heard his motions crackling the twigs of the woodpile, Through the swung half-door of the kitchen I saw him limpsy and weak, And went where he sat on a log and led him in and assured him, And brought water and filled a tub for his sweated body and bruised feet, And gave him a room that entered from my own, and gave him some coarse clean clothes, And remember perfectly well his revolving eyes and his awkwardness, And remember putting plasters on the galls of his neck and ankles; He stayed with me a week before he was recuperated and passed north, I had him sit next me at table, my firelock leaned in the corner.

These are Really the Thoughts of all Men in All Ages and Lands, they are not Original with me,

These are really the thoughts of all men in all ages and lands, they are not original with me, If they are not yours as much as mine they are nothing, or next to nothing, If they are not the riddle and the untying of the riddle they are nothing, If they are not just as close as they are distant they are nothing. This is the grass that grows wherever the land is and the water is, This is the common air that bathes the globe.

With Music Strong I Come, with My Cornets and My Drums,

With music strong I come, with my cornets and my drums, I play not marches for accepted victors only, I play marches for conquered and slain persons. Have you heard that it was good to gain the day? I also say it is good to fall, battles are lost in the same spirit in which they are won. I beat and pound for the dead, I blow through my embouchures my loudest and gayest for them. Vivas to those who have failed! And to those whose war vessels sank in the sea! And to those themselves who sank in the sea! And to all generals that lost engagements, and all overcome heroes! And the numberless unknown heroes equal to the greatest heroes known!

Who Goes There? Hankering, Gross, Mystical, Nude;

Who goes there? hankering, gross, mystical, nude;
How is it I extract strength from the beef I eat?
What is a man anyhow? what am I? what are you?
All I mark as my own you shall offset it with your own,
Else it, were time lost listening to me.
I do not snivel that snivel the world over,

That months are vacuums and the ground but wallow and filth. Whimpering and truckling fold with powders for invalids, conformity goes to the fourth-removed, I wear my hat as I please indoors or out. Why should I pray? why should I venerated and be ceremonious? Having pried through the strata, analyzed to a hair, counseled with doctors and calculated close, I find no sweeter fat than sticks to my own bones. In all people I see myself, none more and not one a barleycorn less, And the good or bad I say of myself I say of them. I know I am solid and sound, To me the converging objects of the universe perpetually flow,

All are written to me, and I must get what the writing means. I know I am deathless, I know this orbit of mine cannot be swept by a carpenter's compass, I know I shall not pass like a child's carlacue cut with a burnt stick at night. I know I am august, I do not trouble my spirit to vindicate itself or be understood, I see that the elementary laws never apologize, (I reckon I behave no prouder than the level I plant my home by, after all.)

I exist as I am, that is enough, If no other in the world be aware I sit content,

And if each and all be aware I sit content.

One world is aware and by far the largest to me, and that is myself,

And whether I come to my own today or in ten thousand or ten million years,

I can cheerfully take it now, or with equal cheerfulness I can wait.

My foothold is tenoned and mortised in granite,
I laugh at what you call dissolution,
And I know the amplitude of time.

Walt Whitman, a Cosmos, of Manhattan the Son,

Walt Whitman, a cosmos, of Manhattan the son,
Turbulent, fleshy, sensual, eating, drinking and breeding,
No sentimentalist, no stander above men and women or apart from them,
No more modest than immodest.
Unscrew the locks from the doors!
Unscrew the doors themselves from their jambs!
Whoever degrades another degrades me,
And whatever is done or said returns at last to me.

Through me the afflatus surging and surging, through me the current and index. I speak the password primeval, I give the sign of democracy, By God! I will accept nothing which all cannot have their counterpart of on the same terms. Through me may long dumb voices, Voices of the interminable generations of prisoners and slaves, Voices of the diseased and despairing and of thieves ad dwarfs,

Voices of cycles of preparation and accretion,

And of the threads that connect the stars, and of wombs and of the father stuff,

And of the rights of them the others are down upon,
Of the deformed, trivial, flat, foolish, despised,
Fog in the air, beetles rolling balls of dung.
Through me forbidden voices,

Voices of sexes and lusts, voices veiled and I remove the veil, Voices indecent by me clarified and transfigured.

I do not press my fingers across my mouth,

I keep as delicate around the bowels as around the head and heart, Copulation is no more rank to me than death is.

I believe in the flesh and the appetites,

Seeing, hearing, feeling, are miracles, and each part and tag of me is a miracle. Divine am I inside and out, and I make holy whatever I touch or am touched from,

The scent of these armpits aroma finer than prayer,
This head more than churches, bibles, and all the creeds.

If I worship one thing more than another it shall be the spread of my own body, or any part of it, Translucent mold of me it shall be you!

Shaded ledges and rests it shall be you!

Firm masculine colter it shall be you!

Whatever goes to the tilth of me it shall be you!

You my rich blood! you milky stream pale strippings of my life! Breast that presses against other breasts it shall be you!

My brain it shall be your occult convolutions!

Root of washed sweet flag! timorous pond snipe! next of guarded duplicate eggs! it shall be you!

Mixed tussled hay of head, beard, brawn, it shall be you!

Trickling sap of maple, fibre of manly wheat, it shall be you! Sun so generous it shall be you!

Vapors lighting and shading my face it shall be you!

You sweaty brooks and dews it shall be you!

Winds whose soft-tickling genitals rub against me it shall be you! Broad muscular fields, branches of live oak, loving lounger in my winding paths, it shall be you!

Hands I have taken, face I have kissed, mortal I have ever touched, it shall be you. I dote on myself, there is that lot of me and all so luscious,

Each moment and whatever happens thrills me with joy,

I cannot tell how my angles bend, nor whence the cause of my faintest wish,

Nor the cause of the friendship I emit, nor the cause of the friendship I take again.

That I walk up my stoop, I pause to consider if it really be, A morning glory at my window satisfies me more than the metaphysics of books.

To behold the daybreak!

The little light fades the immense and diaphanous shadows,

The air tastes good to my palate.

Hefts of the moving world at innocent gambols silently rising, freshly exuding,

Scooting obliquely high and low.

Something I cannot see puts upward libidinous prongs,

Seas of bright juice suffuse heaven.

The earth by the sky stayed with, the daily close of their

junction, The heaved challenge from the east that moment over my head, The mocking taunt, See then whether you shall be master!

It is time to explain myself — let us stand up.

It is time to explain myself — let us stand up.
What is known I strip away,
I launch all men and women forward with me into the Unknown. The clock indicates the moment — but what does eternity indicate?
We have thus far exhausted trillions of winters and summers, There are trillions ahead, and trillions ahead of them.
Births have brought us richness and variety,
And other births will bring us richness and variety.
I do not call one greater and one smaller,
That which fills its period and place is equal to any.
Were mankind murderous or jealous upon you, my brother, my sister? I am sorry for you, they are not murderous or jealous upon me,
All has been gentle with me, I keep no account with lamentation, (What have I to do with lamentation?)
I am an acme of things accomplished, and I am encloser of things to be.
My feet strike an apex of the apices of the stairs,
On every step bunches of ages, and larger bunches between the steps,
All below duly traveled, and still I mount and mount.
Rise after rise bow the phantoms behind me,
Afar down I see the huge first Nothing, I know I was even there, I waited unseen and always, and slept through the lethargic mist,
And took my time, and took no hurt from the fetid carbon.
Long was I hugged close — long and long.
Immense have been the preparations for me,
Faithful and friendly the arms that have helped me.
Cycles ferried my cradle, rowing and rowing like cheerful boatmen,
For room to me stars kept aside in their own rings,

They sent influences to look after what was to hold me.

Before I was born out of my mother generations guided me, My embryo has never been torpid, nothing could overlay it. For it the nebula cohered to an orb,

The long slow strata piled to rest it on,

Vast vegetables gave it sustenance,

Monstrous sauroids transported it in their mouths and deposited it with care.

All forces have been steadily employed to complete and delight me, Now on this spot I stand with my robust soul

Chapter 10

Study Questions and Answers

Q. Write a Brief passage on the life and works of Walt Whitman

Walt Whitman lived from 1819 to 1892. He was one of ten children and was born on New York's Long Island. He worked as a printer, teacher and property speculator. In 1855 he published 13 poems in a collection entitled Leaves of Grass. Over the years, Whitman published fresh editions of this collection, the last one in 1892, each time adding many more poems-eventually it would contain hundreds of poems and some 10,500 lines, making Leaves of Grass the length of a good sized novel.

Whitman set out in Leaves of Grass to write about himself, giving his purpose as: "a feeling or ambition to articulate and faithfully express in literary or poetic form and uncompromisingly, my own physical, emotional, moral, intellectual and aesthetic Personality, in the midst of, and tallying, the momentous spirit and facts of its immediate days, and of current America"

During the American Civil War Whitman served as a nurse in a military hospital, where he caught an infection that weakened him.

In 1873, Whitman moved to Camden in New Jersey, where he stayed until his death. Whitman published other books, but his reputation rests almost wholly on Leaves of Grass.

About the poem The date in the AQA Anthology is mistaken-this poem (according to the Cambridge History of English and American Literature, Volume 16: Early National Literature) was first published in The American in 1880 and reprinted in Harper's Monthly in 1881. By this time, Whitman was settled in New Jersey, where Barnegat lies on the coast in what is today called Ocean County. The title is also "corrected" to the standard UK form-Whitman writes "Patroling" with one "l". This poem comes from a section of Leaves of Grass called Sea Drift-containing poems, inspired by the sea, which explore the mysteries of life and death. It contains two of the most famous of all Whitman's lyrics-Out of the Cradle Endlessly Rocking and As I Ebb'd with the Ocean of Life. Barnegat is on the Atlantic Coast of south New Jersey (between Atlantic City and Jersey City). The wild sea that Whitman describes now draws sailing enthusiasts to Ocean County. Barnegat is on the coast-some way inland lies Camden, where Whitman lived from 1873 until his death. By a curious coincidence, since 1996, Barnegat Bay has been protected as one of the USA's estuaries of national importance-having been nominated for this by a state governor called Whitman.

The Poem in Detail

We are not told who is "patroling" but assume that it is the poet, late at night. The poem is almost a list of details, each line ending with a verb. Mostly these suggest strong physical action or vivid details. It is not clear whether the "dim, weird forms" are natural features, ships or people-but there is a clear sense of nature as massively powerful, threatening man's precarious existence. Whitman suggests the idea of evil spirits by describing the wind as "shouts of demoniac laughter" and seeing "waves, air, midnight" as a savage "trinity"-an image that appears twice. His readers would compare this to the Holy Trinity of Father, Son and Holy Ghost.

He shows the reader how the person "patroling" cannot be sure what is happening out at sea-by the final reference to "dim, weird forms" and earlier in the questions about "that in the distance". Is it "a wreck" and "is the red signal flaring"?

The poet's method

Nearly all of the poems in Leaves of Grass are written in free verse-that is, without formal patterns of rhyme or metre.

Sometimes this gives us little more than chopped prose-prose broken into lines. This poem has a more clear structure-like Old English verse, and the later poems of Gerard Manley Hopkins, the lines fall into two halves, each containing two stressed syllables. The other formal feature is more obvious-each line finishes with a verb ending in "-ing". This is the form called the present participle. This means that the whole poem, set out as a single sentence, does not at any point have a main finite verb.

Among the other technical effects Whitman uses are:

Anthropomorphism or animism-Whitman writes about natural things as if they are features of a person or intelligent creature-such as "muttering" and "laughter". He also writes as if the natural world has attitudes or feelings, with qualifiers like "wild", "fitfully", "fierce", "watchful", "tireless" and "never remitting". (It is not clear whether the "struggling" and "watching" at the end of the poem are also being done by natural things or by real people.)

Images-all of the images are of things that are really there to be seen. But they may also represent other things. Can you find any vivid or memorable images?

Repetition-Whitman writes many things twice, sometimes a whole phrase ("milk-white combs careering", "slush and sand"), sometimes a single word, and sometimes a different form of the same root word.

Q. Comparing Walt Whitman and Ralph Emerson

Walt Whitman is Jay Leno and Ralph Emerson is Ed Hall. Walt takes the instructions announced by Emerson and runs gallantly with them making beautiful and insightful poetry. Walt Whitman and Ralph Emerson spoke out in an age where society was not ready for such dramatic writers. Whitman uses several of Emerson's topics and styles to be that good poet. Whitman elaborates on the characteristics of a poet, freedom, children, and animals.

In order to understand any comparison of the two author's one must first read and comprehend that Emerson's writing are clearly an instruction manual that Whitman adopts in order to become an outstanding poet. Emerson believes we must, "look in vain for the poet whom I describe. We do not, with sufficient plainness, or sufficient profoundness, address ourselves to life, nor dare we chaunt our own times and social circumstances. If we filled the day with bravery, we should not shrink from celebrating it. Time and nature yield us many gifts, but not yet the timely man, the new religion, the reconciler, whom all things await". Emerson is stating how everything can be a poem and a poet can reflect on valuable resources like nature to draw on and write. Whitman clearly uses this guide in order to write his poetry. He agrees that nature is a valuable tool.

In addition, Whitman elaborates that any person and any nature is in itself poet and poem. He thinks America is full of poets. Whitman reflects saying, "I celebrate myself, and what I assume you shall assume, for every atom belonging to me as good belongs to you. I loafe and invite my soul... houses and rooms full of perfumes... the shelves are crowed with perfumes". Whitman expresses himself and how he wants others to take notice and realise poetry is all around.

People want freedom, and this characteristic is a focus in both poet's works. In Emerson freedom is referred to as, "the ancient British bards had for the title of their order, 'Those who are free throughout the world.' They are free, and they make free". Emerson is reflecting how Americans wanted to be free from the British rule. They wrote books and expressed themselves because they wanted others to see their freedom. Whitman also reflects that, " I am a free companion... I bivouac by invading watchfires. I turn to the bridegroom out of bed and stay with the bride myself". Here Whitman is referring to how he is free to take a bride and do whatever he wants. Whitman is referring to a freedom like the Brits who took America and raped the society. Whitman left the bridegroom behind just like America left Britain behind using it as a tool to obtain freedom. Freedom is something every poet should feel in order to obtain the best sense of writing from one's soul.

Another similarity in both works is the references of children who are innocence, trusting, and curious. Emerson thinks that "we seemed to be touched by a wand which makes us dance and run about happily like children". Walt furthers this point by saying, A child said, 'What is the grass?' Fetching it to me with full hands; How could I answer the child?... I do not know what it is any more than he. I guess it must be the flag of my disposition, out of hopeful green stuff woven". Walt looked upon children with amazement and love. Walt uses Emerson's point that children need nature and he teaches children about nature. Emerson believes we, "fill the hands and nurseries of our children with all manner of dolls, drums, and horses, withdrawing their eyes from the plain face and sufficing objects of nature, the sun, and the moon. The animals, the water,. and stones, which should be their toys". Walt, as well as Emerson, realizes children need to be curious and trust the answers of older adults who have more experience.

Moreover, animals are mentioned in Emerson and Walt's passages. "And instantly the mind inquires, whether these fishes under the bride, yonder oxen in the pasture, those dogs in the yard, are immutably fishes, oxen, and dogs, or only so appear to me, and perchance to themselves appear upright men; and whether I appears a man to all eyes". Emerson mentions everything even the dogs and fish. He believes everything is important. Whitman also uses several references to animals, "where the bull advances to do his masculine work, and the stud to the mare, and the cock is treading the hen" The animals work together just like a poet should work together with nature and his surroundings in order to be the best poet. He too realizes that animals are important and that poetry can be written about them. Whitman just expands on Emerson's small references to animals and gives pages of descriptions of animals. Whit thinks that animals are better than humans because they are not like people and do not have the problems and characteristics of humans.

Whitman is a man who truly reshaped literature. He learned from Emerson and drew from Emerson's experiences. Walt realizes that everything is poetry. Perhaps Emerson's plan was to become a Martha Stuart as he gives instructions on how to bake the perfect cake. Unless someone bakes it and uses all the right ingredients then the recipe goes all-wrong. Just like when a poet does not touch in on all the surroundings to draw on composing a poem, the poem is all-wrong. Whitman is more of a free mind and wants others to like him. Emerson on the other hand does not care and only provides the framework while Whitman provides evidence. The two poets are truly an inspiration to all, because Walt Whitman is Jay Leno and Ralph Emerson is Ed Hall!

Q. Comparing Walt Whitman and Emily Dickinson

During the time in American history known as the, several poets began to stray from the traditional methods of writing poetry. Among these poets were Walt Whitman and Emily Dickinson. While these writer's led drastically different lifestyles and had drastically different styles of writing, the messages they presented through their writing were often surprisingly similar. Whitman's poem "Song of Myself, No.6" and Dickinson's poem "This quiet Dust was Gentlemen and Ladies" are examples of pieces which, on the surface, appear completely different, but in fact contain several similarities. Indeed, several similarities and differences can be found between these two poems.

While these works by Whitman and Dickinson are different in many ways, a few similarities can be found between the two. The most obvious of these similarities involves the themes and subject matter of the pieces. Both poems present the idea that life is a continuous and constant circle and that no one is ever really dead as long as he is remembered. Each also suggests that Earth is a living thing which all humans are a piece of in both life and death. Another likeness which can be found in these two poems is the imagery used by the authors. Through Whitman's detailed and vivid description, he allows the reader to form a clear picture of the scene in his head. Likewise, Dickinson use of personification causes the poem to come alive in the reader's mind. Indeed, by observing the themes and imagery found in these two poems, one can see that they do contain some similarities.

Though these similarities do exist, there are also several quite obvious differences between the two. The most noticeable distinguishment involves the length of the poems. While

Whitman's "Song of Myself" is quite lengthy, giving detailed and wordy descriptions, Dickinson's "This quiet dust was Gentlemen and Ladies" is much more concise and to the point. While Whitman tends to leave little to the imagination, Dickinson uses very few, carefully selected words, forcing the reader contemplate the meaning of the poem and create his own image of the scene being described. Another outstanding difference between these poems is the rhyme scheme and meter used. Whitman's poem contains no obvious meter or rhyme, but is written freely and without any apparent structure. Dickinson, on the other hand, uses an abcbdefe slant rhyme scheme, as well as an obvious meter. Without a doubt, the styles of writing used by Dickinson and Whitman in these poems contain several differences.

Certainly, by studying these two poems, one can detect several obvious similarities and differences between the two. While the poems are extremely alike in the messages they present, they are as different as can be in other ways. Surely both of these authors will forever be remembered for their contributions to the American literature of the 1800's and to the poetry of today.

Q. Onomatopoeia and the Doppler Effect in Whitman's To a Locomotive in Winter

Or

Q. Analyse Whitman's To a Locomotive Winter

In his first line of "To a Locomotive in Winter", Walt Whitman indicates why he created this poem. It is a recitative for a Locomotive in winter. A recitative is a passage rendered in style. Whitman uses the technique of onomatopoeia to create a melodic effect reminiscent of the sound of a passing train. The chugging of the engine, the clatter of the track, and the whistle of the train all create a distinct pulsating rhythm. Whitman captures the sound of a train passing by at an exceptional speed. The Doppler Effect is also represented by Whitman in this poem. All of these effects are created in one part of the first stanza of this two stanza poem. The second stanza of the poem consists of a soliloquy to the train. By using the cadence of the train in his depiction, Whitman arouses fervor in the reader which allows for a greater understanding of the soliloquy which follows. Onomatopoeia is used by Whitman in the combination of words rather that in individual words themselves. Only a few words in this poem, such as "roar" and "belching", are individual examples of onomatopoeia. Whitman relies on the formation of words to imitate the pulsating sound of a train approaching on a vibrating track. The rhythm created by Whitman's strong verbs, adjectives and hard consonants resemble that of the train he is describing. He uses many long lines that contain plenty of action or descriptive words to create this rhythm. He also generates this effect using some alliteration, such as "silvery steel" and fix'd in front" These techniques all work together to replicate the sound of a train.

The scientific name of the phenomena emulated by Whitman in this poem is the Doppler Effect. Any sound from a moving object approaching a point moves from a higher pitch to a lower pitch as it approaches and then begins moving farther away. This is a trait common to every sound. The speed and incredible vibrating sound of a train makes this change in tone most noticeable. The first lines of the poem each begin in "Thee". Most lines after this begin in "Thy". In the change from "Thee", "Thee", and "Thee" to "Thy", "Thy", and "Thy" one can almost hear the changing tone of a train's rhythm as it passes by. The Doppler Effect is also captured in the change from the quick, repetitive use of strong, harsh words towards the beginning to more lingering, softer words as the description comes to an end.

The aural effect created by onomatopoeia in "To a Locomotive in Winter" gives the reader a sense of just having been passed by a train. Whitman's use of onomatopoeia in this poem relies more on the formation of words than in individual words that imitate the sounds of a train. He is so precise in his imitation that he replicates the tone change of the Doppler Effect. This makes the soliloquy which follows even more powerful.

I Hear America Singing by Walt Whitman

I hear America singing, the varied carols I hear,

Those of mechanics, each one singing his as it should be blithe and strong, The carpenter singing his as he measures his plank or beam, The mason singing his as he makes ready for work, or leaves off work, The boatman singing what belongs to him in his boat, the deckhand singing on the steamboat deck, The shoemaker singing as he sits on his bench, the hatter singing as he stands, The wood-cutter's song, the ploughboy's on his way in the morning, or at noon intermission or at sundown, The delicious singing of the mother, or of the young wife at work, or of the girl sewing or washing, Each singing what belongs to him or her and to none else, The day what belongs to the day—at night the party of young fellows, robust, friendly, Singing with open mouths their strong melodious songs.

Q. Romanticism in Walt Whitman's Works

Romantics often emphasized the beauty, strangeness, and mystery of nature. Romantic writers expressed their intuition of nature that came from within. The key to this inner world was the imagination of the writer; this frequently reflected their expressions of their inner essence and their attitude towards various aspects of nature. It was these attitudes that marked each writer of the Romantic period as a unique being. These attitudes are greatly reflected in the poem "When I Heard the Learned Astronomer" by Walt Whitman.

Walt Whitman reflects this Romantic attitude in the speaker of his poem. He situates the speaker in a lecture about astronomy that the speaker finds very dull and tedious. Thus the speaker looks past the charts, diagrams and the work that is involved with them and starts to imagine the beauty of the stars alone. Being lifted out of the lecture room, the speaker is freed of his stress and boredom and is able to enjoy the peace and true beauty that the stars embrace.

Varying degrees of Romantic attitude has affected many areas in our lives today. A vast area that Romantic attitude has affected is The Arts. The Arts, composed of many types of genre, are composed and interpreted very different. Some people may look at a painting and imagine extremely different attitudes than the artist who painted it had intended. Another area that the Romantic attitude has drastically affected is fashion. As you glance around you'll probably observe that very few people dress similar and each person has developed their own style of dress. Fashion often reflects a person's attitude towards life and may express the mood that the particular person has, this gives each person a unique quality to distinguish them from the rest of society.

As you can see, in almost every case, the Romantic greatly expressed their attitude towards the beauty, strangeness, and mystery of nature. This attitude gave each Romantic a distinct characteristic that separated them from other Romantics. The Romantic attitude is portrayed in various aspects of our lives today including fashions and The Arts.

Q. A Discussion of The Wound-Dresser and Leaves of Grass

Or

Q. Analyse The Wound Dresser and Leaves of Grass

During the late romantic period, two of history's most profound poets, Emily Dickinson and Walt Whitman, emerged providing a foundation for, and a transition into Modern poetry. In its original form, their poems lacked the characteristics commonly attributed to most romantic poets of the mid to late nineteenth century who tended to utilize "highly stylized verses, having formal structures, figurative language and adorned with symbols". Unique and "eccentric use of punctuation" as well as "irregular use of meter and rhyme" were the steppingstones for this new and innovative style of writing. Even though these two writers rejected the traditional approach, both remained firmly dedicated to their romantic idealism of the glass of water being "half full" opposed to "half empty."

Noted for his frequent practice of catalogs and parallelism, Whitman stirred up much controversy with his first edition of "leaves of Grass" in 1855. Many critics responded negatively to the absence of meter and rhyme for he was the first American poet ever to employ free verse as the basis for his poetic structure.

Unfortunately, this prominent and gifted writer did not

live to see the extent of his poems success and popularity, as well as their impact on other writers. It is clear that Dickinson had a style all her own, however it was not previously recognized due to her reluctance to disclose her work to the public, refusing to give in to Thomas Wentworth Higginson, a literary critic, who suggested that she edit her work from its original form. Although she did not play a key role in influencing the writers of her time, when her work eventually emerged into the mainstream, it was apparent that she "was truly ahead of her time". Her poetry contained highly effective elements such as her tendency to develop figurative language as a way of "adding depth," as well as her "unconventional use of punctuation and capitalization and the brevity of most of her lines and stanzas".

In Dickinson's well known poem, "`Hope' is the thing with feathers—," it is clear that although the structure and presentation of her work displays traces of early modernism, the content of the poem itself revolves around the basis of Romanticism, Her optimistic views are vividly expressed conveying a romantic vibe to her poems, for she sees her surroundings "with the clear-eyed, sometimes mischievous, wonder of a child and breathlessly tells us about them" In this poem, Dickinson capitalizes only the words she wants to stress, paying no attention to where they are in the stanza. She rarely applies any form of grammatical punctuation besides dashes, which are usually found at the end of each line.

"The Wound-Dresser," by Walt Whitman, is a gruesome poem that brings his readers face to face with the cruel realities of war. The wound-dresser is a man who attends to the fatally injured victims of war, and this poem allows the reader to see what he sees, and feel what he feels. For one poor man, who the wound-dresser finds struggling to survive with a bullet through his neck, he replies, "Come sweet death! be persuaded O beautiful death!/In mercy come quickly"

Another is found with "a gnawing and putrid gangrene, so sickening, so offensive," and yet the wound-dresser aided this suffering individual, just as he had to all the others whether it was amputation or merely treating an open wound.

Many critics shunned his poems because they varied so greatly from the flowery and uplifting ones that they had been accustomed to reading. Whitman was one of the first writers to defy the conventual route and opt rather for the eye-opening, horrific images of truth. Most of society had sugar-coated ideas of what the war truly was, refusing to let themselves fathom what was really going on. Whitman's poems hit people like a slap in the face, waking them up from dream land they had previously been living in. The wound-dresser faithfully tries to amputate a man's arm whose "eyes are closed, and face is pale, daring not look on the bloody stump,"

Chapter 11

Critical Analysis

Walt Whitman

Walt Whitman, born in 1819 to a family in Long Island, lived a very humble life before becoming a well known writer. He grew up in a community full of Quakers and followed religion very strictly as a child. Whitman loved reading the works of Ralph Waldo Emerson because he thought he related to Emerson's ideas and theologies which closely corresponded to his own. At the age of 35, Whitman published his first book, Leaves of Grass, which was so successful that it appealed to other known poets worldwide. His talent was a great surprise to many. Whitman's abilities as a poet were unknown because his previous job was working for a local newspaper from which he got fired for being an abolitionist.

It is believed, however, that Whitman's inspiration came from his trip to New Orleans and New York. Whether it was a love affair or the great scenery from the countryside that truly inspired him is unknown; nevertheless this first book was the beginning to an exciting career. Whitman viewed himself as the first real American poet. His poetry was symbolic of freedom and democracy, as well as emotions and beliefs.

Later editions of Leaves of Grass were published in 1856 and 1860. These editions were full of new poems as well as revised earlier ones. At this time, Whitman was the editor of a local newspaper, the Brooklyn Daily Times, in addition to helping is father in carpentry. It was in 1862 when he found out his brother was injured in the war and he traveled South to serve as a volunteer nurse to the military until 1867. During his time as a nurse, Whitman composed several war poems which were published in the 1867 edition of Leaves of Grass. Before his death in 1892, Whitman noted in "A Backward Glance O'er Traveled Roads" that although he was not as successful as he had wished, he hoped that future generations would appreciate his poetry more. His wish came true, and now Walt Whitman is viewed as one of the best poets of all time. Walt Whitman wasn't a very big fan of war. He thought everything about it was negative.

We can see this in his poetry. In "Beat! Beat! Drums!", he expresses his feelings toward war using symbolism. The drums and the bugles are examples of two symbols. He is using these objects as representing war. Whitman starts off each stanza with the same line every time. "Beat! Beat! drums!-blow! bugles! blow!" He uses this symbolism of war to show the effects it has on the world. The drums and the bugles are always interrupting things. This is seen clearly in the first stanza. The drums and bugles are interrupting the church and the farmer can't be peaceful. Whitman continues this symbolism throughout the rest of the poem. Whitman also speaks of how he doesn't like the war in other poems of his.

He does this in "The Wound-Dresser." He speaks of the war as his strangest days. They were long days of sweat and dust. The reader can tell by the explanations by Whitman that he doesn't appreciate war. He also talks about the people who got wounded from the war. He feels bad for them and wants to save them desperately. This shows that he dislikes the war because he felt there was no need for them being injured. If it wasn't for the war, the people wouldn't be that way. He doesn't state these beliefs directly, however it is easy to see through his words. Walt Whitman mentions his dislike of war throughout his poems. He may do this indirectly but his message is abundantly clear. He is obviously anti-war and has only negative aspects of it. He hates the idea of war and shows it in his poetry.

A Defence of Whitman

Whether they have loved or loathed his poetry, each

writer or critic who has encountered "Leaves of Grass" has had to come to some sort of reckoning with Walt Whitman. The Good Gray Poet, the grandfather of American poetry, has been deified by some and labeled a cultural and artistic barbarian by others. While Whitman freely admitted in his preface to the final publication of "Leaves of Grass" that the work was faulty and far from perfect, some critics see no redeeming qualities in Whitman's art. Henry James goes so far as to say, "Whitman's verse...is an offense to art." James chastises Whitman for extolling and exploiting what James feels are truisms. To James, Whitman's poetry is completely self-aggrandizing; it lacks substance and coherence. Through an examination of a specific poem, "The Wound Dresser", the claims of James and other negative critics can be refuted.

The broadest and most general critiques can be dismissed most readily. Henry James accuses Whitman of refusing to deal with challenging moral questions in his poetry. Whitman speaks of the evils of war, suffering, and senseless death in graphic detail in "The Wound Dresser", but to James these evils are obvious targets for lesser poets.

"A great deal of verse that is nothing but words has, during the war, been sympathetically sighed over and cut out of newspaper corners because it possessed a certain simple melody."

James denies Whitman's poetry even a simple melody. Whitman is more an emotional opportunist than a poet. James even claims that Whitman's primary goal is the glorification of the Union army. The poem in question, however, hints at a different conclusion. "(was one side so brave? The other side was equally brave)". In dealing with supposed truisms Whitman's poem begins to ask the question: if the inherent evils of war, suffering, and senseless death are indeed so painfully obvious to you, Henry James, and your world, why are they supported with such fervor? Why in fact do they exist at all? Whitman happens to write from a sincere moral minority of which Henry James is a part. Thus to label Whitman altruistic is to label James as well.

John Jay Chapman levels the most absurd attack on

Whitman: "The man knew the world merely as an outside observer, he was never a living part of it, and no mere observer can understand the life about him."

"The Wound Dresser" is a personal account and reminiscence of Whitman's days as a medic during the Civil War. "The crush'd head I dress, (poor crazed hand tear not the bandage away,) ...Hard breathing rattles, quite glazed already the eye, yet life struggles hard."

These are hardly the words of a passive spectator. Whitman was an active participant in life; life intoxicated him. His poetry reflects his immediate intense sensitivity to the world around him.

This sensitivity is the basis for Whitman's attempt to create a higher level of coherence and meaning in each poem. This Cosmic Sense, as Richard Maurice Bucke terms it, provides a grand unifying theory which pervades and binds all his poetry. Whitman uses an almost structural method building with paradox and antithesis. The dialectics in "The Wound Dresser", youth and age, innocence and wisdom, noise and silence, image and truth, begin to hint at a universal sense gained by the old man in the poem. The poem is a series of gory and painful memories, yet the old man concludes by saying,

"I recall the experience both sweet and sad, (Many a soldier's arms about this neck have cross'd and rested, Many a soldier's kiss dwell on these bearded lips.)". It is precisely this sort of statement, however, that leads Henry James and John Jay Chapman to attack Whitman for lacking any sort of unity or coherence. "We look in vain, however, through your book for a single idea." Whitman's use of paradox and antithesis does differ from structuralism because these elements do not build upward and point to a single idea. These elements extend horizontally in all directions implying both infinity and universality. This is the source of James' frustration.

"No arrangement of Whitman's thoughts can resolve the paradoxes or discover them in a fully coherent pattern. He was incapable of sustained logic, but that should not blind the reader into impatient rejection of the ebb and flow of hisantithesis." James and Chapman complain of Whitman's lack of coherence when in reality they themselves are standing against the tide of a universal unity. James couples his logical attack with one more specific and fundamental. "Art requires, above all things, a supression of one's self, a subordination of one's self to an idea." Whitman's poetry will never be art because he places his own consciousness above ideas or concepts. His poetry is the supreme statement of one's self; it is the essence of Whitman's ego.

To Whitman, however, ideas are in no way subservient. The ideas and images of any poem affect and shape the consciousness of the poet. Therefore, in order for Whitman to attain his ideal of Cosmic Consciousness, the ideas that propel him into such a state must be at the very least equal if not superior to the ego of any one poet. In "The Wound Dresser" a simple but very potent idea is the driving force behind the poem: the sanctity of life and the struggle to preserve it. This idea causes the old man to choose his occupation as a medic and even to enjoy it in some form. Without this idea to motivate and mould Whitman's conscience, he would never have written,

"I never knew you. Yet I think I could not refuse this moment to die for you, if that would save you". As the poem so aptly states, Whitman's poetry exists "in dreams' projections", the very realm of ideas and abstractions. Thus concepts and consciousness become equitable partners in the creation of something larger than the sum of both parts: art. Whitman's art is an amalgamation of coarse reality, paradox, and free floating ideas. Faulty as it is, Henry James is sadly mistaken when he claims that Walt Whitman's poetry is an insult to the very concept of art. At its finest, his poetry is a splendid assimilation of humanity through the eyes of a tender and wise man.

In "On the Beach at Night Alone,"

Walt Whitman develops the idea that everyone has a connection with everything else, including nature. Whitman uses a variety of writing techniques to get his point across. First, the repetition and parallel structure that his poems contain reinforce the connection between everything in nature. The usage of "All" 11 times emphasizes the inclusion of everything in the universe. The sentence structure remains the same throughout the poem, without any drastic change; however, the length of the lines in the poem vary.

In addition, Whitman's' extravagance with his words further illustrates his idea of the Over-Soul. For example, "A vast similitude interlocks all" shows his verbose nature. Whitman does not do directly to the point, but gives every little detail. Most importantly, Whitman's' use of catalogues stands as the most recognizable Whitman characteristic that illustrates his beliefs. These long lists that he uses set the mood of the poem. "All spheres, grown, ungrown, small, large, suns, moons, planets," shows the idea that everything is connected in nature. Similarly, "All nations, colors, barbarisms, civilizations languages." furthermore emphasize Whitman's belief in the Over-Soul.

Although Whitman uses a great deal of structural ways to stress his ideas, he also uses many other ways of delivering his ideas. First of all, Whitman portrays himself as a public spokesman of the masses. The tone of the poem is a very loud, informative tone that grabs ones attention. The emphasis placed on the word "all" adds to the characterization of Whitman as a powerful speaker. Furthermore, Whitman takes part in his own poem.

Participating in his own poem, Whitman moreover illustrates the connection between everything in life. Lastly, Whitman, most of all, celebrates universal brotherhood and democracy. Once again, the inclusion of the word "all" so many times demonstrates Whitman's belief in that everyone is connected no matter what their position is in society. Whitman stresses the fact that all humans are equal in that "All identities that have existed or may exist on this globe" share similar connections with nature. Ultimately, Whitman's belief in the Over-Soul reveals the bond between nature and the universe.

Sight in Camp in the Daybreak Gray and Dim and I Hear America Singing

America the great, land of freedom, home of the brave—each of these phrases has been used to describe the United States of America. Walt Whitman was a man who lived through many tough times in this country, but who would prosper as a poet. He was personally affected by all of the death and destruction that he witnessed during the Civil War. "A Sight in Camp in the Daybreak Gray and Dim" and "I Hear America Singing" have some fascinating similarities but include many differences. Although both poems were written by the same man, he seemed to see America in a different light when writing each poem. Each piece uses different tones and images, but they are tied together by the style of writing and use of America as a main subject. In "I Hear America Singing" and "A Sight in Camp in the Daybreak Gray and Dim," Whitman uses differing tones, images, styles of writing, and even different themes to show the splendors and downfalls that America can bring.

"I Hear America Singing" and "A Sight in Camp in the Daybreak Gray and Dim" have two very different tones about the same subject. "I Hear America Singing," this poem has a very cheerful, happy, and robust tone which is evident even in the title. Whitman describes many different types of people singing "their strong melodious songs." The different trade each person has represents different ethnic backgrounds in the people of America. Whitman writes this poem to show how wonderful America is and how much he loves living here. "A Sight in Camp in the Daybreak Gray and Dim" has a much different tone. During the civil war, Whitman's brother was wounded while fighting. His experiences while working in hospitals full of wounded and dying people inspired him to write such a dreary poem. Whitman's tone throughout the whole poem is solemn and dreadful. Describing three dead soldiers, Whitman seems to write how cruel and unjust people have been in killing the young, old, and even what he sees as "the face of the Christ himself." In each poem, Whitman uses opposite tones to describe America at different times and in different ways. Within these two poems, Whitman does use different tones but he maintains a similar style of writing. In almost all of the poems that Whitman writes he uses free verse. This means that he writes without having any rhyme scheme.

Ordinary words that ordinary people can understand are used in both poems. Whitman did not capitalize random words for stress or use many hyphens to emphasize pauses in either poem. Imagery is also used differently in each poem. In "I Hear America Singing," you can see the people "singing with open mouths." Contrastingly, in "A Sight in Camp in the Daybreak Gray and Dim" he uses the title as a source of seeing the daybreak as gray and dim instead of clear and beautiful. The use of free verse and simple wording make both of these poems alike, but the opposing images he creates set a much more somber mood in "A Sight in Camp in the Daybreak Gray and Dim." "A Sight in Camp in the Daybreak Gray and Dim" contains a somewhat spiritual and patriotic theme.

As Whitman uncovers the blankets of each soldier, he sees a young man, an old man, and a body he sees as Christ. This sight of Christ being dead arouses the thought of the sacrifice that Christ made for all of mankind. A spiritual theme is not seen in "I Heard America Singing." Instead, a theme of the American dream—living happily, in peace, and prospering at whatever one does is evident. "A Sight in Camp in the Daybreak Gray and Dim" also contains a somewhat patriotic theme. The setting is the civil war and three men have died for their country. If so many men, women, and even children had not sacrificed their lives, the American dream would not be at all possible. In choosing the two different themes for each poem, Whitman expressed two contrasting views of the United States of America that he had at different times.

"A Sight in Camp in the Daybreak Gray and Dim" and "I Hear America Singing" have different tones, themes, and images but concentrate on one main subject—America. Whitman wrote using the same style of writing, free verse, and included some of the same themes in both poems. However, these two poems are surprisingly different in that Whitman used opposite tones and themes toward the subject of America.

"A Sight in Camp in the Daybreak Gray and Dim" and "I Hear America Singing" are two unlike poems that have many of the same aspects of writing that are all Walt Whitman.

The Politics of Ethnic Authorship: Li-Young Lee, Emerson, and Whitman at the Banquet Table.

What is it in me would devour this world to utter it?... I would eat it all to utter it...

I would devour this race to sing it... I would eat Emerson, his transparent soul, his soporific transcendence.

Li-Young Lee, "The Cleaving"

In one of his longest and best-known poems, "The Cleaving," Li-Young Lee announces his desire to devour Ralph Waldo Emerson like a steamed fish in a Chinese meal. The reader forgives this breach of table etiquette because, as Lee informs us, Emerson said the whole Chinese race was ugly—he deserves to be eaten. But Lee's poem is more sophisticated and more philosophical than this tit-for-tat scenario suggests. In "The Cleaving," eating is assault, but it is also digestion and assimilation.

Lee brings the butcher's shop close to the banquet table by deliberately playing on the two senses of the verb "cleave" to suggest both chopping up and clinging to, and thus the poem vacillates between the act of rejection and the process of assimilation. Eating in this poem may begin with the butcher's chopping block, but it is ultimately about communion.

The dialectics of Lee's poem reveal a blind spot in contemporary critical theory's discussion of the ethnic author. In valorizing the so-called marginal element in ways that reproduce it as "central" to our cultural concerns, contemporary criticism, in spite of itself, insists upon the segregation of the "ethnic writer" from the "mainstream." As such, we are in danger of patronizingly valuing ethnic writing as a "dynamic" and "colorful" literature of outsiders that brings new "life" to America's tired literary traditions. By insisting on marginality for ethnic authors, we also ignore the dialectical relationship that exists between these writers and the various traditions of American literature to which they, like any other American author, belong. Li-Young Lee's dinner/communion with Ralph Waldo Emerson and Walt Whitman in "The Cleaving" illustrates what is at stake when we approach a given writer as either "Asian American" or "American." Lee's poem shrewdly questions the either/or between these authorial identities.

"ROMANCING THE MARGINS"

We often use the word "marginal" as if it did not undergo its own shifts in meaning, but the shifting relevance of "the marginal" in relation to the larger body of contemporary American literature highlights one of the most remarkable paradoxes of ethnic authorship over the past half century. A broad view of Asian American literary production and consumption over the past fifty years suggests that ethnic writing is no longer marginal, or, to see it another way, that marginality is no longer a negative marker to mainstream literary tastes.

Asian American writers such as Diana Chang, Toshio Mori, Carlos Bulosan, John Okada, and Louis Chu published before the 1960s, but their works fell quickly into obscurity. Even in the wake of the civil-rights movement, authors and publishers saw Asian American writing as a risk. One famous example is Knopf's decision to market The Woman Warrior as nonfiction in 1976, perhaps emphasizing its tour guide status to Chinese culture (which sold well at that time) rather than letting it stand on its strengths as a novel. Also in the 1970s, David Wong Louie reports that he decided to remove the Chinese names from his stories in order to improve their marketability, a decision he made in response to rejections from editors who found his stories "too Chinese".

The marginal status of Asian Americans in the United States was at that time a purely negative factor for publishers. AS a result, most of the Asian American literature published during this period served to satisfy the curiosity of white American readers, and it reinforced the illusion of superiority enjoyed by white culture by presenting Asians as non-threatening and inferior. The Asian American writer was then the tour guide to the literary Chinatown. Elaine Kim, writing in 1982, argues that "until recently, published Asian American writers presented the Asian American experience lightly and euphemistically, even humorously, without significant expression of concern about the manifestations of social injustice". In Kim's view, "publishers and a predominantly white readership" tolerated expressions of "Asian cultures and values, and Asian American values and life styles" when the ethnic writer wrote with racial "self-contempt and self-negation" rather than when the ethnic writer wrote to criticize "problems in American society". In other words, Asian American works before the 1970s were consumed as light appetizers for the American body, which was understood at that time as white/non-marginal, and Asian American writers were not yet invited to the banquet table, much less the communion table.

Since the 1970s the status of the ethnic author within the literature of the United States has undergone a profound change. This change was the effect of both ethnic literary activism and shifts in mainstream literary tastes. Aiiieeeee! An Anthology of Asian American Writers and The Woman Warrior set the table for the publication of more Asian American works and for the invitation of earlier "lost" works to the banquet (e.g., Chu's Eat a Bowl of Tea and Okada's No No Boy). By the end of the 1980s, Amy Tan reached star status with The Joy Luck Club; as a result, writers such as Gish Jen and Gus Lee found the going easier with the larger publishing houses (Dutton paid Gus Lee a $100,000 advance for China Boy and ordered a first print run of 75,000 copies). A story by David Wong Louie about an immigrant couple from China, "Displacement," finally saw the light of day and was reprinted in The Best American Short Stories 1989. In the 1990s, Jhumpa Lahiri won the Pulitzer Prize for her short-story collection Interpreter of Maladies, and Ha Jin won the National Book Award and the PEN/Faulkner Prize for his novel Waiting.

There are many possible explanations for the ethnic author's change in status—we might cite the emergence of a more multicultural education system and curriculum, multiculturalism's success in the "culture war" over the canon, larger economic and cultural processes called "globalization," and other factors. America's appetite for Asian American writing is growing, and this interest is no longer tied to a tourist mentality designed to make white, middle-class readers feel superior. The fact that Asian American writers such as Li-Young Lee receive prestigious literary awards and are included in major anthologies such as the Norton Anthology of American Literature suggests that Asian American works are valued more for their literary quality now than they were in the past.

The rise of the ethnic author, insofar as it represents an "assimilation" of the ethnic author into the larger body of American literature, also implies a consequent shift in the status of "marginality" within American literature. Paradoxically, contemporary literary criticisms emphasis on the marginal has made the marginal central. One prominent example of the critical celebration of marginality is Gilles Deleuze and Felix Guattari's 1986 book Kafka: Toward a Minor Literature. Deleuze and Guattari argue that the writer in the ethnic (and hence linguistic and literary) margins of society occupies the necessary position to rejuvenate the stagnant literary language of the "established" or "major" literature. They argue that marginality "allows the writer all the more the possibility to express another possible community and to forge the means for another consciousness and another sensibility". Deleuze and Guattari are not writing about Asian American writers today; however, their analysis of the ethnic writer is meant to be transportable—Deleuze and Guattari suggest as much when they write that the revolutionary quality of Prague German for Kafka "can be compared in another context to what blacks in America today are able to do with the English language".

If we apply this argument to contemporary American literature, as Deleuze and Guattari suggest we should, we elevate the ethnic author's position and celebrate the heroism of marginalized voices in their struggle against the hegemony of "mainstream" literature, but we also fetishize ethnic marginality, making literary rejuvenation dependent upon ethnic difference and the maintenance of the ethnic author's outsider status.

In order to be articulated clearly, Deleuze and Guattari's model of literary rejuvenation depends upon the literary segregation of "major" and "minor" literatures that reifies difference. In their view, a "minor" literature infiltrates the language and challenges the perspectives of a "major" or "established" literature and thereby revitalizes the major literature. The minor literature "reterritorializes" the major literature, disrupting its hegemonic order and "reterritorializing" it in a new "sense" —thus changing the map or the landscape of the established literature. However, the validity of their theory rests upon the outsider status of the ethnic writer and thereby ignores the influence of the established literature and its various traditions upon that writer. A Czech writer like Kafka may write "like a dog digging a hole" or "a rat digging its burrow" in German literature, but one is left to conclude that German literature does not dig a hole in Kafka. In their emphasis on the ways minority-ness gets into a national literature, Deleuze and Guattari reify the relationship of ethnic authorship to an established, national literature as a one-way street. "Romancing the margins" therefore tends to neglect the dynamic dialectical relationship between an ethnic author and an established national literature, and thus treats the ethnic author as special or extraordinary.

Ethnic authors may draw from cultural codes "alien" to the codes of the established literature, but they likewise draw from the traditions, literary influences, and established codes of the major literature within which they are writing. To put it in Harold Bloom's terms, ethnic authors suffer from the same anxieties of influence as non-ethnic writers. Like other writers, they worry that a hole is being dug in them. In Asian American literature alone there are many examples of the "ethnic" author's interaction with authors from "established" literatures: Walt Whitman in Maxine Hong Kingston's Tripmaster Monkey (the protagonist is Wittman Ah Sing); John

Cheever in Chang-rae Lee's A Gesture Life; Sherwood Anderson in Toshio Mori's Yokohama, California; Sylvia Plath in Patricia Chao's Monkey King; the Bible in Joy Kogawa's Obasan and in Li-Young Lee's poetry and memoir; W. B. Yeats and Greek mythology in Robert Ji-Song Ku's short story "Leda"; W H. Auden, John Donne, John Keats, A. E. Houseman, and many other British poets in Shirley Geok-lin Lim's Joss and Gold; and F. Scott Fitzgerald in Gish Jen's Typical American and the first segment of Russell Leong's long poem The Country of Dreams and Dust. By insisting only on the marginality of ethnic writers, by continually marking them as outsiders to the "mainstream," we are in danger of missing their participation in the various traditions of "established" literature.

To return to Li-Young Lee's banquet table: a consideration of "ethnic eating" in his poetry, particularly in "The Cleaving," will show that the ethnic author is simultaneously the diner and the dinner. Furthermore, we will see that the Asian American writer in contemporary American literature participates in and inherits American literature, that he is not simply a marginalized, heroic voice challenging the status quo. Asian American writers in today's American literature are dialectically engaged with that literature and with its various and disparate traditions. A discussion of cultural eating in Lee's poetry allows us to isolate both the "deterritorializing" function of an ethnic author's writing (as theorized by Deleuze and Guattari) as well as to appreciate that author's dialectical engagement with literary forebears in the established literature.

DEVOURING RACISM

In Li-Young Lee's poetry, eating is a cultural activity that enacts familial and ethnic community. The Chinese meal of rice and steamed fish in "Eating Together" is a metaphor that combines generational continuity with a sense of familial belonging after the death of the poet's father, and this metaphor is juxtaposed with the loneliness of the meal described in "Eating Alone." These poems from Lees first book of poetry, Rose, contextualize eating as a familial activity fraught with personal significance. In a much longer poem, "The Cleaving" (from his second book of poetry, The City in Which I Love You), eating becomes both a sign of cultural communion with other Chinese immigrants (i.e. the larger cultural community) as well as an aggressive weapon against racism in American society and American literature. The poet "transforms words into things capable of competing with food" when, in order to speak as a poet for his community, he "eats" that community and he "eats" Ralph Waldo Emerson and his insulting and reductive remark that the Chinese "managed to preserve to a hair... the ugliest features in the world."

"The Cleaving" forcefully asserts the place of the Chinese American poet in the American literary tradition by simultaneously attacking and embracing that tradition through the Asian American literary trope of what Sau-ling Cynthia Wong calls "the big eating hero." Regardless of cultural contexts, eating is an image of both domination and acquiescence. As Wong reminds us, "ingestion is the physical act that mediates between self and non-self, native essence and foreign matter, the inside and the outside." Deleuze and Guattari similarly argue that eating, like speaking, is a fundamental act of deterritorialization of the Other that ultimately reterritorializes the space of the Other through the activity of "the mouth, the tongue, and the teeth". The difference between writing and eating for Deleuze and Guattari is that writing reterritorializes language as something more "capable of competing with food", whereas eating merely deterritorializes.

Eating, in any case, allows the speaker in "The Cleaving" to mediate between his own voice and the American literary tradition. The poet expresses the seemingly divergent actions of attacking and embracing through his use of the verb "cleave." The verb "to cleave" encompasses opposing possibilities: to "split" or "divide by force", and to "adhere closely," "hold fast," or "cling". In the poem, Lee writes that change resides in the embrace of the effaced and the effacer, in the covenant of the opened and the opener. Like the sharp-edged cleaver wielded by the Chinese butcher, the poem "coaxes, cleaves, brings change" through violent images of eating and devouring; the teeth also functioning as a kind of cleaver. Writing within the Chinese tradition of the conquering hero, the poet in "The Cleaving" is the "big eater": like Brave Orchid in The Woman Warrior, who vanquishes life-threatening ghosts through eating, the poet is driven by "necessity" to ingest all forms of nutrition, no matter how unpalatable they may seem to the reader. The speaker ingests the brain of the duck and the head of the carp. He also expresses a desire to eat the butcher, the Chinese race, Ralph Waldo Emerson, and even death itself. As these descriptions attest, becoming a big eater is not simply a matter of eating what one must to survive but actually learning to enjoy as delicacies the parts that others may simply discard as inedible. According to Wong, big eaters in Asian American literature are defined by ban ability to eat unpromising substances and to extract sustenance, even a sort of willed enjoyment, from them; to put it symbolically, it is the ability to cope with the constraints and persecutions Asian Americans have had to endure as immigrants and racial minorities".

The sixth stanza of the poem launches into a frenzy of big eating that speaks of both the poem's response to racism as well as its function as poetic utterance. The poem's pace is driven by the quick transition from one "food-item" to another: fish, butcher, bodies, features, hairs, Emerson, and the carp's/ Emerson's head. Although the poet expresses his desire to eat in the conditional voice, the steady repetition of the monosyllabic and aggressive "eat" hurls the reader from one image to another:

What is it in me will not let the world be, would eat not just this fish, but the one who killed it, the butcher who cleaned it. I would eat the way he squats, the way he reaches into the plastic tubs and pulls out a fish, clubs it, takes it to the sink, guts it, drops it on the weighing pan. I would eat that thrash and plunge of the watery body in the water, that liquid violence between the man's hands, I would eat the gutless twitching on the scales, three pounds of dumb nerve and pulse,

I would eat it all to utter it. This segment describes more than simply eating a fish: the fish is not sitting idly on a plate, cooked and ready for consumption. The fish is alive and vigorous, and it is that vigour, that "violence," that the speaker wishes to absorb: "I would eat that thrash/and plunge, that liquid violence." There is something vital in the fish that the speaker seeks to obtain, in much the same way that traditional Chinese eating relates the properties of the eaten to the properties of the eater. This traditional concept brings Lee's poem into conversation with that tradition but also, again, with other Asian American texts. In Lee's poem, however, the "thrash," "plunge," and "liquid violence" relate to vitality (as does the image of the "liquid violence/between the man's hands," which may also suggest sexual potency); but they also relate to death: the fish, after all, is in its dying throes. As the stanza develops, the presence of death and the speaker's reaction to it become central. The speaker's attraction to the fish's "twitching" death under the butcher's club is burdened with meaning. Eating the struggles of the fish (the "thrash" and the "plunge") in its dying throes is like eating the struggles of the immigrant community.

I would eat it all to utter it. The deaths at the sinks, those bodies prepared for eating, I would eat, and the standing deaths at the counters, in the aisles, the walking deaths in the streets, the death-far-from-home, the death-in-a-strange-land, these Chinatown deaths, these American deaths. I would devour this race to sing it.... The death of the fish leads the speaker to consider other deaths around him: "the standing deaths/at the counters" are the butchers and fishmongers of the Hon Kee Grocery; the deaths "in the aisles" are the customers; "the walking deaths in the streets" are connected to the "Chinatown deaths," that is, the streets of Chinatown surrounding the grocery; and "Chinatown deaths" are immigrant deaths ("far-from-home" and "in-a-strange-land"). Finally, these deaths of immigrants from Asia are "American deaths': they occur in America, but more importantly, the line suggests that leaving one's country to live and die in America is an American experience. The next line confirms that these are Asian immigrants whom the speaker wishes to ingest: "I would devour this race to sing it". The struggles, the thrashing and plunging, of the immigrant Chinese are the result of anti-Chinese sentiment, as the next segment suggests:

I would devour this race to sing it, this race that according to Emerson managed to preserve to a hair for three or four thousand years the ugliest features in the world. I would eat these features, eat the last three or four thousand years, every hair. And I would eat Emerson, his transparent soul, his soporific transcendence. The quotation from Emerson's journals is the point at which Lee most explicitly enters into a conversation with the American literary tradition. For now, however, I will discuss Lee's emphasis on the quotation's racism, thus bracketing for the moment the literary and poetic tradition Emerson represents as well as the context of Emerson's journal entry. The speaker's response to Emerson's racist remarks is central to the entire poem. The poet contrasts his own poetic utterance, the speaker's ability to speak, with the muteness of the fish, which as we have seen above stands for the Chinese immigrant: the gutless twitching on the scales, three pounds of dumb nerve and pulse, I would eat it all to utter it. The response of the Chinese immigrant to racism has been a "dumb" struggle: the immigrant thrashes and plunges but remains unable to articulate a response to the discursive power behind popular, literary, and institutional racism. The speaker responds with a discursive feast modeled after the big-eating heroes of Chinese legends: "I would eat this head,/ glazed in pepper-speckled sauce."

The fish's head comes to represent both the immigrant community (whose "features" and "hairs" the speaker says he would eat) as well as Emerson's racist comments, the "opaque" eyes of the fish head reminding us of the "transparent eyeball" of Emerson's philosophy? Perhaps the idea of eating these negative comments would strike some American readers as an odd gesture. Swallowing hardship for some might be a courageous act that reveals one's mental toughness, but it also carries connotations of acquiescence, of giving in. Yet, in Chinese American literary tradition, swallowing hardship, or "eating bitter," is often represented as a heroic act. According to Wong, disagreeable food puts to the test one's capacity to consolidate one's self by appropriating resources from the external environment, to convert the seemingly useless into the useful, refuse into nutrition. Physical survival is incompatible with a finicky palate; psychological survival hinges on the wresting of meaning from arbitrary infliction of humiliation and pain; survival of family and the ethnic group not only presupposes individually successful eating but may demand unusually difficult "swallowing" to ensure a continued supply of nourishment for the next generation. The speaker in "The Cleaving" turns the "seemingly useless into the useful" when he eats Emerson's racist remarks.

Rather than cringing and retreating from them, he "devours" them, much the way that he devours the fish's head ("with a stiff tongue lick out/the cheek-meat"). The speaker openly relishes the fish head, describing his experience as "sensual". This ravishing enjoyment is an act of defiance in Bakhtin's sense of the carnivalesque—an overturning of hegemonic and hierarchical order, a response to the age-old argument that Chinese eating habits mark them as barbaric and inhumane. As with his response to Emerson's racist statement, the speaker embraces the notion of the champion eater; he does not adopt white American eating habits but makes his pride in his own culture's customs his weapon. That the speaker's eating is more than an individual response is suggested by the manner in which he consumes the fish's cheeks: "the way I was taught, the way I've watched/others before me do". The speaker eats in a cultural way; he has learned this eating from his community.

Thus, while those who came before him may have been able to devour only a literal fish in this way, the speaker meshes "ethnic eating" with linguistic skill and poetic discourse to devour racist discourse. In Lee's poetry, cultural eating is not always expressed in violent terms, despite the carnivalesque and grotesque imagery described above. In his first book of poetry, Rose, Lee exalts the communal and relational significance of eating in a Chinese family, a significance that he expands to the immigrant community in "The Cleaving." His poem "Eating Alone" describes his loneliness as he tends his garden and thinks of his recently deceased father. The loss of his father is so poignant for the young poet that he imagines his father waving to him in the garden, only to realise, he says, that it was "the shovel, learning where I had/left it." The poem then concludes with a stanza describing a Chinese meal that he prepares and consumes alone: White rice steaming, almost done. Sweet green peas filed in onions. Shrimp braised in sesame oil and garlic.

And my own loneliness. What more could I, a young man, want. The final line's sardonic tone is achieved through the juxtaposing of the poet's father's absence from the garden and his implicit absence from the table. There is no joy in the "bare," "cold,/brown and old" garden without his father's presence. The illusion of his presence merely increases the loneliness the poet describes at the table. The tide of another poem in Rose, "Eating Together," provides an intertextual juxtaposition with "Eating Alone." In "Eating Together," the father is still absent, but the community of family around their Chinese meal remembers the father as the conveyor of tradition and, significantly, as no longer alone.

In the community of family, the poet is not lonely, and neither is his father. The family continues the tradition of eating together. Moreover, the mother has taken the father's place, as signified by her eating the sweetest meat nestled in the trout's head. In "The Cleaving," this same love of community through the communion of cultural eating is contrasted with the violent eating required in devouring racism. In his paean to the Chinese immigrant in stanza five, the poet says of his fellow Chinese immigrants that they are

happy, talkative, voracious at day's end, eager to eat four kinds of meat prepared four different ways, numerous plates and bowls of rice and vegetables, each made by distinct affections and brought to table by many hands. Significantly, the cultural eating of the family in "Eating Together" opens to the cultural eating of the immigrant community in "The

Cleaving." Cultural eating is as much an image of revolt against racism as it is a statement of community and, as we will see below, of transcendence.

Transcendental Eating: "The Cleaving" is a poetic cleaver that carves a space in American literary tradition, with Emerson standing for the overt marker of that tradition. In some sense it would be more accurate to say that the poem "hacks" a space: hacking describes the action of a cleaver, and perhaps it more clearly describes the speaker's voracious attack on Emerson. Yet, as discussed above, Lee makes deliberate use of the verb "cleave" to suggest both hacking and adhering, splitting and joining. This same process is inherent in the analogy of eating: we attack by cutting, biting, chewing, swallowing, and digesting, but through this attack we also absorb the nutrients of what we eat; we reterritorialize it. What we eat, in this sense, becomes a part of us. The opposite actions of devouring and nourishing, and of deterritorializing and reterritorializing, are thus necessary to the speaker's response to Emerson, which is implicitly linked to this line toward the poems end:

Change resides in the embrace of the effaced and the effacer, in the covenant of the opened and the opener. By linking these lines with the speaker's response to Emerson, I wash to suggest that the poem is not an outright rejection of Emerson and the philosophy of transcendentalism. While eating Emerson seems overtly and violently to disassociate the speaker from Emerson and his influence, as a "food" substance Emerson also becomes a nutrient for the speaker's poetic utterance (though I will later question the poem's reconstruction of Emerson). The poem suggests therefore that positive "change" require(^?^?^es, as in expanding the horizon of consciousness and the reader's horizon of expectation, an "embrace" and a "covenant" between the racialized self and the racist Other. Thus, while it may appear that Lee has set Emerson up as a straw man, what he expresses in the poem belies a deep-seated indebtedness to Emerson. The poem explicitly rejects Emerson's racist remarks and philosophy of transcendentalism, making no distinction between the two.

However, I believe it is necessary to make the distinction. First, the poet rightly objects to Emerson's inflammatory attack on the Chinese. There can be no denying that the remarks are inappropriate and ignorant. But, given a fuller picture of Emerson's life and of nineteenth-century thinking on race, we can at least contextualize them and perhaps better understand them. Emerson entered these comments on the Chinese in his private journal at the age of twenty during a period in which, as Robert D. Richardson Jr. describes, he was in a "gloomy and petulant" mood. His information about the Chinese came from one secondary source, a book he had just read called Journal of the Late Embassy to China.

Richardson describes Emerson's early journals as "mostly dross and largely unoriginal". Emerson's own, often self-parodic, comments in the margins suggest that he saw some of his own jottings as crude. His early journals are also full of tastes, opinions, and statements that would be completely inverted later in life. Richardson notes that "among modern poets he idolized Byron and made fun of Wordsworth, tastes he would later reverse. His college writings, like his college life, were full of contradictions. His long poem "Indian Superstition' was a Southey-inspired tirade against the Hindu religious tradition he would later come to admire". Emerson's comments on the Chinese race are indeed "petulant" and dismissive, but the fervor of his tirade against the Chinese, whom he had never personally encountered, might be regarded as "comic," as Richardson suggests. His exclamation, "I hate Pekin!" is over-exuberant and ridiculous.

Given the breadth and depth of Emerson's mature writing, it might well be unfair to boil him down to one racist comment recorded in a melancholy period of his youth. On the other hand, we might also note that this kind of racialized discourse was common to nineteenth-century thinkers, as unacceptable as it may appear to us today, and that Emerson's mature writing reflected his culture's understanding of race and character. In his essay on race (originally published as a chapter in English Traits in 1856), Emerson writes, "on the English face are combined decision and nerve, with the fair complexion, blue eyes, and open and florid aspect. Hence the love of truth, hence the sensibility, the fine perception, and poetic construction". The positive traits of English culture, Emerson believed, were literally written on the face of the Englishman. Emerson furthermore explained the success of English imperialism in racial terms: "It is race, is it not? that puts the hundred millions of India under the domination of a remote island in the north of Europe".

Emerson's insistence that the English race owed its "success" to its hybridity connects these observations to the journal comments quoted in "The Cleaving": "The best nations," wrote Emerson, "are those most widely related; and navigation, as effecting a world-wide mixture, is the most potent advancement of nations.... Everything English is a fusion of distant and antagonistic elements". True to his belief in "evolutionary humanism, based on the pre-Darwinian theory of the French naturalist, Lamark", Emerson argued that the more advanced races were those that experienced the broadest range of contact with other races. His argument against the Chinese race twenty-seven years earlier was based on what he perceived to be its purity: that the Chinese race "managed to preserve" its features explains why he claimed in the same journal entry that the Chinese empire enjoyed "a Mummy's reputation". (In "The Conservative," Emerson refers to the lack of regeneration through reform as "the Chinese stagnation of society".) Emerson's argument reflects the general American and British sentiment against China's protectionist policies regarding trade, a sentiment that led to the Opium Wars of 1839-42 and 1856-58.

In "The Cleaving," Lee explicitly contradicts Emerson's journal comments by valorizing the immigrant race's fluidity and variety. The butcher, by the end of the poem, is described as having a "Shang dynasty face" which, as Zhou Xiaojing suggests, is a response to Emerson's comment about the static nature of the Chinese for the past three to four thousand years. This Shang dynasty face is, in the speaker's imagination, transformed into an "African face with slit eyes", suggesting a hybrid blending of races. Furthermore, he transgresses gender boundaries, as well, with the phrase, "he is my sister". The speaker's valorization of the immigrant race's hybridity and variety responds to Emerson's claim that the Chinese race has "managed to preserve" itself over the centuries, but it joins with Emerson in privileging the hybrid over the pure. In addition, the speaker reads the butcher's physical features in much the same way that Emerson reads the English face. The butcher reminds the speaker of a northerner in the "boniness" of his face, "clear from the high/warlike forehead/to the sheer edge of the jaw". At the same time, the "moodiness" of his looks and the way "his face poised" suggest to the speaker that he is a southerner. Unlike the Emerson of the 1824 journal entry, the speaker sees variety in the Chinese race, but because the distinctions are inscribed in the butcher's physical features, they serve to re-inscribe Chinese racial biases regarding northern and southern Chinese in much the way Emerson re-inscribed racial biases in English Traits.

At a deeper and more positive level, "The Cleaving" enters into dialogue with the humanism and universalism of both Emerson and Whitman. Judith Kitchen, in a review of Lee's poetry for The Georgia Review, claims that "The Cleaving" "eschews the need for transcendence". She does not elaborate on this point, so one is left to speculate that, for her, the poem's statements about Emerson and his "soporific transcendence" constitute a rejection of transcendentalism. But the question remains: What does Lee mean by calling Emerson's philosophy a "soporific transcendence"? I believe that the phrase is meant to convey the ethereal qualities often associated with transcendentalism.

In other words, the speaker sees Emerson's transcendentalism as a mystical philosophy devoid of action and empirical validity. By "soporific" the speaker may be suggesting that Emerson's is a non-active philosophy, hence marked by lethargy, or that belief in transcendentalism leads to a dulling of one's awareness of reality. Thus, in comparison, the transcendence that describes the metaphysics of "The Cleaving" is expressed in physical and aggressive terms. We are "bodies eating bodies, heads eating heads," and "as we eat we're eaten", summing up the interconnectedness of all beings not in mystical but in physical terms. However, the poem misconstrues Emerson if its complaint against his philosophy is based on a distinction between active transcendentalism (illustrated in the violent, aggressive transcendence of "The Cleaving") and inactive or purely mystical transcendentalism (supposedly illustrated by Emerson's writings). Although Emerson's philosophy owed much to mysticism, his was by no means a soporific transcendentalism. As Edward L. Ericson writes in his introduction to Emerson on Transcendentalism:

Despite the mystical strain in Emerson's philosophy, or perhaps because of it, he recognized that the action gives birth to the thought, providing the American mind with its unmistakable signature: "The preamble of thought, the transition through which it passes from the unconscious to the conscious, is action. Only so much do I know, as I have lived." Besides the basic relation between physical action and mystical thought, as described here, Emerson's philosophy cannot properly be construed as causing lethargy or leading to inaction. According to Ericson, while metaphysical idealism is often considered a conservative philosophy, allied to the status quo, in Emerson it attains an antiauthoritarian, evolutionary outlook.

It affirms a spiritual conception of democracy in which each person writes within his or her own heart the living scripture of personal worth and self-reliance. One could argue that serf-reliance and the kind of tenacious individualism that have come to be associated with America are the direct legacies of Emerson's thinking and writing on individual action. We might see little difference between Emerson's transcendentalism and the interconnectedness of Lee's immigrants through eating if we consider the way Perry Miller once described Emerson's notion of interconnectedness;

Emerson... assert that should he ever be bayoneted he would fall by his own hand disguised in another uniform, that because all men participate in the Over-Soul those who shoot and those who are shot prove to be identical, that in the realm of the transcendental there is nothing to choose between eating and being eaten. To say then that Lee "eschews the transcendental" because the speaker in his poem wants to eat Emerson and calls Emerson's philosophy "soporific" is to miss the essential point that Lee's poem becomes what it seems to eschew. As seen in the quotation from Miller, a victim in Emerson's transcendentalism sees himself in his attacker, and one who eats is at one with what is eaten. This is precisely the kind of transcendence portrayed in "The Cleaving."

In the poet's words, we are "bodies eating bodies, heads eating heads." The transcendental relatedness of all beings is moreover present in the poem from beginning to end through identification and resemblance. "The Cleaving" begins with the speaker's observations on the Chinese butcher in the Hon Kee Grocery, a man whose face resembles the speaker's face and whose actions resemble those of an old woman: "He gossips like my grandmother, this man/with my face". The poem therefore begins with an act of identification but also with a broadening of the scope of resemblance. Not only does the man look like the speaker and gossip like his grandmother, but we are told that his "sorrowful," "warlike," bony face resembles a nomad from the Gobi regions of northern China, yet in his "light-handed calligraphy" on receipts and his "moodiness" he resembles a "Southerner from a river-province". Moreover, the speaker says, "he could be my grandfather;/come to America to get a Western education/in 1917". Personal history and ethnic history are thus located in this one man, in whom the speaker also sees himself.

The Chinese immigrant community from which the speaker descends is the beginning point for the poem's transcendental foundation. By the end, this identity opens up to all immigrants: The sorrow of his Shang dynasty face African face with slit eyes. He is my sister, this beautiful Bedouin, this Shulamite, keeper of Sabbaths, diviner of holy texts, this dark dancer, this Jew, this Asian, this one with the Cambodian face, the Vietnamese face, this Chinese I daily face, this immigrant, this man with my own face. The butcher therefore stands for the Other in whom the poet sees himself, and in their shared humanity, they are not only connected, they are the same. "Was it me in the other I loved/when I loved another?" he asks. But the face he sees also extends through the Asian diaspora (Asian, Cambodian, Vietnamese, Chinese), through the Middle East, and even hybridizes race and gender ("African face with slit eyes. He is/my sister"). The poem constructs the immigrant community as a united family that transcends borders and boundaries. In her discussion of this poem's dialogue with Emerson, Xiaojing Zhou suggests that Lee broadens the topic broached by Emerson by bringing to it a marginalized immigrant perspective: Lee's response to Emerson's words brings his narrowly conceived generalization to dialogue with multiple and heterogenous specificity presented in the poem.

The validity of the assumed universal truth in Emerson's remarks, acquired through transcendental consciousness, is challenged within a wider cultural horizon and from a different point of view. I concur that Lee's attack on Emerson opens the conversation to a larger context, one that includes those who have been relegated to the margins of American society by racialized and racist discourse. However, in claiming that Emerson's comments were "acquired through transcendental consciousness," Zhou seems to be submitting to the same reductionist view of Emerson that the poem does.

Zhou claims that "Emerson's transcendental generalization about the whole people becomes dangerously limited". I agree that Emerson's generalization is dangerously "narrow"; however, what is transcendental about Emerson's generalization? In equating the young Emerson's racist comments with his entire philosophy, Zhou fails to recognize the ways in which Lee's poem, perhaps unwittingly, embraces Emerson's philosophy. Zhou rightly claims that "Lee's 'telling' of the Chinese-American immigrants' experiences in his poems involves the processes of self-exploration and self-invention" and that through his poetry Lee reveals that "Chinese-Americans can remake themselves in images of their own invention". What she neglects to recognize is how Emersonian these claims are.

"A Many-Membered Body of Love": Eating the Body Electric: Thus, for all its violent eating and grotesque devouring, the metaphysics of "The Cleaving" is Emersonian. The poet, furthermore, communes with his American literary forebears through the poem's celebratory mood, reminiscent of Walt Whitman and his brand of transcendentalism. Through "The Cleaving," Lee enters a dialogic relationship with Emersonian transcendentalism that is similar to the relationship between Whitman's poetry and Emerson's philosophy. According to Jerome Loving, one "of Whitman's achievements in his first edition of Leaves of Grass was to advance Emersonianism or transcendentalism by contradicting it".

While Whitman's poetry maintained a transcendentalist perspective that God is immanent in nature and in the human soul (encapsulated, for Emerson, in the rather disembodied notion of the Oversoul), his poetry departed from Emerson's transcendentalism in its language and philosophy of the body. Rather than seeing the body as merely "an emblem of the Soul" or as a "world of senses" that must be transcended in order to become "whole again in the mind of God", Whitman celebrated the body as soul. In the twenty-first stanza of "Song of Myself," Whitman writes, "I am the poet of the Body and I am the poet of the Soul". Similarly, in the closing lines of "I Sing the Body Electric," the poet equates the body with the soul, thereby breaking down the distinction between the two: "O I say these are not the parts and poems of the body only, but of the soul,/O I say now these are the soul!". This poem in particular established Whitman as "the poet of the body" and distinguishes his transcendentalism from Emerson's. Like Li-Young Lee, Whitman continued Emerson by challenging him in an Emersonian way.

In a strikingly similar fashion, "The Cleaving" glories in the Chinese immigrants' physical bodies. Their physical features and their diversity become the window to their collective soul. The speaker delights in the bodies he describes; he "longs" for these "bodies/and scents of bodies". Even in describing their inadequacies ("straight/or humped, whole, manque, quasi") and stereotypical differences from the white race ("jut jaw... wide nose... thick lips"), the speaker insists that "each pleases." This pleasure is reminiscent of Whitman's paean to the human form in "I Sing the Body Electric," in which some stanzas read like an anatomy lesson in their detailed descriptions: "Head, neck, hair, ears, drop and tympan of the ears/... The lung-sponges, the stomach-sac, the bowels sweet and clean,/The brain in its folds inside the skull-frame". As with Lee's "cleaving" paradox, Whitman mixes seemingly incommensurable vocabularies of poetry and dissection. Moreover, the poet's contemplation of "the brain in its folds inside the skull-frame" is echoed by Lee's meditation on the duck's brain, which the speaker picks out of "the skull-cradle". Lee's poem expresses identity with the immigrant community in terms of their shared blood; despite physical differences, they are "brothers and sisters by blood". In Whitman's poem, the speaker identifies with humanity, in one instance with that of a black slave being sold at auction:

Within there runs blood, The same old blood the same red-running blood! There swells and jets a heart, there all passions, desires, reachings, aspirations. In much the same way that the speaker in "The Cleaving" identifies with his immigrant community, Whitman's speaker identifies himself with the bodies he describes in the very first lines of "I Sing the Body-Electric":

I sing the body electric, The armies of those I love engirth me and I engirth them, They will not let me off till I go with them, respond to them, And discorrupt them, and charge them full with the charge of the soul. In these lines, the speaker reveals two concerns that become central to the poem: one is his sense of shared humanity ("the armies of those I love engirth me and I engirth them"); the other is his responsibility to his fellow human beings to "respond to them," to "discorrupt them," and to "charge them full with the charge of the soul." In this second purpose, the poet sees himself as speaking for the entire human race, through this poetic utterance to free it from "false" notions of corruption. He is a poet/prophet who will return honour to the human body and the interconnectedness of humankind. "The Cleaving" shares with Whitman's poem this expressed desire to unite, to inspire dignity, and to give utterance:

What is it in me would devour the world to utter it?... I would eat it all to utter it... I would devour this race to sing it.

The ultimate goal of eating in Lee's poem is poetry. The bodies of his immigrant community as well as the racial slurs of the white majority nourish the poet in the same way that fish, pig, and duck nourish the physical body. He must internalize everything—good, bad, or neutral—in order to have poetic control of everything. His poem does not discard the immigrant community as a burden, neither does it retreat into Chinatown in the face of discrimination. Rather, his poem speaks in an American poetic voice through a motif that affirms the ethnic community.

We must recognize, however, that the line "I would devour this race to sing it" echoes but distinctly alters Whitman's declaration, "I sing the body electric." Whitman celebrates the physical body, glorying in its form and in its reproductive and hence life-affirming powers. Lee, on the other hand, celebrates the Chinese immigrant body by declaring his desire to devour it as though it were food. To grasp the subversive and transformative potential of Lee's language, we turn to Bakhtin.

In Bakhtin's conception of literature, each utterance is a site of dialectical struggle: "within the arena of almost every utterance an intense interaction and struggle between one's own and another's word is being waged, a process in which they oppose or dialogically interanimate each other". "I would devour this race to sing it" is an utterance that allows us to appreciate Bakhtin's point of view. This one line from "The Cleaving" is the site of several dialogues elaborated by the entire poem. "Devour," as we have seen, is highly charged with cultural significance. The word signifies not only the "big eating" heroism of Chinese folklore but also the struggles and successes of Chinese immigrants in America to survive hardship and to swallow—in order to overcome—racist oppression.

Moreover, the word devour brings to mind the

carnivalesque eating central to Bakhtin's Rabelais and His World, which, as Zhou argues, helps to explain Lee's emphasis on grotesque eating imagery (e.g. "bodies eating bodies, heads eating heads") and grotesque physical features (e.g. the "jut-jaw" and the backs "humped, whole, manque, quasi"). According to Zhou, Lee's "celebration and descriptions of all sorts of physical features, including those that verge 'on utter grotesquery', can be understood as a subversive strategy like what Bakhtin calls... 'the carnival-grotesque" image".

For Bakhtin, carnival humour, carnival feasting, and images of the "grotesque body" function in literature to deconstruct and overturn the prevailing hierarchical power structure. Devouring the Chinese race, licking cheek-meat from the "armored jaw" of a carp, sucking down the brain of a duck—to a Euro-American audience, these are all forms of grotesque eating that oppose standard, "mainstream" American foodways and hence stand in opposition to mainstream culture.

What makes the line "I would devour this race to sing it" carnivalesque is the Whitmanesque, celebratory nature of that eating: devouring, the line suggests, is necessary to singing. This celebration of the grotesque, like the carnival spirit described by Bakhtin, seeks to "liberate from the prevailing point of view of the world, from conventions and established truths, from cliches, from all that is humdrum and universally accepted". The poem does not retreat from stereotypes or racist remarks nor does it pretend "assimilation" by adopting what might be called "normal" American behaviour.

Rather, the poem embraces its own culture and, in its participation with Whitman's celebratory singing and with Emerson's transcendental interrelatedness, endeavors to expand the reader's horizon. What Bakhtin writes of the carnival spirit in literature can be applied fully to "The Cleaving": "This carnival spirit offers the chance to have a new outlook on the world, to realise the relative nature of all that exists, and to enter a completely new order of things". "The Cleaving" echoes a Whitmanesque love for humanity but achieves this tone through the Asian American motif of big eating. In this way, as the poet says, he "cleaves to that which cleaves me", which if taken as an expression of a minority poet and a minor literature in relation to the mainstream tradition, suggests that the boundaries drawn by those who would denounce his "ugly features" can be transgressed and the map of the territory redrawn.

However, the politics of ethnic authorship do not begin and end with the poet's marginal status. Lee's poem both contests and participates in the literary vision represented by Emerson. In his strong association with both his own ethnic community and his literary forebears, Li-Young Lee complicates the relationship between "ethnic" and "mainstream" authorship.

"A Thousand Willing Forms": The Evolution of Whitman's Wounded Bodies.

For much of the past 150 years, critics have dismissed Walt Whitman's fiction as mediocre at best, painfully beholden to the cliches of its time and largely irrelevant to the brilliant poetic innovations that would follow in its wake. Even Whitman once expressed his "serious wish to have all these crude and boyish pieces quietly dropp'd in oblivion." Yet it's possible to see many of the guiding concerns of Leaves of Grass—the enigma of intimacy, the aftermath of injury, the predicament and potentiality of social adhesion—manifest in these early tales.

But even if it's possible to find traces of Whitman's later brilliance in his early mediocrity, why is it useful to search for them? This paper is fueled by the belief that these textual searches illustrate something more surprising than an obvious commonality of authorship. With their heavy-handed tragedies and hackneyed sentiments, Whitman's early stories show an authorial consciousness coming to terms with the specter and the possibilities of violence: violent plot twists, violent intimacies, violent change. Violence becomes an important catalyst for the embodied empathy that charged Whitman's poetry with such sympathetic force.

From Schoolboys to Soldiers: Proto-Rumblings of "Drum-

Taps"In general, Whitman's early stories begin preciously rather than precociously, with mannered sound effects ("'Ting-a-ling-ling-ling!' went the little bell...") or sentimentalized pastoral scenes: "Just after sunset, one evening in summer—that pleasant hour when the air is balmy, the light loses its glare, and all around is imbued with soothing quiet.... " These cheery openings are inevitably punctured—and rather quickly—by the sinister narrative devices that follow: innocent youths are corrupted by alcohol or greed, beautiful young women are stricken with vague illnesses, boys are destroyed by sadistic power figures or malicious rabble-rousers, and poets and maidens find their integrity challenged at every turn.

It is not hard to find the early ancestors of Whitman's stylistic signatures in these stories: his attachment to parenthetical asides, his bold use of omniscient roving narrators, and even an occasional arresting image (blossoms on a tomb, fingers clutching a body) nestled amidst the predictable paraphernalia of his generic milieu. But even his crudest strokes of sentiment—sensationalized plot twists, secrets sharpened by melodrama—gesture towards an evolving sense of the importance of violence to the project of empathy.

In these gestures, Whitman was certainly not alone. Nineteenth-century American authors were active agents inside a shifting cultural understanding of empathy. Increasingly, this shift marked a departure from the axioms of Enlightenment thinkers like Adam Smith, who deemed empathy something accomplished by "the imagination only," because our "senses will never inform us of what [the wounded man] suffers," and towards a sense of empathy as something mystical, visceral, and inescapably embodied, what Elizabeth Barnes terms "a kind of fleshly sympathy." Glenn Hendler echoes this characterization of the shift as one that abandoned Enlightenment principles of mediated cognitive empathy—imagining oneself into the experience of another—in favor of a vision of empathy as something immediate and volatile, less easily controlled: "The mediation between a distanced observer and the sufferer is always at risk of collapsing." Michael Moon examines the specific nature of this "collapse" in Whitman's work, understanding it as a breakdown permitting the double-tiered "radical embodiment" that makes his work so arresting. As Whitman dissolves boundaries between the bodies of his fictional figures, he manage to dissolve boundaries between the bodies of his readers and the body of the text. Moon is one of the only Whitman scholars who has attempted a serious reading of the early prose. His search for resonances across genres allowed him to articulate Whitman's achievement of this "radical embodiment" in more naunced terms—as an essential element of his poetics that had been fomenting and crystallizing beneath the crude surfaces of his prose.

In the 1855 Leaves of Grass, Whitman frames the wounded body as a locus for radical declarations of empathic personal effusion: "I am the wounded slave," his speaker famously declares in the poem that would become "Song of Myself," "I wince at the bite of the dogs... I am the mashed fireman with breastbone broken." There is an arrogance to these demonstrations of sympathetic immersion, and an explicit dismissal of more discursive strategies of identification: "I do not ask the wounded person how he feels... I myself become the wounded person". But these empathetic engagements, however bold and deeply felt, remain discreet and fleeting: "Agonies are one of my changes of garments," he says, and they ultimately leave him "painless" after their multiple outfits of suffering—"exhausted but not unhappy".

The speakers of "Drum-Taps," Whitman's cluster of Civil War poems, find their empathic "exhaustion" more overpowering. Sympathy becomes more than a catalogue of "garments," agony more than a costume: these speakers find themselves consumed by others' wounds, their very boundaries dissolved by the suffering they encounter. Their acts of identification necessitate the kind of complete collapse that Hendler and Moon describe. The speaker of "The Wound Dresser" finds that wounds function as apertures rather than spectacles, fissures that demand he travel "deep, deep" into another injured body. He cannot simply sympathize from a distance, apprehending "clotted lint... matter and blood" as the materials for yet another hypothetical costume. Instead, he feels the growing urge to implicate his own body in the wounded soldier's suffering, hoping not simply for identification but also for the irrational possibility of substitution: "I could not refuse this moment to die for you, if that would save you."

There is a great distance traveled between the "garments" of Leaves and the wounds of "Drum-Taps." In these post-War poems, empathy demands more than passing fits of exhaustion. It overpowers Whitman's speakers rather than simply offering them the possibility of temporary empathic transcendence. The tragedy of the Civil War offered itself as an aesthetic crucible, allowing Whitman to re-articulate the links between violence and embodied empathy in more urgent terms. As Robert Leigh Davis argues, the "instability" of the Civil War was something that Whitman welcomed as "restorative," a chance to redefine the nation's political enterprise and "make possible the emergence of what is not yet named or known."

The presence of war as an external event—a tragic condition rather than simply a set of mediated choices—lent the empathy of Whitman's war poems an urgency that the sympathies of Leaves lack. They seem more like acts of imaginative innovation—breathless leaps across traditional boundaries of class and circumstance—rather than genuine articulations of the "agony" that true identification would yield. They leave his speaker "exhausted but not unhappy," energized by his empathic capacities even while he is dismayed by the suffering they access. The stark, unchosen tragedy of the Civil War called for an empathy entirely distinct from these aesthetic forays. The external insistence of circumstance is exactly what the early stories prefigured, their plots studded with dramatic events that left Whitman's protagonists forced into postures of empathy they could not have chosen for themselves. Michael Warner has examined Whitman's early fiction—especially his temperance novel Franklin Evans—as writing engaged in an "extended treatment of dialectic between self-mastery and self-abandonment." This tension between control and abandon, as it appears in the early fiction, is a useful lens through which to examine the divide between the speaker of Leaves—arrogant, roving, blustering—and the agonized effusive sojourns of Drum-Taps. This is essentially a clash between the self-mastery necessary to mediate the sympathetic exchange and the self-abandonment necessary to be overwhelmed by it. In Whitman Possessed, Mark Maslan argues for the importance of involuntary responses to Whitman's poetics. He uses the idea of the "involuntary" to link together Whitman's sexuality and his creativity, arguing that "poetry and sexual desire alike violate his identity in order to express themselves through him."

What shifted between the bodily ventures of Leaves and the bodily entanglements of Drum-Taps? And how do the early stories illuminate this shift? Whitman stresses the importance of bodily knowledge in the 1855 Leaves, but many of his celebrations of embodiment focus on epistemological exploration rather than interpersonal empathy. The "child" in the poem that would become "There Was a Child Went Forth" learns through the porousness of his physical form: "the first object he looked upon and received with wonder or pity or love or dread, that object he became/And that object became part of him". But these objects function like the "garments" of agony and fear that have already appeared: they matter, certainly, but are easily supplanted. The primacy of each object is dislodged by the object that follows.

The physical engagement of the "wound-dresser," on the other hand, necessitates less transient bodily entanglements. His own body registers contact with the wounded bodies around him as a "burning flame" in his breast that will not dwindle. Wounds become mediums through which speakers effuse into the bodies of dying soldiers, plunging "deep, deep" into their pain. Jimmie Killingsworth discusses Whitman's vision of physical connection as a form of "mystical passage that go beyond identification... and enact a kind of interpenetration." This interpenetration—the " one another's actual flesh and fluids"—is a useful way to chart the evolution of Whitman's bodily empathy.

While the speaker of Whitman's 1855 version of "I Sing the Body Electric" declares that "the bodies of men and women engirth me, and I engirth them" this assertion lacks the visceral "interpenetration" that Killingsworth stresses. The situation of the poem—an expansive gesture towards collectivity—is too peaceful to inspire the urgency that fuels bodily communion in Drum-Taps, where extraordinary circumstances breed extraordinary acts of empathy. Katherine Kinney notes that few of the poems in Drum-Taps "contain extended catalogs in which the poet's use of parallelism and repetition creates unity in multiplicity," largely because the circumstances of these poems demand that their speakers remain "embodied in a specific time and place." Their speakers are denied the disembodied imaginative leaps of Leaves, but they are offered another opportunity—the chance to inhabit bodies within the boundaries of their poems, and to connect with other bodies from inside their own.

Kinney uses Whitman's prose writings about the Patent Office Hospital to analyse his departure from the expansive sympathetic inventories of his early poetics. The Patent Office represented an architecture of display, offering a veritable "catalogue" of wounded bodies that Whitman's war poems reacted against. He frames wounded soldiers within particular dramas rather than collective displays. His early stories bear traces of this impulse to generate empathy from dramatic situation rather than aesthetic organization. They use rudimentary tropes to create external conditions that will force their characters into empathy, an empathy fueled by tragic urgency rather than aesthetic abandon. Their melodrama stumbles towards the situational urgency that the Civil War ultimately provides.

As Killingsworth argues, the "physical eloquence" of Whitman's poetry "revives dead metaphors" with its unflinching visceral innovations, but Whitman's concern with these tropes runs deep into the awkward adolescence of his oeuvre. It is a concern whose genesis and evolution is worth investigating—not primarily to excavate some value from the early prose, but to contextualize Whitman's relationship to the war, as a national catastrophe and a poetic subject, in terms of some of his most enduring concerns. The Civil War did not overturn Whitman's poetics of national adhesion and celebration, it gave him the chance to rediscover an old idea—the potentiality of violence and its aftermath—in more resonant and original language.

His formulaic early stories do have moments in which they betray their author's restless conceptual sensibilities and his penchant for complication. Even in their slickest melodramatic guises, moments of violence manage to exert an eerie and resounding impact through the margins of these stories and the crevices between their cliches. Flogging a Corpse: The Horror of Distance in "Death in the School Room. Whitman's first piece of published fiction, "Death in the School Room," initially appeared in The Democratic Review in 1841. The story sketches a single incident of misguided corporal punishment under the despotic school-house tyranny of a sinister teacher named Lugare. Lugare is quickly banished to the ranks of caricatured villainy. One need only witness the way he "bulge out his nose and cheeks with contempt" to imagine his transformation of the classroom into a "place so often made the scene of heartless and coarse brutality, of timid innocence confused, helpless childhood outraged, and gentle feelings crush'd". He appears as a Frankensteinian monster cobbled together from contemporary tropes—full of fierce glances, sarcastic vocal mannerisms, and (as a didactic parenthetical suggests) "many ingenious methods of child-torture". His victim is a "slight" boy named Tim Barker, whose "good-humor'd expression" betrays a "countenance... too unearthly fair for health" and a past riddled with shamelessly straightforward pity tags—a dead father, a bout of childhood sickness, a mother with whom he duly "struggle on".

When Lugare accuses Tim of fruit thievery, the story unfolds in a fairly predictable manner—the omniscient narrative goes to awkward pains to insist the boy did not commit the crime while Lugare refuses to listen to the boy's protestations of innocence. The story's final moments are devoted to a histrionic portrayal of Lugare's punishment—he brings his rattan "down on Tim's back with a force and whacking sound which seem'd sufficient to awake a freezing man in his last lethargy," and then (without pausing to assess the damage), he strikes again and again, "ply his instrument of torture first on one side of the boy's back, and then on the other". After a few minutes of this frenzy, the story finally delivers on the promise of its title, though it is clear that Tim has actually been dead for a while—his classmates and teacher simply presumed he had fallen into a sudden, anxious slumber. This is where the narrative becomes most interesting: readers do not witness Tim's death, they only witness Lugare's belated discovery of his death: "his eyes were turn'd up, and his body was quite cold".

This staging of revelation displaces the story's primary tragedy: its keenest horror is not that Lugare has killed his pupil, but that he does not realise that he has killed him, and thus keeps on "flogging a corpse". This is a more interesting source of dramatic effect—not simply functioning as a depiction of violence but as a depiction of the ways in which violence blinds us to the suffering of others, creating distance between bodies and obstructing their awareness of one another.

This horror is not principally about violence, it is about the failure of empathy—in its crudest form—and the breakdown of interpersonal sentiency. This vision of horror summons the work of two distinct theorists of bodily experience, Maurice Merleau-Ponty and Elaine Scarry, both interested in the possibilities of bodily empathy and the predicament of bodily alienation. Though Merleau-Ponty believes in "variations of belonging in the world, undivided between body and consciousness," he also believes it is just as important to realise that someone's body never has "quite the same significance" to another as it does to itself. This perpetual slippage—the gulf between two feeling individuals—creates an impetus for translating the pain of another into something internally felt, but it also means that agony can be kept at a distance by someone's willfully limited gaze. Scarry finds these willfully limited gazes inescapable and chilling. In her discussions of torture, an apt reference for a teacher well-versed in numerous methods of "child-torture," Scarry asserts that "the distance separating [torturer and tortured] is probably the greatest distance that can separate two human beings." She argues that this distance is a product of the torturer's utter lack of awareness: he is "free of the pain originating in the agonized body so near him. He is so without any human recognition of or identification with the pain that he is not only able to bear its presence but able to bring it continually into the present, inflict it, sustain it, minute after minute, hour after hour." The narrative emphasizes this lack of recognition when it depicts Tim's punishment as a blindly ritualized repetition of motions: "blow follow'd blow," inflicted by a "brutal wretch" who does not even wait "to see the effect of the first cut" because he is capable of remaining so terminally oblivious to the bodily agonies of his young victim.

Scarry's observations suggest that Whitman's ending is more innovative than first impressions might suggest. His conclusion is not simply invested in arousing readers' sympathies for an injustly murdered boy, it is interested in forcing them into contact with a situation in which one human being is utterly unaware of the suffering of another. Readers are even implicated in this lack of awareness, because the narrative does not allow them an understanding of Tim's death that is more accurate or specific than Lugare's. The story effectively subjects its readers to a state of empathic disenfranchisement—we are only allowed to witness Tim's corpse when it's already turning cold, and we are not granted access to any internal view of his suffering. This narrative exclusion offers a formal enactment of the obliviousness that it portrays. Of course, readers are granted more knowledge than Lugare from the outset—because they know from the title that Tim will die—and so their exclusion from any interior perspective is coupled with an urgent desire to understand his suffering. Because readers are privileged with more information than Lugare, the schoolteacher's obliviousness creates an empathic vacuum for them to fill. The subtleties of this ending complicate some of Whitman's more predictable tropes. Lugare dons another hackneyed guise of villainy as he investigates Tim's body, his outstretched limbs "quiver like the tongue of a snake," but the narrative quickly disrupts this caricature: Lugare's strength "momentarily fail him," and we sense that the trope of snake-demon has been momentarily deflated as well. For a moment, Lugare is transformed from a demonic creature into a fallible human being, a man briefly paralyzed by the horror of what he's done. Drum-Taps explores similar dimensions of injury—its impact and its aftermath—from a richer set of perspectives, examining the ways that wounded bodies spark moments of unsettling empathy.

For Whitman, violence was an important element all along, though the Civil War forced his preoccupation onto a larger cultural stage. Most of the speakers in Drum-Taps, of course, are healing injured bodies rather than injuring them, but the context of the war itself—in which men ostensibly joined together by one national body were destroying each other's bodies—meant that Whitman's depictions of healing were tinged with an awareness of the violent processes that made this healing necessary in the first place.

In poems like "The Wound Dresser," encounters with injured bodies become channels of access into the pain of others: beneath the dresser's "impassive hand... deep in breast," there is "a fire, a burning flame" that echoes the pain of his patient. Even the language of their engagement suggests modes of connection that bridge the distances separating bodies in the school-room. The aching cadences of this assertion of action—"I dress a wound in the side, deep, deep"—gives a sense of linguistic struggle. The strain in its repetition of the long vowels of "deep, deep" formally mimics the intensity of the desire to achieve entry into what lies "deep" within. It's possible to hear the urgency of that desire in Whitman's repeated words, as the speaker follows the "deep, deep" opening of the wound into another interiority, eventually finding a powerful kinship in the felt experience of another's pain—a kinship that carves out a space for gentler sensations of intimacy: the memory of soldier's arms "cross'd and rested" around his neck, or the lingering feel of their "kiss" on his "bearded lips".

The idea that empathy might manifest itself as an embodied echoing—a kind of "burning flame" to match the soldier's pain—shows up throughout Whitman's work. Even "Death in the School Room" makes stilted gestures towards this embodied correlative, calling our attention to physical parallels between the body of the torturer and his victim. Lugare's mounting horror is inscribed upon a "countenance" that has turned to "leaden whiteness," beaded with "great globules" of sweat coming "from every pore in his face". These descriptions are reminiscent of Tim's manner during his accusation, when his silent anxiety is rendered in terms of corporeal response: "The perspiration ran down his white forehead like rain-drops". The evacuation of expression and the sublimation of expression become shared expressions between these two figures.

These physical correspondences are legible upon a sensory register of inhuman objects—"wooden," "leaden," "raindrops"—that suggest that Lugare's empathic failures have not only objectified his victim, they have objectified him as well. Merleau-Ponty discusses the breakdown of phenomenological empathy with similar language, suggesting that a limited gaze can "transform into an object" and that "the objectification of each by the other's gaze is felt as unbearable... because it takes the place of possible communication." This process of reciprocal objectification effectively displaces any meaningful communication in the narrative as well. The story's final tragedy of misapprehension thrusts the paraphernalia of Lugare's abuse into sharper relief: because he can only see Tim as a "wooden" object, a receptacle for punishment, he himself becomes little more than an object in Tim's phenomenal awareness as well, just an extension of the "ratan" he wields so viciously.

The opacity of Tim's meek and reticent manner—betrayed only by small signals of pallor and perspiration—is a recognizable trope that Whitman often forced upon their misaccused martyrs. For Whitman, it appears most offensively in Arrow-Tip, a character in "The Half-Breed" who often lapses into the stock racial profile of an "apathetic" and expressionless Native American. But while Lugare's horror echoes Tim's stoicism—his "leaden whiteness" reminding us of the pale muted manner of his defenseless victim—Arrow-Tip's stoicism is paired with its opposite: the "phrenzied contortions" writ across the face of his would-be savior, Peter Brown. Brown is the only man who can save Arrow-Tip from death, and his failure to do so makes him feel indirectly—but power fully and viscerally—implicated in the execution. In one story, a boy's stoic expression becomes a strange channel of embodied evocation, while in the other, the victim's stoicism becomes a point of contrast for the expression of true empathy: Brown's sympathetic seizures.

At first glance, Tim seems like the generic incarnation of an archetypal innocent, but the story's final turn shows Whitman playing with this trope, revealing that Tim's final display of "wooden" stoicism is actually a sign that he's lost consciousness for good. When his passivity is mistaken for expressionless slumber, the narrative seems to be indulging in a kind of morbid joke—transforming this symptom of stylized predictability into a much more literal symptom of death itself.

The story's villain subverts one trope with another: the benevolent mentor is displaced by his sinister doppelganger, the abusive schoolteacher. In the zeal of its social consciousness, the story articulates a didactic aesthetic goal: that the "old-fashion'd school-maste, with his cowhide, his heavy birch-rod... will be gazed upon as a scorn'd memento of an ignorant, cruel, and exploded doctrine". This concern with societal institutions recurs throughout Whitman's poetry, as the cultural implications of his poetics grew less overtly awkward and more organically expansive. "Brave Hands Pressed Forward": Agents of Rescue in "The Fireman's Dream" and "Shirval: A Tale of Jerusalem" Whitman's enduring concern with mentorship—both authorial and pedagogical—also informed his model of the poet as a mentor for his future readers.

The particular horror of "Death in the School-Room" is inspired by the same sensibility that articulated such admiration for benevolent figures of authority and aid in stories like "The Fireman's Dream" (with its glorification of rugged civil servants) and "Shirval: A Tale of Jerusalem" (with its depiction of an otherworldly agent of resurrection), or poems celebrating a variety of societal provisions and societal governance. The sinister teacher Lugare is a vision of social authority gone wrong, while the wound-dressers and democratic leaders of later poems offer visions of social authority and engagement gone right—figures who are actually fulfilling their obligations to other members of society.

"The Fireman's Dream," first published as an unfinished fragment in the New York Sunday Times in 1844, offers an occupational counterpoint to the nefarious Lugare: its protagonist rises to the call of duty with predictably superlative bravery. Violence deepens and commemorates his valor rather than undermining it: he even suffers a traumatic head injury in the service of his fellow citizens, claiming their physical peril as his own physical burden. In turn, these citizens offer a series of physical reactions to his wounds—stretching out their hands in aid. Violence provides the occasion for communally embodied empathy: "involuntary exclamations... burst from the spectator's lips" and "a thousand willing forms and brave hands pressed forward to drag the stricken down bodies of their comrades." Sympathy and aid are corporeally manifest, not just rendered in the abstract language of ideas, intentions, or sentiments, but thrust forth as an array of "forms" and "hands."

In contrast to these earthly saviors, mortal "forms" with mortal limbs, the "Being" at the centre of "Shirval: A Tale of Jerusalem" is distinctly unearthly, an otherworldly Christ-figure with supernatural powers. Whitman's obscure retelling of the Lazurus story from the Gospel of Luke first appeared in the March 1845 issue of Aristidean. Though it imports both its subject and its language from a Biblical register, it shows

Whitman refining his vision of bodily redemption. This Christ-like "Being" allows him to explore the possibilities and limitations of hierarchical salvation—a manner of depiction he ultimately discards in favor of a more democratic poetics, empathy predicated on social equality and shared corporeality.

In moments of healing and empathy throughout "Drum-Taps," humans find solace and sympathy from other humans—flawed, weak, full of echoes of their patients' vulnerability and suffering—rather than superhuman creatures like the Being, a re-Christened Christ-figure without flaw or blemish: with a "beautifully clear... face" and "eyes... blue as the sky above" who "beamed forth benevolence and love". Even his physical features are suggestive of worlds beyond the realm of mortal physicality and his "mortal look of sympathy," though it is purportedly "mortal," does not partake of any of the "agony and death" it gazes upon. It remains perpetually distanced with its "beautifully clear" countenance, reminiscent of Whitman's evocation of the "disdain and calmness of martyrs" in the 1855 Leaves.

The Being remains distinct from more powerfully Whitmanian healers: figures who are unwilling to transcend the suffering of others, who find themselves implicated and embroiled in this suffering instead. These are the men who find they cannot raise fallen soldiers from the dead, and must commit—instead—to honoring and identifying with those who have fallen. "Vigil Strange I Kept on the Field One Night" embodies this vision of elegiac provision. During the course of a battlefield burial, its speaker reconciles himself to the impossibility of resurrection. He spends long "hours" holding vigil over the body of his "son and comrade," but his final act of commemoration is one that resists the urge to reverse this death: he " him where he fell", consecrating his death rather than defying it.

A similarly anti-ressurectional vision of mourning is offered in Whitman's most famous elegy, "When Lilacs Last in the Dooryard Bloom'd," whose lyrical instrument—the "hermit thrush"—offers another example of embodied identification with the body of another. The thrush's song is called the "song of the bleeding throat," gesturing towards an elegiac poetics that demands some degree of suffering from those who commemorate the dead. Scarry argues that this kind of physical pain is actually "the equivalent in felt-experience of what is unfeelable in death." Patricia Yongue suggests that the speaker of "Lilacs" wants to implicate himself in the process of violence as an expression of empathy. She points to the breaking of the lilac sprig as an attempt to "respond to violence with his own violence." This speaker embraces the potentiality of violence, as regenerative force and commemorative mode, rather than trying to refute or nullify its impact.

This "bleeding" song testifies to Whitman's enduring faith in non-discursive channels of empathy and remembrance. The occasions of his Civil War poems often involve some unspoken inheritance of bodily anguish. As William Aarnes argues, these moments of inheritance bring Whitman's speakers into contact with the "utterable" truths of other bodies and their bravery, what Whitman himself called the "free margins" beyond articulated experience. In the later prose of Specimen Days, he emphasizes the limits of speech as an expression of empathy: "in the main [chamber of the army hospital] there is quiet—almost a painful absence of demonstration". It is as if the "absence" of sound is necessarily "painful" because it forces the body of the observer to experience viscerally the pain it cannot audibly discern. It is the bodies of the soldiers that communicate their trauma most eloquently, with "pallid face" and "dull'd eye," and—conversely—it is physical touch that proves most conducive to healing: "the magnetic touch of hands the expressive features" of nurses.

Whitman's struggle to document the war is perpetually confronting the possibility that words cannot fully evoke its horrors—or that they could evoke without truly invoking, summon their object without truly overwhelming their subjects. Timothy Sweet finds evidence of this futility in Whitman's blood-stained war notebooks, texts that literally "bear traces" of the violence they have abstracted into figurative language. Sweet argues that they testify—more directly than language ever could—to the "violated human body which cannot be represented." But what if we allow ourselves to view Sweet's "violated human body" as Whitman did? Sweet's "bloody" margins become "free margins" full of the possibility to create channels of empathy outside of traditional discourse, using the body—rather than simply the mind—as a vessel. Moon finds these marginal avenues crucial as well—to Whitman's prose as well as his poetry—remarking that he uses his technique of "radical embodiment" to engage in "projecting liminal spaces," summoning bodies to inhabit cultural margins full of homoerotic desire or violent intimacy.

The presence of this violent intimacy is what divides Whitman's truly mediocre early stories from those tales that prefigure his poetic innovations. A story like "Shirval" fails to depict its savior's empathy in resonant terms, largely because this empathy remains sequestered to the territory of expository sentiment. It never comes alive between bodies, and the Being ultimately achieves his resurrection with words instead of physical touch. The most poignant moments of the story are its most viscerally specific, when those who have found comfort in the Being's miracle " upon the ground and ben their faces on earthworn sandals". The story gleans a brief moment of power from this haunting image, which is fraught with simultaneous invocations of intimacy and distance: the onlookers remain, importantly, beneath him as they kiss his sandals.

The "Hideous Object" of Violence: Empathic Mimicry and Possession in "The Half-Breed" The Being who resurrects young Shirval from the dead represents one end of a continuum of characters in Whitman's fiction—characters who manifest various levels of culpability. The Being is wholly without blemish or guilt; he simply offers an entirely superhuman grace. But his grace depends upon the violence that necessitated his healing in the first place. The schoolteacher Lugare defines the opposite end of this spectrum—his violence is what necessitates empathy, but he can offer very little of this empathy himself. The middle ranks of this spectrum are populated by characters like Peter Brown, whose empathy is fueled by the fact that he feels implicated in the circumstances of another man's death, even if he is not legally or morally responsible for it. Arrow-Tip, the stalwart defendant and resident Native American caricature of the tale, has been accused of murdering Peter Brown, who finds out belatedly that his physical presence could instantly exonerate Arrow-Tip and save him from execution. But Peter cannot offer aid in time, and so his sympathy for Arrow-Tip—manifest across his "wild and ghastly visage" —is driven by a sense of circumstantial responsibility.

Without meaning to, he has become complicit in another man's wrongful execution, and this complicity prompts an agonized experience of deeply—almost cartoonishly—embodied identification with the hanged man. His face displays the "phrenzied contortions of a madman in his worst paroxysm," a kind of disfigurement reminiscent of the "hideous object" of the corpse hanging from the scaffold. His body even resembles the newly-dead man in its physical impotence: "his limbs fail him" as he pantomimes the obsolete gestures of his rescue. When Brown's "head vibrate to and fro, like the pendulum of a clock", his body effectively mimics the swinging motion of the corpse itself. In these parallel demonstrations of bodily suffering, traditional boundaries of race are punctured: the body of the white man mimics the body of the half-breed.

Brown crumples into "phrenzied contortions" that powerfully foreshadow the embodied sympathies of Whitman's poetry, where empathy is not a choice but an involuntary response to the sight of suffering. Arrow-Tip's death, and the grotesqueness of its spectacle, give rise to an empathy so urgent that it overwhelms its subject with a kind of expressive violence commensurate to the occasion. Peter Brown's contortions are not the gentle tears or moist eyes of fictional tropisms; they testify to an experience of "violation" worthy of Maslan's term, overtaking his physical body in a way that connects him more forcefully to the broken body of the deceased. Waking Dreams and Quivering Hearts: The Evolution of Remorse in "One Wicked Impulse" Nowhere in the early prose does empathy take more wrenching form than in "One Wicked Impulse," a hysterical tale of violence and remorse that Whitman published in the Democratic Review in 1845. The story's protagonist, Philip Marsh, is positioned in an important place on the culpability spectrum discussed above—he is wholly responsible for another man's death but deeply remorseful about his "wicked impulse" and its single casualty: a sinister lawyer stabbed in a moment of drunken anger. Marsh is neither supernaturally benevolent nor unequivocally callous, effectively yoking together Lugare's capacity for anger and Peter Brown's capacity for empathy.

His guilt gives the story its pulse: a series of disembodied dream-visions that recall the "cold roll of the murder'd man's eye, as it turn'd up its last glance into his face" and the dying man's "shrill exclamation of pain— all the unearthly vividness of the posture, motion, and looks of the dead... pursued him like tormenting furies". There is an enduring asymmetry in this mode of remorse because these slivered memories of his victim's body remain stubbornly disembodied, experienced in his mind rather than his flesh. Not only are they described as "waking dreams" that are "unearthly" in their composition, they never involve contact with an actual injured body—as is the case for Lugare and Tim, or Peter Brown and the "hideous" hanging corpse of Arrow-Tip. In Maslan's terms, they never fully "violate" Marsh by implicating him in the physical experience of pain. Instead, they stay quarantined within the nightmarish landscape of his intangible conscience. The only physical correlatives to Marsh's remorse are so conspicuously and obtrusively symbolic—"red roses" meant to conjure Marsh's "bloody hands" (along with a metonymic pedigree that extends back to Lady Macbeth)—that they can only offer meager visceral impact.

Because the initial stages of Marsh's remorse remain so abstract, his tale comes off as melodramatic and histrionic. It is only the later stages of his narrative that offer glimpses of a more sophisticated reckoning with suffering. Marsh's immediate response to injury, in its sweeping sentiment and stark melodrama, provides a remarkable point of contrast for the visceral gravity of Whitman's poetics: the wound-dresser sensing his way "deep, deep" into his charge, or the soldier-speaker of "A March in the Ranks Hard-Prest," who becomes aware of the suffering of wounded men as an inescapably sensory presence all around him. This speaker registers injury in terms of a highly visceral epistemology, smelling "ether" and "the odor of blood" as he watches soldiers in "the death-spasm sweating" or "bleeding to death" as "little steel instruments the glint of the torches" and—with a kind of instrumental metonymy—invoke the specter of amputation. Katherine Kinney argues that this speaker's perception of the hospital "remains a disjointed collection of image, smell, and sound" that does not allow him "to recognize humanity" because his "powers of perception, on which depend his ability to feel and sympathize, are so diminished by disorientation and fatigue."

But Kinney fails to acknowledge the ways in which the speaker's gaze—infused with so much weariness—actually affords closer approximation of what the soldiers themselves experience. His "ability to feel and sympathize" is powerfully manifest in his perceptual disorientation, and his fractured awareness allows for more authentic engagement than orderly descriptions would have permitted. If the scene made more sensory "sense," it would have kept everything suspended at colder aesthetic distance.

The final gestures of the poem, in which a "dying lad... calmly close" his eyes and the speaker departs to "speed forth to the darkness" suggest a concluding moment of bodily identification. The darkness beyond the boy's closed eyes becomes an abyss that the speaker inherits as he returns to his own darkness, the night-march that continues past the church-hospital and away from the incident itself. This darkness becomes a point of commonality as these two figures share a deeply embodied encounter with mortality—one dies while the other is permitted access into the depths of a stranger's inner dark.

The original version of "One Wicked Impulse" grants Marsh similar entry into an experience of shared darkness, a moment of bodily encounter textured by the visceral empathy so absent from the early stages of his remorse. The story's original conclusion delivers a pointed anti-hanging message, steering Marsh towards narrative salvation by forcing him into the devoted service of New York City's cholera victims. He goes out like a "merciful spirit... wiping the drops from hot brows, and soothing the agony of cramped limbs". Though this passage likens him to a "spirit," his care-giving is deeply corporeal and fundamentally mortal, as he "cool... hot cheeks with his own hands and lips" amidst the squalor of "noisome alleys and foul rear-buildings". His physical body becomes implicated in the suffering of others—"his eyes moist with tears of sympathy" as he "inhale peril at every breath'—and it is this physical involvement that satisfies his "engrossing wish to cancel, as far as he could, the great outrage he had committed".

These acts of bodily provision gesture towards Maslan's principle of "involuntary" involvement. Though Marsh has chosen to administer aid to the sick (despite the fact that one keenly feels the tyranny of authorial sensibilities guiding his choice), he cannot choose—or control—the ways that his body will be implicated in these ministrations. Vapors of contagion encroach upon his "inhalations" and sickness threatens the boundaries of his body. As is true for the speakers of "Drum-Taps," things happen to the bodies of healers that cannot be controlled, and this relinquishing of agency is what deepens and authenticates their acts of empathy. Maslan describes this "devotion to the soldiers as involuntary—the result of an unnamed external force having seized control of and taken his body as sacrifice."

In glimmers, Philip Marsh does prefigure the "sacrificial bodies" of Whitman's poetic speakers in important ways, though this prefiguration is obscured by the cumbersome layers of melodrama that shroud his care-giving in sentimentality. This sentimentality is compounded by the story's final turn, whose neat predictability eventually disappoints: Marsh achieves his "crowning act of recompense" by caring for—of all people—the sickly son of his murder victim. This redemption, however forced, does manage to push Whitman's ideas about embodied empathy even further than other early stories. When "Philip's heart quivered as if some harsh instrument had cut into it," he is subjected by a direct visceral echo of the sensations his victim must have felt when he was stabbed to death in the chest. Just as the "leaden whiteness" and "globules" of sweat across Lugare's brow recall his victim's pallor and perspiration; just as the "pendulum" of Peter Brown's swinging neck mimics the "hideous object" of the swinging corpse; so do the specific—almost clinical—pangs of Marsh's heart resurrect the physical impact of his crime, finally inscribing an abstract remorse onto the body responsible for the crime.

The initial execution of the deed itself is rendered in strikingly bodily terms: "the arm of the murderer thrust the blade, once, twice, deep in his enemy's bosom!". In this act of impulsive violence, the "arm" of the murderer is given more syntactical responsibility than his mind, and so it seems natural that his sympathy would have to manifest itself in the flesh before he could approach "recompense." It is as if—for the first time—Marsh is living through the experience of committing his crime. During the murder, he is "possess'd" by a "fiendish rage" that effectively displaces his own gentler nature, and so it seems appropriate that he would need to be "possessed" by some physical sensation to displace the "rage" that overwhelmed his better nature in the first place.

Merleau-Ponty posits that every man's "possession of own time is always postponed until a stage when may fully understand it," and we see this process at work with Marsh, who can only reclaim the "time" of his violence once his own heart "quivers." Maslan's language intersects Merleau-Ponty's theory in the denouement of this process: in effect, Marsh can only begin to "possess" this moment when it takes possession of him. Written years later, "The Artilleryman's Vision" presents a more aesthetically sophisticated depiction of the memorial aftermath of violence. This poem documents the subtleties of interior awareness, fingering recollections that stay in the "fantasy unreal" of the mind's-eye rather than manifesting in the flesh. But while "One Wicked Impulse" feels mired in the ineffectual texture of its protagonist's sympathy, "The Artilleryman's Vision" is able to dramatize the futility of its speaker's empathic impulses in deeply moving terms. The poem reads like a prescient lyrical case study in post-traumatic stress disorder, spoken by an artilleryman who is still haunted by the afterglow of "vari-color'd rockets" and "suffocating smoke," even though the "wars are over long" and he is lying in bed with his wife. We see that these memories are habitual as we witness the speaker's unsuccessful efforts to ignore their grimmest offerings: "And ever the hastening of infantry shifting positions.../(The falling, dying, I heed not, the wounded dripping and red I heed not, some to the rear are hobbling)".

Though the poem's primary pathos lies in the brutality of how these memories of war encroach upon this speaker's consciousness, there is also something tragic about the distance between his body and the experience of war: the disembodied nature of his retrospective engagement also keeps him distanced from his own potential for empathy. He cannot fully "heed" the "falling, dying... the wounded dripping" even though we can sense that their existence still pains him, as they are thrust into prominence by their parenthetical quarantines.

"The Child and the Profligate": An Early Draft of the "Pugilistic Art"

In "The Child and the Profligate," the crippling aftermath of the past—the "vari-color'd rockets" of prior horror—actually deepens the protagonist's capacity for empathy. The plot of this early story, first published in the New World in 1841, develops one of the earliest figurations of homosocial intimacy in Whitman's entire canon. The story hinges upon the striking bond forged between an innocent youth and the mysterious stranger who comes to his rescue in a bar-room brawl. When young Charles is hit by a "one-eyed" sailor, the fashionable stranger, who is certainly "no stranger to the pugilistic art" himself, intervenes with sudden force and deep conviction. He offers physical defence, "shelter" in his bed, and ultimately lasting friendship and monetary support. Like the speaker-healers of Whitman's poetry, who are inspired into empathy by an involuntary compulsion, the stranger finds his own "rage... uncontrollable". He is overwhelmed by the impulse to intervene—"violated" by this impulse and thus re-defined by it.

Appearing as a kind of cosmopolitan deus ex machina in his spotless linen suit, Langton is not inspired by a direct sense of remorse towards the boy but by a more generalized sense of moral failure. He is later identified as "a dissipated young man—a brawler—one whose too frequent companions were rowdies, blacklegs, and swindlers". He has seen his share of vice—indeed, the "New York police officers were no stranger to his countenance" —but his benevolent impulses towards the boy are not beholden to any simple arithmetic of guilt and reform. This ensures them a certain integrity and grants Whitman the liberty to suggest something larger and more generous about the human capacity for empathy: it does not have to be beholden to some tally of wrongdoing and responsibility, as it was for characters like Peter Brown.

Because readers only learn about Langton's many vices after his intervention, we initially read his actions as natural instincts rather than guilty compensations—products of basic human impulses rather than any situational desire for "recompense." The narrative seems invested in building up the mystery of this empathy, rather than translating it into some predictably reductive arithmetic of shame and remorse. The story steps out of its own dramatic flame to ask: "Why was it, too, that the young man's heart moved with a feeling of kindness toward the harshly treated child?"

This acknowledgment of the mystery of empathy—and the refusal to immediately undercut this mystery—suggests a primal "wish to love and be loved" that foreshadows Whitman's poetry, in which the hunger for connection is an essential human trait. The stranger's instant attachment to this vulnerable boy is portrayed as an innate human impulse rather than a strategic narrative device, and Whitman is eager to insist that "no scrap of this is sentimental fiction; ask your own heart, reader, for endorsement to its truth". Langton's empathetic impulse is sharpened into focus by the dramatic pause of a "strange" and "silent" human tableau: "In the middle of the room stood the young man, in his not at all ungraceful attitude—every nerve out, and his eyes flashing brilliantly. He seem'd rooted like a rock; and clasping him with an appearance of confidence in his protection, clung the boy".

The stranger's intervention becomes a performance that commands attention, and the theatricality of his empathy evidences a certain contagious engagement: just as the stranger's sentiments are "uncontrollable," so the rest of the "company" cannot help but " from their seats... for a moment breathless but strain'd positions". The rest of the room has become engaged in the boy's plight through the medium of visual spectacle, witnessing with "strain'd" bodies the outrage that has become externally legible on the body of the stranger—in his taut "nerves" and "flashing" eyes.

The entangling of these two male bodies, their "clasping" and "clinging," creates a physical precedent for their night of shared "shelter," when Charles sleeps with his "arms around " and his "cheek rested on his bosom". This physical intimacy prompts less tangible unions of mind and heart, as the profligate begins to consider his future "interwoven with the youth". The incident is striking for the ways in which it prefigures those celebrations of embodied homosocial bonding that appear throughout Leaves of Grass, particularly the lusty eroticism of the "Calamus" cluster and the hospital comradery of "Drum-Taps" and Specimen Days.

The physicality of these moments—one body clutching another body in the bar, or in the bed—is ultimately more poignant than the predictable expressions of empathy that follow them. The stranger ends up funding Charles' education, rescuing his mother from destitution, and saving himself from a life of vice through these acts of altruism, but even the narrator acknowledges the perfunctory nature of these concluding strokes, admitting, "It needs not that I should particularize the subsequent events of Langton's and the boy's history" because these events are already common features of the redemption-story genre. The story finds more resonance in the physical connection between these two men than it does in the narrative machinery surrounding their intimacy, a framework encumbered by the sentimental arc of a hard-working young boy and a mother wracked by "the sickening idea of her own poverty".

The opening pages of the story depict embodied sympathy in terms of recognizable tropes: tears are shared, blood is spilt, and Charles' "passionate fit of weeping" become "pangs" in his mother's breast. Here are faint preludes to the poignant reciprocity celebrated by Whitman's poetics, but they are faint preludes indeed. It is the intimacy between Langton and Charles that becomes innovative and surprising, defying traditional (especially nineteenth-century) strategies of classification and categorization with its intertwining of illicit intimacy and violent energy. As Moon notes—in his classic study of the story against Whitman's 1855 Leaves—the leit motif of fluids throughout the story (sweat, tears, liquor, rivers) becomes an aqueous correlative to its project of "eroding and dissolving... boundaries" between the bodies of its characters.

In Whitman's prose, it can be difficult to distinguish between the early traces of an evolving authorial sensibility and the ghost-limb relics of generic inheritance—tropes and narrative appendages that Whitman employs even though one senses that he did not fully believe in them. When do teary eyes cease functioning as sentimental tropes and start exploring more interesting facets of embodied sympathy? When do incidents of violence transcend the territory of melodrama and start prefiguring a more sophisticated poetics of injury and healing?

Exploring Whitman's early taxonomy of empathic variations does not require us to dull our critical sensibilities or elevate his early fiction—clearly stilted in its language and heavy-handed in its concepts—to the level of his poetry. It simply means acknowledging that Whitman's creativity was full of missteps, flaws, and inconsistencies, those same dimensions of selfhood that his later poetry would celebrate so eloquently. It means recognizing the stamina of his faith in the human potential for empathy—even, or especially, in the aftermath of violence—and his commitment to exploring the forms this empathy could take: the costumes it might wear, the exuberant variety of bodies it might inhabit, and the infinite channels of conception and expression it might follow.

1863 Letter from Ralph Waldo Emerson about Walt Whitman.

By Lee Ann Potter

Biographers have called Walt Whitman "America's most influential and innovative poet" and some have even called him "the greatest of all American poets." But in the winter of 1862-63, even as he was gaining a reputation as a talented poet, Whitman was forty-three years old, volunteering as a nurse in Union hospitals, and looking for a steady job in the nation's capital.

Whitman's desire to work for the government in Washington, D.C., had much to do with the Civil War. In December 1862, a few days after the Battle of Fredericksburg, Whitman checked the casualty roster in his New York newspaper and saw a name that resembled that of his younger brother. His brother was George Washington Whitman, and the roster read "G.W. Whitmore." So, the elder Whitman immediately went to Virginia in search of his brother.

In Fredericksburg, Whitman did find his brother, who was alive, having sustained only a superficial facial wound. But rather than returning home immediately, Whitman sent a telegram telling their family that George was safe and that he, Walt, had decided to stay for a few days, as his help was needed.

The battle had resulted in nearly 18,000 casualties on both sides. The bodies of the dead needed to be buried and the wounded needed attention. Whitman assisted with both tasks. He spent time attending wounded soldiers, often writing down their messages to their families. He also wrote a letter to his own mother, telling her that he might look for work in Washington, D.C.

The federal bureaucracy during these years was growing.

In the 1830s, there were 20,000 federal employees; by the end of the Civil War, there were 53,000; and by the mid 1880s, there were 131,000. Whitman knew that while government jobs were available, the so-called "spoils system" still dictated who was hired (and would for another twenty years until the passage of the Pendleton Act). Under this system, many officials obtained their positions, not because of special skills, but because of whom they knew. So, Whitman wrote to his friend, the American transcendentalist Ralph Waldo Emerson, and asked him to write letters of recommendation on his behalf to the secretary" of state and the secretary of treasury, who were both acquaintances of Emerson.

Emerson's handwritten letter to Salmon P. Chase, secretary of the treasury, dated January 10, 1863, is featured in this article. In it, Emerson described Whitman as a man "of strong original genius" who was "self-relying" and "large-hearted." He described Whitman's writings as "more deeply American, democratic, and in the interest of political liberty than those of any other poet," He stated that if the government had work that Whitman could do, "it may find that it has called to its side more valuable aid than it bargained for."

The government did indeed have work that Whitman could do, and for the next eleven years, "Whitman was a public servant in three different cabinet departments—but never in the Treasury Department. Initially, he worked part-time as a copyist in the army's paymaster office. Then, in early 1865, he went to work as a clerk in the Indian Bureau of the Interior Department. However, his time with the Interior Department was short-lived. In the spring of that year, the new secretary of the interior, James Harlan, sought to abolish all non-essential positions, and to dismiss any employee whose moral character was considered questionable. Learning that Whitman was the author of the controversial volume of poetry, Leaves of Grass, Harlan dismissed him in late June.

Through personal connections in other agencies, Whitman immediately secured a position as a clerk in the busy and evolving attorney general's office. The Judiciary Act of 1789 had established the office of the attorney general, but it was not until 1870 that Congress passed the Act to Establish the Department of Justice and made the attorney general the head of the department. The brand new Justice Department was involved in issues such as patent infringement cases, disputes over Reconstruction, and challenges to legislation—such as the Chinese Exclusion Act, the Civil Rights Act of 1875, and the Ku Klux Klan Act of 1871.

As a clerk in the attorney general's office for nearly nine years, Whitman's tasks varied. Initially, he assisted in the preparation of pardon requests from Confederates, and later he copied documents for delivery to the president and cabinet members.

During the war years, while employed by the federal government, Whitman continued his volunteer work in the Union hospitals—there were more than thirty of them in the district, some in government office buildings, including the U.S. Patent Office. He would often run errands for the soldiers and help them write letters home. Whitman estimated that he visited between eighty thousand and one hundred thousand sick and wounded soldiers.

His personal time was also spent on his poetry During his years of government service, Whitman published such famous works as "When Lilacs Last in the Dooryard Bloom'd" and "O Captain! My Captain!" that reflected his wartime experience.

His career as a federal government employee ended following a stroke in 1874 that left him partially paralyzed. That year, he moved to Camden, New Jersey, where he lived until his death on March 26, 1892.

Dear Sir,

Mr. Walt Whitman, of New York, writes that he is seeking employment in the public service in Washington, and perhaps some application on his part has already been made to yourself.

Will you permit me to say that he is known to me as a man of strong original genius, combining with marked eccentricities, great powers and valuable traits of character: a self-relying, large-hearted man, much beloved by his friends;

entirely patriotic and benevolent in his theory, talks, and practice. If his writings are in certain points open to criticism, they show extraordinary power, and are more deeply American, democratic, and in the interest of political liberty, than those of any other poet.

A man of his talents and dispositions will quickly make himself useful, and if the government has work that he can do, I think it may find that it has called to its side more valuable aid than it bargained for.

With entire respect, Your obedient servant,

R. W. Emerson

Honorable Salmon P. Chase Secretary of the Treasury

Audience Terminable and Interminable: Anne Gilchrist, Walt Whitman, and the Achievement of Disinhibited Reading

Anne burrows gilchrist was introduced to walt whitman's poetry in 1869 by her friend william michael Rossetti, and the effect was galvanic. She read him first in Rossetti's own expurgated Poems of Walt Whitman and subsequently in the complete 1867 edition of Leaves of Grass, which Rossetti gave her. Her letters to Rossetti on Whitman so impressed him with their fervorous insight that he urged her to publish them as a counteractive to the squeamishness, outrage, and plain misunderstanding that so widely characterized the poet's early reception. Gilchrist's "A Woman's Estimate of Walt Whitman" appeared in the Boston Radical in 1870, and in 1871, with Rossetti's help, she initiated a correspondence with the poet himself. Widowed with four children, Gilchrist had discovered in Whitman's poetry the object of her desire, and she not only wanted him to know it, she wanted him. After five years of intimations, Gilchrist took action in 1876, announcing her imminent move across the Atlantic to be near him. Whitman, of course, balked at first ("I do not approve your American trans.settlement"). But, upon finding her behaviour less than predatory, he warmed to her presence just as she quickly adjusted her comportment to his sexual unavailability, and their friendship lasted until her death, back in England, in

1885. Whitman was fond of being fond of her, measuring out heaps of preposthumous and posthumous praise to Traubel and others. At times his praise rings with some of the sad falsity of his later years (the rebuff of John Addington Symonds, the claims of illegitimate children, etc.), a falsity ravened by later biographers and critics bent on retrospectively constructing for him a fundamentally heterosexual, if unfulfilled, life. But there is no doubting the genuineness of Whitman's affection for Gilchrist, or his appreciation of her critical acumen, especially with reference to his own poetry. Indeed, her disinhibited reading of the poems, and of the poet in the poems, called the serious bluff of addressivity central to the poet's own eroticism. In Gilchrist, Whitman had precisely not found his "match." Instead, he found a reader willing and able to take seriously his ambivalent offers to rescind the fictionality of address.

"A Woman's Estimate of Walt Whitman" still reads as a marvelously unencumbered appreciation of Whitman at his best: his conviction of the debt poetry owes to the dignity of the common; the rhythmic sophistication of poetry that rewards, not the counting of syllables, but the ear willing to turn to new music; and especially his frank and fearless language of instinctual and bodily life in both men and women. Gilchrist's essay was a love letter, and—just in case Whitman had not noticed—she followed it up with more private avowals of the transformation wrought upon her by Leaves of Grass: "I never before dreamed what love meant," she writes in her first letter to Whitman in 1871. She tells him the story of her happy but erotically unsatisfying marriage to Alexander Gilchrist, and his death in 1861. Since then, she explains, she has had "much sweet tranquil happiness, much strenuous work and endeavour raising my darlings", without much sense of the loss of sexual love. But then:

In May, 1869, came the voice over the Atlantic to me—O, the voice of my Mate: it must be so—my love rises up out of the very depths of the grief and tramples upon despair. I can wait-any time, a lifetime, many lifetimes—I can suffer, I can dare, I can learn, grow, toil, but nothing in life or death can tear out of my heart the passionate belief that one day I shall hear that voice say to me, "My Mate. The one I so much want. Bride, Wife, indissoluble eternal!" It is not happiness I plead with God for—it is the very life of my Soul, my love is its life. Dear Walt. Three weeks went by, and, having heard nothing back from Whitman, Gilchrist wrote to him again:

I that have never set eyes upon thee, all the Atlantic flowing between us, yet cleave closer than those that stand nearest and dearest around thee—love thee day and night.... Do not say that I am forward, or that I lack pride because I tell this love to thee who have never sought or made sign of desiring to seek me. Oh, for all that, this love is my pride my glory. Source of sufferings and joys that cannot put themselves into words. Besides, it is not true thou hast not sought or loved me. For when I read the divine poems I feel all folded round in thy love. Part Robert Browning to Whitman's Elizabeth Barrett ("I love your verses with all my heart"2), part Clytie to Whitman's Helios ("Not more do the things that grow want the sun"), Gilchrist not only snaps her fingers in the face of contemporary interdictions against women's direct sexual pursuit of men, but also runs the risk-dangerous in any era-of acting on libidinal investments made in distant objects. It is difficult to read without making such investments at least occasionally. One falls in love with a Gwendolen Harleth or a Tom Outland, or craves contact with a writer who seems to have some special insight into oneself.

Gilchrist was neither the first nor the last to pursue Whitman with affectional designs. But few of his contemporary readers combined such critical acumen with such uncommon disinhibition and personal daring. It is no small measure of her insight as a reader of Whitman that her deployment of the often effusive conventions of romantic correspondence comport so well with his own prescriptions for the annihilation of distance through writing and reading-too well, indeed, for Whitman's perfect comfort. Some of her solicitations are as embarrassing to read now as they must have been frightening for Whitman to read then. For example, she tells him flatly in her second letter, "I am yet young enough to bear thee children, my darling". His response to this long letter is brief but gentle. It urges her to rest content with his poems:

My book is my best letter, my response, my truest explanation of all. In it I have put my body and spirit. You understand this better and fuller and clearer than any one else. And I too fully and clearly understand the loving letter it has evoked. Enough that there surely exists so beautiful and a delicate relation, accepted by both of us with joy. Whitman says "my best letter, my response, my truest explanation" as if to say "my best defence" against a breakdown of the very protocols of decorous reading it has been his avowed project to dismantle. The "enough" is devastating to Gilchrist ("like a blow on the breast to me"), not only because it is a rebuff to her amorous advances, but also because it is an attempt to inhibit her way of reading-a way of reading she thought she had learned from Whitman. Unlike the auditors in Shelley's "Defence of Poetry," "entranced by the melody of an unseen musician, who feel that they are moved and softened, yet know not whence or why," Gilchrist does know, and she continues to feel that she knows, despite Whitman's slightly panicky efforts to neutralize the ideas the conviction of such knowledge gives her) In letter after letter she persists, not only in offering herself up quite literally as wife and prospective bearer of his children, but also, quite fairly, in calling him on his doctrine of poetic transubstantiation:

If it seems to you there must needs be something unreal, illusive, in a love that has grown up entirely without the basis of personal inter course, dear Friend, then you do not yourself realise your own power nor understand the full meaning of your own words, "whoso touches this, touches a man." Is the book, or is it not, an embodiment? And if it is, then why is Whitman's programme for contact with his reader so frequently subverted by forms of inhibition expressed as warnings? "You will hardly know who I am"; "forever reject those who would expound me"; "I understand your anguish, but I cannot help you"; "I depart as air"; "To touch my person to some one else's is about as much as I can stand"; "I will certainly elude you". It is not just because Gilchrist was a woman that her advances were frightening. On some level Gilchrist knew this, and in calling Whitman's bluff she may have experienced an enhancement of the erotic excitement of her pursuit of a man whose desires had yet to be clearly settled in relational terms.

Gilchrist's letters to Whitman between 1871 and 1876 are almost uniformly faithful to the rhetoric of unrequited love, holding intensely to that fine line between paranoia (she complains of feeling "restless, anxious, impatient" waiting for his replies to letters she fears he never received) and erotic entreaty ("above all, longing, longing so for you to come—to come and see if you feel happy beside me"). She sometimes lapses unselfconsciously into fantasies of being Whitman's mother, and she occasionally strikes a delusional note of omnipotence ("you will want me.

You will not be able to help stretching out your hand and drawing me to you"). But the most pronounced tendencies, as the years pass, are the tempering of her libidinous designs (at one point she projects their consummation into the afterlife) and the compensatory plan to move to America with at least three of her children to be as close as possible to Whitman, in whatever loving capacity he will tolerate. Though never fulfilled in the way she hoped, Gilchrist's singular relationship with the poet speaks the more general desire both to take seriously and to critique seriously some of Whitman's more audacious claims about audience, and to evaluate poetry's role in overcoming both social and psychic constraints, not least because, to his surprise, Whitman's verse actually did have the seductive effect he claimed it might.

Ralph Waldo Emerson repeatedly called poets "liberating gods" at a time when there was a high degree of confidence in poetry's efficacy as an agent of social change. The rise of associationism in antebellum America and the astonishing proliferation of reformist institutions helped to generate and disseminate widely the versifications of conscience, piety, grievance, smugness, sympathy, and rage that occupied writers of all sorts. Poetry itself became an object of reform, as more and more women, for example, commodified as well as diversified their literary output for periodicals, anthologies, and annuals devoted in whole or in part to the plight of slaves, children, the ill, the laboring classes, and women themselves. But the question of just what sort of liberation poets might effect in their own and in their readers' lives not only remained open but grew sore as a wound in a literary culture that thrived on, even as it sought to combat, human misery.

Emerson was not alone in casting an increasingly skeptical eye on the rate at which the publicity of such misery continued to outstrip the pace of the good that could be done. Nor was he alone in noting the perversity of Romantic celebrations of an American landscape pocked and stained by the violence of individual greed and national rapacity. In 1848, the annus mirabilis and horribilis of its political era, Emerson lectured in Great Britain and Europe amid widespread unrest and uncertainty, while in America, too, the union of freedom with justice could seem either gloriously imminent or thoroughly chimerical depending on who you were and where you were, from Beacon Hill to Sutter's Mill, and from Seneca Falls to Guadalupe Hidalgo.

The victory over Mexico and the consequent ramping of sectional tensions over slavery, the passage of the Fugitive Slave Act, "Bleeding Kansas," and other preliminaries to national collapse overtook and largely extinguished the brightness of reformist energy and turned the national literary project from one of melioration into one of mourning. Whitman's own exuberant version of a Hegelian-Emersonian faith in freedom as self-development gave way, in the atmosphere of the Washington hospitals especially, to a soberer view of the intimacies that could be expected to matter, in poetry and in life. Nevertheless, Whitman managed substantially to sustain the demanding and often flirtatious addressivity of Leaves of Grass through and beyond the Civil War, in successive editions-even in one that escaped his editorial control.

Rossetti based his Poems of Walt Whitman on the fourth edition of Leaves of Grass. He was an early and highly sympathetic champion of Whitman in England and brought out this first English edition with the hope that a wider readership could be trained to see beyond what he acknowledged, on the basis of others' previous complaints, to be Whitman's "very serious faults" of crudeness and impropriety. "Whitman," Rossetti insisted, "is a poet who bears and needs to be read as a whole, and then the volume and torrent of his power carry the disfigurements along with it, and away." Yet Rossetti did not think his English readers could swallow Whitman whole, so he expurgated Leaves, "omit entirely any poem which could with any tolerable fairness be deemed offensive to the feelings of morals or propriety in this peculiarly nervous age". The mechanisms of defence, that is, that Rossetti understands to be motivating his own falsifications of the text are social, rather than personal, in nature; these are the mechanisms that soon came to be called "Victorian" and that were mythologized under that name. The "peculiarly nervous age" in which he situates his editorial project is, moreover, a spatial as well as temporal situation-the situation of England, specifically, as opposed to the situation of America. England, for Rossetti, represents an inhibiting force brought to bear on Whitman's uncensored humanistic avowals:

knows of no reason why what is universally seen and known, necessary and right, should not also be allowed and proclaimed in speech. That such a view of the matter is entitled to a great deal of weight, and at any rate to candid consideration and construction, appears to me not to adrait of a doubt; neither is it dubious that the contrary view which a mealy-mouthed British nineteenth century admits as endurable, amounts to the condemnation of nearly every great or eminent literary work of past time. Rossetti was, of course, aware that Whitman's reception in America had been anything but universally approving. Yet the author of what is, as he puts it, "incomparably the largest performance of our period in poetry" is also in his view "the founder of an American poetry rightly to be so called". Rossetti's phrase "mealy-mouthed British nineteenth century" reviles the canon that the American Edmund Clarence Stedman would soon definitively establish as the very "course of British poetry during the present reign." Not only does Rossetti stand Whitman, as an essentially American poet, in opposition to the "mealy-mouthed British" who will not speak of things openly and honestly, but he also implies that American poetry is fundamentally the work of a single poet. Stedman, in sharp contrast, characterizes Victorian poetry as the work of many hands. As Joseph Bristow observes, Stedman's Victorian Poets "remains one of the most inclusive pieces of research ever to map English poetry between the mid-1830s and mid-1870s."

Whitman stands apart from the aggregate of English poetry. But, according to Rossetti, he is "saved from isolation by the depth of his Americanism". It is an Americanism, moreover, that he predicts will trump the British Victorian enshrinement of what Bristow calls "the spatial ideologies of empire". "His voice," Rossetti says of Whitman, will one day be potential or magisterial wherever the English language is spoken-that is to say, in the four corners of the earth; and, in his own American hemisphere, the uttermost avatars of democracy will confess him not more their announcer than their inspirer. Democracy, in other words, means the domain in which everything is "allowed and proclaimed in speech," and that domain is invoked by Whitman—a voice not only singularly iconoclastic but also uniquely reviled in Rossetti's time by most of his American readers, yet which would paradoxically assume the stewardship of freedom throughout a global imperium no longer British but American.

Rossetti saw his task in Poems of Walt Whitman as "paving the way towards the issue and unprejudiced reception of a complete edition of [Leaves of Grass] in England". Whitman, however, did not think the end justified the means. In 1871 he wrote to the London publisher F. S. Ellis proposing the publication of "a full edition of my poems, Leaves of Grass, in England under my sanction.... I make this proposition not only to get my poems before the British public, but more because I am annoyed at the horrible dismemberment of my book there already and of something worse." Ellis did not think the time was ripe. But less than a month later Whitman received his first letter from Anne Gilchrist, who seemed ripe enough, offering not merely to love Whitman but to publicly sacrifice herself for him, to "joyfully bare her breast to wrest the blows aimed at her beloved." She told him she deeply regretted allowing Rossetti to convince her to publish "A Woman's Estimate of Walt Whitman" anonymously: "It has been very bitter and hateful to me this not standing to what I have said as it were, with my own personality". She wanted to say everything, not anonymously or to Whitman alone, but publicly-to speak from a place of disinhibition that would constitute not a retreat from social life, but rather an enhanced, more fully democratized sociability.

Gilchrist highly prized Whitman's poetics of disclosure and amplitude. In "A Woman's Estimate," she celebrates his "fearless and comprehensive dealing with reality," his "utmost faithful freedom of speech." And in her letters to him she aspires to a linguistic transparency of her own: "I would if I could lay every thought and action and feeling of my whole life open to thee as it lies to the eye of God". Gilchrist's responsiveness to Whitman's poetry makes this wish more than a mere romantic convention. It turns such conventionalism into ethical aspiration. What indeed would the world be like if people could say everything to one another?

Disinhibition is the politico-linguistic project of Leaves of Grass. Its aim is to incite a rapport with its audience that will help further to disseminate both the poet's and the reader's affectional presence in the world. When Gilchrist picks up Whitman's book and finds this aim directed at her, her response is to fall in love and to imagine a life of erotic fulfillment that would not only be more than a matter of words, but would be the embodiment of democratic principle:

If the poet's heart were not "a measureless ocean of love" that seeks the lips and would quench the thirst of all, he were not the one we have waited for so long. Who but he could put at last the right meaning into that word "democracy," which has been made to bear such a burthen of incongruous notions? "By God! I will have nothing that all cannot have their counterpart of on the same terms!" flashing it forth like a banner, making it draw the instant allegiance of every man and woman who loves justice. For Gilchrist as for Whitman, the terms of the rapport of democracy are erotic terms ("heart," "love," "lips," "thirst"), and thus they resound with the many senses of the word "term" itself, which Whitman plays with promiscuously: the spatial and the temporal, the gestational and the necrotic, the relational and the linguistic, the measured and the immeasurable. "For me," he boasts in "Starting from Paumanok," "an audience interminable":

With firm and regular step they wend, they never stop, Successions of men, Americanos, a hundred millions, One generation playing its part and passing on, Another generation playing its part and passing on in its turn, With faces turn'd sideways or backward towards me to listen, With eyes retrospective towards me. Prognosticating literary immortality is a game any author can play more or less anxiously with himself. But when the terms of this prediction are understood to be ontogenetic rather than phylogenetic, the game has two players and the stakes go up enormously. Generations to come may, in some attenuated sense, continue as an "audience" to harken back to Whitman. His poems may survive as texts and be read by certain individuals from time to time. Discursive traditions may continue to reflect the influence of his works well beyond the point of identifiability. But when it comes to the individual reader, continuity of audience is far more precarious. Is it desirable or even possible to prolong the experience of reading into something interminable? How much good can reading Whitman do you, and how do you know when you have exhausted the possibilities?

Whitman's singular practice of revision and edition makes these important questions, not only about reception, but also about revisionary technique-that is, about the way Whitman seeks to make himself intelligible to others. He subjects himself to a long-term task called Leaves of Grass that invites readers to do the same. Part of the lure is the thrilling prospect of competition over who will have final control over the resolution of that task. Gilchrist's "A Woman's Estimate of Walt Whitman," her later essay on Whitman, called "A

Confession of Faith", and the other artifacts of their correspondence (not just letters but also books, pictures, newspapers, a ring, etc.) constitute the record of one such competitive alliance, an alliance that survives Gilchrist's erotic disappointment but is therefore also constituted by the traumatic alienation of her desire.

Gilchrist never exhibited an inclination to stop reading Whitman. Her letters to him refer to his books—often "the Book"—as being always with her. But if it is, as she at one point claims, "an effort to me to turn to any other reading," it is not because she has found satisfaction in reading him. "And if you say, 'Read my books, and be content—you have me in them,' I say, it is because I read them so that I am not content". Born of frustration, this language is also deeply playful. Does "I read them so" mean "I read them because I do have you in them"? Or does "so" mean "to such a great extent"? Or does "so that" mean "in order to feel that"? In her ambivalence, Gilchrist understood "the Book" to be the form in which her alienated demand (her desire for Whitman himself) returned to her, and would keep returning, again and again.

Gilchrist's letters to Whitman from the point of her 1879 move back to England to her death in 1885 include one that she wrote shortly after obtaining a copy of the 1881-82 edition of Leaves from British publisher David Bogue. Like everyone else, Gilchrist had strong views on Whitman's new arrangement of the poems:

I find a few new friends [that is, poems] to love—perhaps I have not yet found them all out. But you must not expect me to take kindly to any changes in the titles or arrangement of the old beloved friends. I love them too dearly—every word and look of them—for that. For instance, I want "Walt Whitman" instead of "Myself" at the top of the page. Also my own longing is always for a chronological arrangement, if change at all there is to be; for that at once makes biography of the best kind. What deaths, dear Friend! At the end of this passage, Gilchrist is still talking about poems. The "deaths" are the effect of new revisions and arrangements that have taken from her some of her "beloved friends." But she also means the accumulating deaths of her human friends and contemporaries: Darwin, Dante Gabriel Rossetti, Edward Carpenter's father, and especially her daughter Beatrice, who killed herself in 1881. And she is anticipating her own death:

As for me, my heart is already gone over to the other side of the river, so that sometimes I feel a kind of rejoicing in the swelling of the ranks of the great company there. She longs, as she puts it in "A Confession of Faith," to be "going somewhere." This phrase, which she adopts from the openly atheistic mathematician and philosopher William Kingdon Clifford, assumes importance not only in "A Confession," where it is repeated and celebrated as "the meaning... of all our perplexities," but also as the title of Whitman's 1887 elegy for her. Whitman composed this elegy on the back of a letter from newspaper editor Charles Marseilles, who had written to ask when and where Whitman's "recent oration on Lincoln" would be published. Whitman drew a canceling line through the letter and turned over the paper to write his poem. Thus the artifact seems to make the poem into a kind of countersign of national mourning, lending the phrase "going somewhere" the attractiveness of a password out of the dispirited, static memorialism of the postwar years, to which the aged Whitman himself was an influential contributor. Though it is not a particularly fine poem, the manuscript version differs sufficiently from the Variorum printing as to warrant its reproduction here:

"Going Somewhere" My science-friend—my noblest woman friend, (Now buried in an English grave—and this a memory-leaf for dear love's sake,) Ended our talk—"The amount and sum of all we know—of old or modern learning, intuitions deep, Of all the Histories, Geologies—of all Astronomy—of Evolution, Metaphysics all, Is, that we are bounding, speeding slowly, surely, Life, life an endless march, an endless army, The world, the race, the soul, the universe, All onward bound-all surely going somewhere." The poignancy of this elegy has less to do with the occasion of Gilchrist's death than with the opportunity Whitman makes of her disappearance for shoring up, through the figure of prosopopoeia, the fictionality of address Gilchrist had worked so hard, and had desired so strongly, to prove that Whitman had rescinded. Yet one can still share some of the exhilaration drawn by Gilchrist and undoubtedly by Whitman too from the Clifford passage:

Suppose all moving things to be suddenly stopped at some instant, and that we could be brought fresh, without any previous knowledge, to look at the petrified scene. The spectacle would be immensely absurd. Crowds of people would be senselessly standing on one leg in the street looking at one another's backs; others would be wasting their time by sitting in a train in a place difficult to get at, nearly all with their mouths open, and their bodies in some contorted, unrestful posture. Clocks would stand with their pendulums on one side. Everything would be disorderly, conflicting, in its wrong place. But once remember that the world is in motion, is going somewhere, and everything will be accounted for and found just as it should be. Just so great a change of view, just so complete an explanation is given to us when we recognize that the nature of man and beast and of all the world is going somewhere. In this allegory of disinhibition, all functioning is lowered to the point of total cessation so that the meaning of the world can be revealed as a diametrical opposition to everything remaining where and as it is. The frustration of aim renders the world not only frozen but "absurd," without order, without value. No object aimed at can be extrapolated from the frozen view; the goals and destinations of the people of the crowds are as unintelligible as they must be manifold. Just where all this is going is irrelevant. What matters, Gilchrist exults, is the going itself."

"Going somewhere!" That is the meaning then of all our perplexities! That changes a mystery which stultified and contradicted the best we knew into a mystery which teaches, allures, elevates; which harmonizes what we know with what we hope....... Going somewhere! And if it is impossible for us to see whither, as in the nature of things it must be, how can we be adequate judges of the way? how can we but often grope and be full of perplexity? But we know that a smooth path, a paradise of a world, could only nurture fools, cowards, sluggards. It is hard not to discern in these effusions the trace of Gilchrist's erotic disappointment in her relationship with Whitman. For one thing, the colloquialism "going somewhere" is so evocative of romantic proposition ("So, is this going somewhere?"). And one can readily imagine the perplexities endured by a passionate female pursuer of Whitman-public champion of female disinhibition but not its private encourager. Whitman himself must have seemed, finally, a way "full of perplexity" for her, and what is truly remarkable, and exemplary, about her reading of Whitman is its affirmative, indeed generative, engagement with the remoteness of his allure.

In January 1889, almost four years after Gilchrist's death, Whitman asked Traubel to read aloud a copy of his first letter to her—the letter that, in responding to her sexual aggressivity, attempted to establish their epistolary relationship on other terms, to say for them both what would be "enough." After Traubel finished, Whitman launched into a lengthy meditation, with eyes closed, on his life's many enemies ("the worst enemies that ever were") and his relatively few but glorious friends. It was his turn to be effusive: "when I turn about and look at my friends—the friends I have had: how sacred, stern, noble, they have been: the few of them: When I have thought of them I have realized the intrinsic immensity of the human spirit and felt as if I lived environed by gods."

"They don't need to be named to you," he tells Traubel. Yet he names a handful anyway, all men: Edward Dowden, John Addington Symonds, William O'Connor, John Burroughs, John Swinton, William Michael Rossetti, Thomas Harned, T. W. Rolleston. "Then," says Traubel, "he referred to his letter to Mrs. Gilchrist: 'The substance of that letter—its feel: what it starts out to say to her: oh! with a few words taken out and put in—it would do for any one of you!'"

The combination here of plangency and ruthlessness is startling. This is one of those innumerable places in With Walt Whitman in Camden where one would give almost anything to see the expression on Traubel's face. (It is, of course,

Traubel's great gift to Whitman's readers that we almost never can.) With nearly the same breath, Whitman delivers an impromptu ode to some of his closest friends, names them, does not forget to imply that Traubel is one of them, and then wipes away their individuality like water over sand. Perhaps he has suddenly been struck by the impression that he is their audience, that he is the one now "turn about" to look back at his friends with the "eyes retrospective" he imagined the future would be turning on him.

What assurances does he crave here from his (particular, yet to him interchangeable) friends that might in some way be like the assurances we desire from Whitman as his (embodied, yet to him anonymous) readers? Does the shared desire to receive assurances from one another exhaust the possibilities of disinhibited reading? If we could speak to Whitman now, what assurances would we want most to give him? That the social and psychic constraints we have learned from him to deplore have been overcome? Or that an unrelinquished commitment to the mythology of Victorianism, known to us still by the resistances that accompany our most ardent hankerings after the experience of transformation, promises him an audience without end?

Ivor Gurney's Creative Reading of Walt Whitman: Thinking of Paumanok.

IVOR GURNEY wrote most of his poetry in his twenties and thirties, between 1916 and 1926, both before and after his incarceration in a mental hospital in 1922. After 1926 his condition declined, and with it his creativity, and he died finally in 1937 from tuberculosis, long separated from the world of serious intellectual exchange. In this decade of poetry writing, Whitman became a progressively more important influence, helping him to reach beyond the forms and modes of Georgianism. As Patrick Kavanagh observes, Gurney "is not a Georgian poet who 'broke down' but one who consciously, though unprogrammatically, broke away [from Georgianism] and was, as far as he knew, on his own, fortified by his beloved Whitman." Gurney's nuanced reading of Whitman deserves careful consideration, both in itself, and as a contribution to our understanding of the interaction of English and American culture in the 1910s and 1920s. He responded profoundly to Whitman's concern for vernacular speech, his rugged egalitarianism and mysticism, his quest for the "illimitable," but for all this his reading was not uncritical. The following essay studies various aspects of Gurney's engagement: how Whitman was mediated to him through music; the experience of reading whitman in the trenches of the First World War; how Whitman's example grew on him in the postwar years; the interpretation of certain crucial poems; and Gurney's final "conversion" to Whitman in 1925. While D. H. Lawrence's view of Whitman, in Studies in Classic American Literature, is well known from this period, the contention here is that Gurney's reading of Whitman is worthy of equal regard.

The composer-poet first encountered Whitman significantly through music. He may have read whitman as a child—the evidence is tenuous—but, once he began his studies at the Royal College of Music in the autumn term of 1911, he moved into an environment where both the name and the poetry were prominent. The leading English composers of this period were very taken with Whitman. Both Sir Charles Stanford, Gurney's main tutor at the college, and Hubert Parry had made settings of Whitman, seeing in him "a liberation from jingoism, prudery and prejudice." There was also, for example, Frederick Delius's Sea Drift (composed 1902-1903, performed 1908 onwards), a setting of an extract from "Out of the Cradle Endlessly Rocking" for baritone, chorus, and orchestra.

The work that most affected Gurney was Ralph Vaughan Williams's A Sea Symphony, composed 1903-1909, and premiered in 1910 in Leeds, which uses Whitman texts to create an orchestral-choral tone poem of the sea of Elgar-like grandeur. Gurney went to its first London performance in February 1913, and Marion Scott, his confidante, recalls seeing him in a group with Herbert Howells and Arthur Benjamin, "almost speechless from the shock of joy the music had given them, and all trying to talk at once in their excitement." In listening to performances on three subsequent days, he paid close attention to the relationship between musical effect and words, and he refers enthusiastically to the symphony in his letters.

Vaughan Williams's selection of texts comprised "Song of the Exposition", "Song for All Seas, All Ships", a shortened version of "On the Beach at Night Alone," "After the Sea-Ship," and extracts from "Passage to India." As James Day observes, "The final design perceives as a vast natural force both separating and uniting the continents, deep, majestic, and ostensibly limitless, the arena for human endeavour and achievement and the symbol of man's never-ending spiritual quest to reach out for, explore and understand the unknown, both within himself and in the universe at large." In his 1920s poetry Gurney often associates whitman and the sea, in "Of the Sea," for example, in Best Poems, and in the fine, late "Going Outward"—Whitmanesque both in theme and manner—which speaks of "the rough-breasted kind/Vasty affection of swift-lilting ocean". The Whitman that Gurney encountered in A Sea Symphony was not a political or a sexual Whitman, or a Whitman of energetic vernacular speech, but primarily a sublime whitman of spiritual aspiration. This is influential for his long-term view. In "Walt Whitman," another late poem, he says that in Whitman "thought to clear-of-thought/Always vowed".

In February 1915 Gurney volunteered for the army; he was drafted into the 2nd/5th Gloucester Regiment, trained with it for over a year in England, and was deployed in France in May 1916. For the next seventeen months he experienced the full rigors of war, until he was finally invalided out after being caught in a gas attack in September 1917. His reading of Whitman through much of this period—seemingly involving several different editions, sent to him by Marion Scott—is well documented in his letters. In September 1915, while still in England, he writes to Ethel Voynich:

Walt Whitman is my latest rediscovery, and he has taken me like a flood. One of the greatest of teachers. And as a poet, he among others has this enormous virtue—that when he has nothing to say, you may divine it a mile off. A marked copy may be read in half an hour; but oh, what gorgeous stuff it is!... On Death he says the supreme word. On the making of men also.

On the Open Air and its revelations....

The titles of his poems will be a complete inspiration to a sensitive musician in tune with his spirit.

"Ethiopia saluting the Colours"
"To the leavened soil they trod."
"Darest thou now O Soul"
"Thou Mother with thy equal Brood."
"Out of the Cradle Endlessly rocking'"
"Song for all Seas, All Ships."
"Year that trembled and reeled beneath me."

A month later, to Marion Scott, this vivid appreciation continues: "The good of Whitman may be condensed in 20 pages, but O, what a score! He is either absurdly unpoetic; or a prophet, speaking high things in high words. A greater and more balanced than Tolstoi—yes, on twenty pages he is that."

After this, both in the trenches and out of them, we see an ongoing contest between judgment and enthusiasm. On 29 June 1916 he vividly recalls A Sea Symphony, a passage in the second section ("Song for All Seas, All Ships"), and writes out the musical notation to the phrase he particularly likes: "Indomitable, untamed as thee." On 1 August 1916 he worries about the "raw" or unformed nature of Whitman's verse, and then sweeps away his own caveats: "Shouldn't I just like to talk on 'This Compost' or 'A Sight in Camp'; on the man who could write Bach-like openings like 'Word over all, beautiful as the sky." On 16 August he praises Whitman over Keats and Shelley: "Walt Whitman is my man however, and I want to write in music such stuff as 'This Compost'"; and on 28 August, to Ethel Voynich, he gives a chatty but revealing assessment of Robert Bridges's anthology The Spirit of Man, attacking what he sees as the effete, upper-class bias of the selection: "it is a good book, though very far below what it might be. Why all that Shelley and Dixon, and Hopkins or what's his names of the crazy precious dictions? About one third of the book is worth having, some of it foolish merely. The Greek stuff is sometimes nonsense. The French trite and dull. Where is Wordsworth, Stevenson, Whitman, Browning?" His evolving attitude has something in common with Hopkins's view of Whitman's "savage" quality, and with Tom Paulin's admiration of his "vernacular energy." The comment takes life from a knowledge of The Spirit of Man anthology itself, in particular its gracious and often archaized translations of the Greek classics. In September 1916, Gurney remarks: "Any fool can do better than WW, save at his best. Who can equal him then, or what better teacher is there?"

The allusions in the letters make clear that Gurney was no secondhand reader of Whitman: he experienced him in the immediate context of life and death, often surrounded by the ugliest exigencies of war. His lists of his favourite Whitman poems are moving when considered from the perspective of an individual soldier facing the horrors of the trenches, and indeed Drum-Taps's stark descriptions of battlefield incidents are an obvious influence on some of his own battlefield poems. But the encounter here is primal, psychologically immediate. Whitman is a "Master", but also a "teacher," someone helping him to live his life; there are, for example, hints that reading him helped with the day-to-day struggle to face death and injury. Calamus was one vehicle through which he could understand his own experience of comradeship, particularly as before the war he had a tendency to shyness and inhibition: "You will be glad to hear however that as a personality I am rather popular in my company. It pleases me this, as so I know myself nearer Walt Whitman's perfect man; equal to shepherd and President; equal and familiar."

Gurney's memories of these reading experiences are as significant as the experiences themselves. In the 1920s we can see that the recollection of how and in what ways Whitman was important to him in the trenches became fused with his emotional attitude towards him in the present. "Whitman" is one of the themes on which his mind snags. In the poetry his allusions to Whitman are most prominent in the middle of the 1920s, particularly in 1925—in other words, they culminate just before the end of his effective period of writing. It is at the moment when the nature of his own poetic development becomes clear to him that Gurney wants to return and write in Whitman as his founding father, his crucial source.

Gurney's reading of Whitman, from September 1915 onwards, precedes his own first great period of creativity as a poet, the writing of the poems in 1916 that made up his first published volume, Severn and Somme. The preface to that volume contains an important, if covert, allusion to Whitman. Here Gurney is both self-conscious about appearing before the public for the first time as a poet, and self-conscious about his class position, a "Common Private"; the allusion to whitman partakes of this complex tentativeness. As a whole the preface affects an offhanded charm and naivete in terms of syntax and vocabulary ("terrible thing," "great little book," "lad," "jolly," etc.), while at the same time it wants to be proud of the fact that it introduces the work of an ordinary soldier (as opposed to a member of the officer class). To use an appropriate Whitman phrase, it has a "fraternizing" bent, its style opposed to "the inertness and fossilism making so large a part of human institutions." The allusion to "Song of Myself" should be viewed in this context. Presumably Gurney knows that the phrasing will seem awkward to those who do not know Whitman, and also from a more conventional viewpoint:

I fear that those who buy the book, to get Information about the Gloucesters will be disappointed. Most of the book is concerned with a person named Myself, and the rest with my county, Gloucester, that whether I die or live stays always with me—being in itself so beautiful, so full of memories; whose people are so good to be friends with, so easy-going and so frank. The forms and moods of the poems comprising Severn and Somme are, by and large, conventional and Georgian, and Whitman is not very evident. This said, he is not invisible. His presence would be more obvious if, as Gurney had wanted, the volume's title had been "Strange Service," for this would have placed emphasis on the one truly Whitmanesque poem, a beautiful and intense meditation on the poet's love of the "secret beauty" of Gloucestershire and the river Severn, and through them, of England. "Strange Service" bears comparison with Hardy's "Drummer Hodge": in both the sense of place is so strong that it almost upsets a conventional patriotism. What has he (a Gloucester lad born and bred) to do with the fields of Flanders?

There are several Whitmanesque features. The most obvious are the address to England as a "mother"; the "enfolding seas" that protect England (reminiscent of "cool-enfolding death" in "When Lilacs Last"); and the open, unrhymed stanza form. In the poetry that Gurney produced over the next years we can see the example of Whitman growing on him. By and large, his work is at first contained within the modes and gestures of Georgianism; only gradually does he free himself. War's Embers, his second volume of poems—and the only other one published in his lifetime—is in many respects more conventional as a whole than Severn and Somme, though it does contain the exquisite lyric "Old Martinmas Eve," whose "moon, one tree, one star" echoes "Lilac and star and bird". In 80 Poems or So (submitted for publication in 1922, but not accepted) Whitman is becoming a more significant implicit presence, but still not one that should be exaggerated. It is in the poems forming Rewards of Wonder (typed up and put into reasonably final form in 1924) that Gurney's use of longer lines and a generally freer sense of form really begin to tell, and it seems no accident that it is here that we encounter his first great poem on an American theme, with Whitman at its centre.

This poem, "Thoughts of New England," was probably first drafted in 1921, the date of the earliest manuscript, and—within the generally hazy chronology of Gurney's work—it gives us a moment we can reasonably identify as marking his emergence from Georgianism. As it becomes better known, it will certainly provoke more debate concerning Anglo-American literary relations in this period. George Walter, who has edited the drafts, speaks of the poem's almost "endless" revision as indicating that Gurney "is truly unable to drag himself away... and move on to producing new material. This might be another way of saying that he recognized how important the poem was to the development of his imagination. "Thoughts of New England "was published twice in 1924, in January in J. C. Squire's London Mercury, and in Second Selections from Modern Poets, also edited by Squire. (This is the main version referred to here.) After this, however, Gurney went on rewriting and, probably in July 1924, produced a "3rd version," which he considered "twice as long—twice as good."

In "Thoughts of New England" Gurney is rethinking his attraction to the American literary tradition, represented centrally by Whitman, but also by Thoreau, Longfellow, Lowell, Hawthorne, and Holmes. The setting is a fine dusk in autumn in Gloucester, England, with the poet wondering about dusk in New England, and thinking also about the Hoare family from Gloucestershire, some of whom emigrated to America in the seventeenth century. Perhaps almost unconsciously, the implicit issue for Gurney here is whether he himself can become a kind of Pilgrim Father of art, crossing over into a new imaginative space that he associates with America. His conflicting instincts can be most clearly seen in some of the lines added to form the third version. The poet imagines contemporary New Englanders brooding over their history, and then identifies with some of the earliest settlers in their immediate experience of a new land:

They watched the Massachusetts land, and thanked God to come Into a free land, might be their all-loved home, Save for the newness of all things, and never the flames Of old story suddenly bursting out from the deep loam, and thought how worship here might have its course.... But where was Gloucester tower standing above the alive Valley of spring, and where was Tewkesbury to be known? (Crying rough rebukes to the straining uncomprehending horse) Thanking so much, after the waste of dangerous-pass foam—Regretting so much the age hallowed beauty, and the sha or triumphs of battle, that to the older earth continual cleave? The identification with the settlers' homesickness is revelatory, making apparent the symbolic and personal nature of these lines: can Gurney cross over into the new imaginative space that is America, given its apparent lack of historical resonance? This dilemma is particularly clear in lines 36-59 of the published version of 1924, in their rhetorical over-insistence and in the vividness with which they evoke local history and ancient association. Here the details of history crowd in: the Domesday Book was commissioned from Gloucester in 1089; William I held court there; it was the scene of Henry III's coronation: "Are there not crowns of England old/That first in Gloucester's Abbey showed their gold?". It is only after this recognition of the pull of the "older earth" of England that the poet can acknowledge his attraction to the "new lands":

But nevertheless one would go very willingly At the year's turn, where Washington or Lincoln walked, Or praise Drum Taps or "This Compost," and hear talked Speech of Lowell, of Hawthorne, or Holmes and be Pleased with citizenship of Gloucester or Worcester And companionship of veterans or veterans' sons Of the Wilderness or Richmond, see the old guns That set Chattanooga's thronged woods astir; Or woke terror in steadfastness with red anger. Just as this picture of America is gathering force, there is a regress: "But not for longer than the strangeness lasted" the "strangeness" of new imaginative territory. The rhetorical effect here repeats a similar effect in the opening lines. There the image of the peaceful evening in England is balanced by the similar evening in New England: even the newspaper boys, selling "our Citizen" and the Massachusetts Times, form a parallel.

Suddenly: "But those no historied ground of Roman or Danes./What are the streets that have no memories,/That are not underset by ancient rubbish?". Thoughts of America are thrust aside by recollections of Gloucestershire's Roman, Danish, and medieval past. (Gurney often recalls the fact that Gloucester was a colonia, i.e., one of the most important centers in Roman Britain.) "Ancient rubbish" is an ambivalent collocation, showing the depths of the issues that are unconsciously at stake. How crucial are historical and imaginative continuities? and how difficult a process is it for the poet to draw real sustenance from the past? Whitman features prominently towards the end of the third version:

The New World has qualities, Her great own, But the Old not yet decrepit or worn is grown, And brick and timber of age five centuries known Are consolations for bare poverty enough Against New York, where they say Opera is brilliant And the bye-ways with five-dollar notes are strown. (For all the glory of Whitman in his words surge and plan). (1924 draft version, ll. 88-94) While from one perspective, then, Whitman is crucial, from another he appears cut off from history (specifically English history) and separated from tradition, the kind of tradition represented metonymically by the five-centuries-old buildings. (The measure of time is not innocent, but an approximate reminder of Gurney's love of the English Renaissance, particularly the dramatists.)

Yet, even with this in the balance, the direction of the syntax is clear, and the third version is bolder than the published one: "brick and timber of age five centuries know/ Are consolations... For all the glory of Whitman in his words surge and plan." Putting in the commas reveals how the vividness of the nouns undermines the explicit meaning: " words, surge, and plan." Rhetorically at least, and evidently more than rhetorically, the ancient buildings and what they symbolize are not really proper "consolations" for the absence of Whitman's energy and skill. Gurney experiences a real desire to reach out beyond his imaginative and literary origins in the native tradition; it is only the strength of this temptation that makes him indulge in heavy restatements of an ancient English past. "The New Poet," "Walt Whitman," and "To Long Island First" carry forward Gurney's argument with himself. We do not know the dates at which these poems were first written or conceived, nor indeed the order of their composition, only that all three seem to have been transcribed in final form in early 1925.

Considerations of style would certainly place them after "Thoughts of New England," which is the important point here. "Walt Whitman" occurs in a typescript called "In Praise of Poets. Poems of the States," some dated March 1925. The writers celebrated show the expanded nature of Gurney's interest in America: there are poems on Thoreau, Irving,

Hawthorne, J. Burroughs, Longfellow, Lanier, J. R. Lowell, Oliver Wendell Holmes, Emerson, Jack London, Frank Norris, Whittier, Fenimore Cooper, and Mark Twain. Despite this variety, Whitman is still the central object of concern. In "Thoreau," for example, "After Whitman, Thoreau in France was my praise". "The New Poet" occurs in a typescript called "Six Poems of the North American States," again dated 1925; and "To Long Island First" comes from a typescript headed "Poems to the States. March 1925."

Considered as a group, these poems reenact the dilemmas about rootedness and adventure evident in "Thoughts of New England." That poem manages to balance within itself the contrary instincts of attraction and repulsion to the imaginative space that is America and Walt Whitman. Now such instincts split apart, and are starkly opposed. Whitman's preeminence is taken for granted—it is only because he is so potentially influential that he requires to be challenged—but the attitudes towards him vary significantly. "The New Poet" presents a limiting, heavily qualified view of Whitman. "Walt Whitman" is still critical, but more deeply engaged. "To Long Island First" is a paean, and clearly intended to act as the opening to a collection or sequence, probably Gurney's very own Leaves of Grass. The assessment of Whitman's value in all three poems is bound up with the issue of Gurney's relationship with poetic tradition and history.

"The New Poet" whom Gurney envisages—the poet he himself wants to be—will move decisively into the new space of America (this space is both literal and symbolic). He will take up what is in many ways a Whitmanian and centralized stance, alert to the myriad of ordinary lives across the States, responsive to Whitman's "divine average": "let him sing/Of all the States, let his home be the Town watching/Mississippi flowing southward with names untold,/And waters numberless hidden in Her flowing". But there is a qualification: "More honouring Masters old than one Walt Whitman". This is a jolt. The tone of "one Walt Whitman" is wittily deprecating rather than a putdown, but it still indicates a limiting view. It is not enough for Gurney that the poet should "respectfully credit" the European past. He wants to extend Whitman's own democratic inclusiveness into history, so that the new poet will draw on "Greece, Rome, middle England and the all-honouring/Provinces of France, and the Indian tradition". As in T.S. Eliot's "Tradition and the Individual Talent", the future can only be forged from a deep engagement with the past.

In "Walt Whitman" the struggle with Whitman is part of Gurney's own struggle with his personal past, the horrors and comradeship that he had experienced in the First World War. Whitman, the poet who might help him into a creative future, is also bound up with his painful memories of the trenches. In this sense the poem is broken-backed: the tensions of attraction and repulsion noted in "Thoughts of New England" come to the fore in a way that demands that they be resolved. Line by line, the poem's opening veers between praise and blame:

With more knowledge of the poetic things, of the manly things But with no knowledge of Greek care in fashionings: Forging out great thought like Beethoven, yet caught In ignorance, not honouring makings of generations. Not square to form of truth; thought to clear-of-thought Always vowed—the maker, the companion of true kings, (Whose page is coloured with earth's and his heart's blood). This is a threefold reiteration of the same point: Whitman fails in "fashioning," in "making," in issues of "form." Yet what is brought against these criticisms strives powerfully to overcome them. The second half of the poem finds further justification for Whitman in the responses of Gurney's comrades during the war and in his own responses when reading Whitman in the trenches.

His fellow soldiers really appreciated Whitman's "courage, colour or master-in-action mood". The homely image that follows is maybe suggested from blacksmithery (picking up on "forging" in line 3) or perhaps from cricket: "What 'Song of Myself,' or 'Drum Taps' or 'Brooklyn,'/ 'Calamus,' or 'Paumanok' strikes out or clean misses/Is best known by those who have to Death's face gone". This is an awkward, if beautiful, apologia: Gurney knows the high cultural and/or English view that Whitman is rough and unformed, and struggles with it. The tension leads to a situation where he can cross over the symbolic barrier, and enter wholeheartedly the new American space. "To Long Island First" is the poem in which he achieves this.

It recounts the experience of buying a copy of Leaves of Grass—sometime before the First World War from a secondhand bookstall in Gloucester. The literal details enact a symbolic and psychological meaning: the weight of the European and English past that has acted as an inhibition is now seen in perspective. The opening line might better end with a colon, for it implies that what follows is an introduction to a series of poems, and that its statement is in some sense complete in itself: "To Long Island first with my tortured verse". This is the moment of crossing over from England to America, of turning away from a backward-looking mindset. "Tortured" connects with the image of himself in the poem as a "hesitater" (an image already used in "Walt Whitman," 1. 12). Gurney's verse is "tortured" because of his mental sufferings in and out of war, and also because it is enclosed within classical-and English-rooted tradition: it needs new spaces, and—the poem implies—it needs to move into an arena of greater spiritual energy. On the bookstall "I saw, brown 'Leaves of Grass'...". Literally the pages of the book are brown and discolored, but symbolically it is not alive in England, its meaning about life deadened in the wrong cultural atmosphere. Then, Gurney brings it alive through his wholehearted reading:

Remember how on a Gloucester book-stall one morning I saw, brown "Leaves of Grass" after long hesitation (For fourpence to me was bankruptcy then or worse) I bought, what since in book or mind about the dawning On Roman Cotswold, Roman Artois war stations, Severn and Buckingham, London after night wanderings, Has served me, friend or Master on many occasions Of weariness, or gloriousness or delight. Emotional hesitancy or diffidence seems ludicrous, part of a wider emotional disablement that is now being healed. The list of the places where he either read or remembered Leaves of Grass is the historical past to which Whitman helps to give a future. Gurney particularly liked the hills forming the western edge of the Cotswolds with their Roman remains. The "war stations" in Artois were the site of Julius Caesar's campaigns against the Gauls and of Gurney's service in the First World War. These many-times-fought-over lands are a symbol of a "tortured," self-involved European past. But now, to counter this, there is the memory of reading Whitman: "At first to puzzle [over Whitman], then grow past all traditions/ To be Master unquestioned—a book that brings the clear/Spirit of him that wrote, to the thought again here".

This is a bold assertion, a contradiction of one aspect of "Walt Whitman." It no longer seems important that Whitman is weak in "form" and "fashioning," or unheeding of tradition; he transcends "all traditions" in order to create a way into the future. This assertion is amplified in the close of the poem where Gurney makes the gesture of dedication that he refused in "Thoughts of New England": "Briton, I am also Hers [i.e. New England's]/... have more than Virgil for meditations". A past symbolized by Rome, a present symbolized by Severn, Buckingham, and London, can now be joined by a future symbolized by the regions and towns of America loved by Whitman. Whitman becomes Gurney's way into his own poetic future, his means to draw together his respect for the past and for tradition with his desire to move forward into a new poetic space. This point of transition was both symbolic and literal. References to Whitman, with varying kinds of significance, now become more frequent in the poetry.

In the poems that Gurney grouped together under the heading Best Poems, all written down between November 1925 and April 1926, there are twelve explicit allusions to Whitman as well as many other moments when his presence can be felt in less obvious or implicit terms. "O Tan-faced Prairie Boy," "Picture of two Veterans" (originally "Dirge for two Veterans"), and "Drum Taps" all pay homage to their counterparts in Whitman. In the elegy "To the memory of Alan Seeger," Gurney sees it as almost painfully ironic that, while he knew Whitman, a dead American poet, so well, he knew nothing of a live American poet sharing with him the horrors of the trenches: "Carrying Walt Whitman in my haversack or at my back—/ Or in a pocket-knowing nothing of Alan Seeger, name or fame... only/Walt Whitman was with me my thought as a sentry lonely".

Other references, to times after the war, identify Whitman as a constant source of reading and inspiration ("A London memory," "I saw Her soul," "Love," and "Happy is he, Ulysses"). The well-achieved "Of the Sea" hinges on an allusion to "In Cabin'd Ships at Sea." "Humility—and Her friend" mentions "Whitman set clear to music", probably a reference to Vaughan Williams's A Sea Symphony. Perhaps the most poignant allusion of all occurs in the stark "Of Death." This catalogues the "bare misses" of war: a shell "hitting middle from body" of a comrade; another shell exploding so close, while he was shaving, that it made his hand shake. It openly acknowledges the daily fear of incapacity, the injury that would stop him being a "maker". But the fear of death itself is quickly salved: "Death? Bach drew me out of such fear; Whitman,/Beethoven's deep soul triumphing above far Orion".

By now, and particularly if we look back to "Walt Whitman," the meaning of Whitman to Gurney becomes clear. It is a meaning that he has gradually clarified for himself over time. In aesthetic terms, form and truth in art are supposed mutually to illuminate each other: form are there to communicate and reveal. But Gurney is worried about the priorities in the relationship: "With more knowledge of the poetic things.../But with no knowledge of Greek care in fashionings." Children will understand the subject matter of a sonnet but not its prosody or rhetoric. Even student readers will look at issues of truth, morality, or revelation before they will consider issues of form. (Reading, say, The Rape of the Lock, it is easier to get students to think about Pope's analysis of vanity and the corruption of the beau monde than to think about how he uses the heroic couplet.)

But Gurney, in a thoroughly Whitmanesque way, backs the instinct of the apparently naive reader. He interrogates this relationship, and, because of his sense of the limitations of Georgianism, decides that form cannot be prioritized over truth, that "fashioning" is less important than "knowledge of the poetic things." This instinct was there from early on, and his understanding of music and musical composition may have fostered it. So, receiving from Marion Scott a copy of a sonnet by Rupert Brooke—a poet for whom he generally expressed some admiration—he says this: "The Sonnet of R.B. you sent me, I do not like.

It seems to me that Rupert Brooke would not have improved with age, would not have broadened, his manner has become mannerism, both in rhythm and diction." (This comment just precedes, or coincides with, his "rediscovery" of Whitman in September 1915.) The important opposition here is between "mannerism" and "inspiration." Two years later, his deep reading of Whitman and the composition of Severn and Somme behind him, he generalizes more explicitly: "a work of Art never should be greatly praised for its perfection; for that should set off its beauty, and its beauty or truth should be the chief impression on the mind. To praise a thing for its faultlessness is to damn it with faint praise." In his late Whitman poem "As They Draw to a Close", he says simply, in a Whitmanesque parenthesis: "(O, it is not that I have been careless of the fashioned formal songs!)".

Form needs to be flexible, not too self-consciously concerned with itself. Presumably in this instance Gurney is remembering Whitman's "Spirit That Form'd This Scene": "Was't charged against my chants they had forgotten art?/To fuse within themselves its rules precise and delicatesse?". The corollary of this position—to continue using Whitman's terms—is that poets have to be alive to "the joyous, electric all"; they have to show a wide sensitive responsiveness to people, events, nature, and art—an intelligent, discerning passion. The enemy is emotional staidness or ennui, particularly as related to the comfortable or overly conforming bourgeois life.

This last is indeed a theme that Gurney explores more and more through the late 1910s and the beginning of the 1920s. As in Rewards of Wonder, Gurney's engagement with Whitman begins significantly to grow, so his attack on the "polite" comes to the fore. In the denatured life criticized in "When the Sun Leaps Tremendous" the people of the city "keep shameful soft beds in brick/And slate erections polite, set far too thick./Sleep because others sleep, and have regular meals". In "Blighty," remembering returning to England from the trenches, Gurney hates "restrictions, order and politeness and directions". "The Bargain" deplores the genteel houses taking over the beauty of the countryside, which "will stand there and look polite—with folk polite/Where sedges stood for the wind's play and poet-delight". "If Ben Jonson Were Back" contrasts the playwright's engagement with robust life with present middle-class etiolation:

The poets have polite friends and family circles And say the right things and go early and polite to bed, Never talk of Elizabethans—nor drink wine red Nor glory in great talk till the dawn makes new glory shown. They follow not his ways, and they live half-dead. (Elsewhere, in "The Silent One," "politest" is used to terrible effect to describe the "finicking" upper-class accent of the officer.) All this is leading more and more to the Gurney outlined above, and Whitman is clearly the main influence on these attitudes. In 1926, after a burst of writing in September, Gurney's mental condition deteriorated, and this point is often seen as a watershed, the moment when his schizophrenia began to impair his creativity in a serious way. Now the natural empathy and creative engagement that any artist feels for previous artists and exemplars began to take on a strange form: Gurney actually became some of his heroes.

At various times, as psychosis took greater hold, he thought he was Shakespeare, Hilaire Belloc, or Beethoven; and now, at various times, he paid Whitman a similar compliment, in some sense wanting to become him. He "revised" and "corrected" poems by Whitman, writing over the originals to produce his very own Whitman poems. Only one of these late works has been published, but it is such an extraordinary restatement of his Whitmanism that it deserves careful attention.

P.J. Kavanagh sets "As They Draw to a Close" at the end of Collected Poems because it is evidently a late work and because its quality makes it worthy of such a prominent position. It is a response to Whitman's "As They Draw to a Close," in Songs of Parting, and it is sufficiently problematic to have caused Kavanagh some heartache as an editor.

The poem completely assimilates a Whitmanian stance: it praises "democracy," and "courtesy," and ordinary passionate men and women ("men and women of the two-fold asking," i.e. those who have had the banns read in church in anticipation of marriage). In Selected Poems Kavanagh is unsure how to deal with it, and adds a footnote claiming that "in this poem Gurney writes in the voice of Walt Whitman." This would be one way of accounting for the references to "Leaves of Grass" and to "the soul American or Yankee". In Collected Poems he backtracks somewhat: now he simply describes the poem as in the "manner" of Whitman, and as Gurney's "apologia for himself." Given the poem's quality, and given the argument outlined above, we can surely be more definite. "As They Draw to a Close" is not deranged or "mad" in any meaningful sense. It is a reworking of Whitman's poem, a translation, what Basil Bunting would call an "overdraft," or perhaps (to use an appropriately musical term) a "variation on a theme by Whitman."

Certainly it reprises the theme and structure of Whitman's original in a remarkable way, taking over at least six phrases directly: "As they draw to a close", "Of what underlies my songs", "the precedent songs", "winds of the north", "the seed I have sought to plant in them", and "compacted". But the emphases of Gurney's version are his own and are different from Whitman's: for example, in lines 10-11 he concedes a lot more than Whitman in terms of what he considers the weaknesses or failings of his own work. He also refers to his own Leaves of Grass, a work about which, at this time, we can only conjecture. Kavanagh is fair-minded, but perhaps misses one possibility: "Gurney wrote much verse in the manner of Walt Whitman, including his own 'Leaves of Grass' referred to here, of which there are fragments in the Ivor Gurney Collection in Gloucester Library." But this presupposes that only material explicitly marked "Leaves of

Grass" in the archive was intended by Gurney to be part of this work. In fact, it would seem much more likely that his "Leaves of Grass" would have comprised an arrangement of many of the poems we have now grouped as Rewards of Wonder, Best Poems, and The Book of Five Makings. Perhaps his opening is even a hint of the threefold division he envisaged for the work: "As they draw to a close,/These songs of the earth and art, war's romanzas and stern".

"To Long Island First" would then, logically, have been the opening poem. When, in line 21, Gurney speaks of what his poetry has done to "the soul American or Yankee" we can surely accept that he is writing symbolically rather than "in Whitman's voice," for the ending of the poem is a beautiful recouping of the argument advanced above. Whitman has helped Gurney escape from what is overly genteel and debilitating within the native tradition, so that he has found a freer, more open "American" voice, and a more forward-looking attitude in creative terms. Gurney is here addressing his own "precedent songs":

When you were launched there was small roughness in the touch of words, A woman's weapon, a boy's chatter, a thing for barter and loss: But I have roughed the soul American or Yankee at least to truth and instinct, And compacted the loose-drifting faiths and questions of men in a few words. We may note simply the extraordinary eloquence of these lines. Though the exact date of composition is unknown, everything points to this poem being one of Gurney's last and most complete avowals to the "Master" and "teacher" he loved. STEFAN HAWLIN

Marching with Walt Whitman.

Fired from his government job for writing about his love of men, the great gay poet would have marched to end policies like "don't ask, don't tell" What would Walt Whitman have thought about that prize example of inside-the-Beltway folly "don't ask, don't tell"? I'm pretty certain I know—not only from my experience writing Walt Whitman: A Gay Life, but also my experience as one of Uncle Sam's soldiers.

In the mid 1970s, when I was just coming out, I paid my first visit to the nation's capital, courtesy of the U.S. Army. I was a clerk in the Fifth Judge Advocate General's Reserve Detachment, based at the Presidio of San Francisco, and we were encamped for two weeks at the University of Virginia in Charlottesville. (The Army's JAG school was on the campus.)

During my free weekend I made a beeline for Washington. I couldn't believe how many military haircuts I saw in the first gay bar I entered in Georgetown. (Military buzz cuts really stood out then.) I hooked up with a soldier there who said he worked at the Pentagon for a gay two-star general. He gave me a grand tour, and we ended up at a three-floor bar that thrived practically under the eaves of the then-new J. Edgar Hoover Building. Even to a visitor from laissez-faire San Francisco, the capital gay scene seemed relaxed and wide-open. Having hung out with Whitman for several years now, I've been trying to imagine how the poet—who exulted "I hear America singing" and who had a penchant for shouting from the rooftop—would have reacted to the military's policy of the zipped lip. He would have ridiculed it, for sure. The first three words in the first poem of the first Leaves of Grass edition of 1855 are all that is needed to explode the skulking, dishonest, un-American rationale of "don't ask, don't tell": "I celebrate myself." These three simple words are even more fundamental to the pursuit of happiness than e pluribus unum. What use is celebrating if one cannot tell about it?

Whitman spent his entire career untying the tongue of America and encouraging the freedom of personal speech. The very phrase don't tell—which is exactly synonymous with don't speak—would have offended him deeply as a contradiction of the First Amendment.

"How beautiful is candor!" Whitman wrote in his 1855 Leaves preface, and he also said great poets should be known by their "perfect personal candor." That is also how great nations—and all human beings—should be known. But suspiciously not inquiring and fearfully not telling make candor impossible. No American poet has written more potently of the thick-plated hell of the closet (read his "Calamus

40" or "Song of the Open Road"), and the closet is what the military policy perpetuates. And no poet has written more glowingly of the joys of truthfulness to oneself and about oneself. "It is time to explain myself," he says in "Song of Myself." For the gay or lesbian member of the armed forces, that time never comes.

Did Whitman experience something like the purse-lipped bigotry that animates "don't ask, don't tell"? Without a doubt. The smarter homophobes of Whitman's day read between his lines and hit the ceiling. One reviewer, in 1855, said Leaves of Grass was a "gathering of muck" filled with "gross obscenity." Then he ended his review by quoting the 19th-century Latin legal euphemism for sodomy: peccatum illud horribile inter Christianos non nominandum. This translates as "that horrible sin not to be named among Christians." You can't get more pointed than that!

Later, in 1865, when Whitman was working in Washington as a clerk at the Department of the Interior, Secretary James Harlan himself rifled through the poet's desk and came upon a copy of the most exuberantly "out" of all Leaves editions. This was the third edition of 1860, which contained the 45-poem "Calamus" sequence about Whitman's love for a man. Harlan, who was a former professor of mental and moral science from Iowa, sacked the poet the next day, saying, "I will not have the author of that book in this department."

Years later Whitman dismissed Harlan gently: "He was only a fool: there was only a dim light in his noddle." One can only think, now, that a lot of noddles with dim lights in them came up with "don't ask, don't tell."

Finally, what would have riled Whitman most about the policy is the simple motive of exclusion that animates it. "My gait is no faultfinder's or rejecter's gait," he announced in "Song of Myself," and he reiterated this quintessentially open-armed philosophy in private when he said to a friend: "Allowing a place for every man's personality, idiosyncrasy the keystone to the arch of my teachings." Unlike the Pentagon, Leaves of Grass, Whitman insisted, "has room for everybody." He famously asserted, "The United States themselves are essentially the greatest poem." I have no doubt that he would cast a glum eye on "don't ask, don't tell" and conclude that the current draft of America's poem-in-progress needs more revision. Whitman was the champion schmoozer, cruiser, and convivial gossip among American poets. He loved the "curious questioning glances—glints of love!" he saw while idling on Broadway, his favourite thoroughfare. He was always reaching out, across the page, to touch his reader. He was, as I wrote in my biography, in the literal sense the most touching of all poets, the most caressingly engaged with his fellow Americans. And he was our great professor of intimate secrets. "Come! Vouchsafe to me what has yet been vouchsafed to none," he cajoles in his short poem "To You." "Tell me the whole stow," he demands. Don't tell? The admonition would mystify and infuriate him!

Whitman was our supreme compassionater and warm embracer. "I will infold you," he assures his reader. So I am quite convinced that, were he alive, he would have been in the crowd on the Mall in Washington to listen to Marian Anderson sing, "my country, 'tis of thee," and he would have been present, later, under his beloved Abraham Lincoln's melancholy gaze, to hear Martin Luther King Jr. tell about his dream.

Nor do I doubt that the dedicated nurse in the Civil War hospitals of Washington would have visited the Vietnam Memorial and shed some tears. And surely he would have come to Washington, not so many years ago, to wander among the AIDS quilts spread out on the Mall. And will his spirit be present at the Millennium March on Washington?

Don't ask.

TIME LINE/GAYS IN THE MILITARY

1778 Lieutenant Gotthold Frederick Enslin is dismissed from the military after being found in bed with another soldier, making him the first known person discharged from the U.S. Army for homosexuality.

1919 The military revises the Articles of War to make sodomy a felony, The same year a sting operation conducted at the naval station in Newport, R.I., leads to the arrest of 20 sailors on morals charges.

1943 The military issues regulations barring gay men and lesbians from serving in the armed forces on the basis of their sexual behaviour.

1957 The Crittenden Report, a 639-page summary of an investigation undertaken by the Navy, says there is "no sound basis" for barring gays from the military as a security risk, The report goes so far as to conclude that "there is some information to indicate that homosexuals are quite good security risks." The military suppresses the report for nearly two decades.

1975 Air Force sergeant Leonard Matlovich sues the military for reinstatement after being discharged because he is gay, Eventually, a federal judge orders his reinstatement, but Matlovich accepts a settlement of $160,000 to end the case, The lawsuit is the first in a series of discharges challenged by gay and lesbian personnel, including Army sergeant Perry Watkins, Army Reserves sergeant Miriam Ben-Shalom, Naval Academy midshipman Joseph Steffan, and Navy petty officer Keith Meinhold.

1981 As the Carter administration winds down, Deputy Secretary of Defence Graham Claytor revises the military's policy to declare that "homosexuality is incompatible with military service," whether or not the service member acts on his or her sexual orientation.

1992 The General Accounting Office says that nearly 17,000 men and women were discharged between 1981 and 1990 for being gay.

1993 At the very start of his first term, President Clinton seeks to lift the ban on gay service personnel, The uproar in Congress is so strong that he is forced to back down, "Don't ask, don't tell" is crafted as a compromise.

1994 Army colonel Margarethe Cammermeyer is ordered reinstated in the National Guard by a federal court,

Cammermeyer, who served in Vietnam as à nurse and won a Bronze Star, becomes the subject of a television movie starring Glenn Close.

1999 Former senator Bill Bradley, who is seeking the Democratic presidential nomination, tells The Advocate that if he is elected, he would allow gay military personnel to serve openly, Three months later, after President Clinton says the current policy is "out of whack," Vice President Al Gore says he also would lift "don't ask," Leading Republican presidential candidates, including Texas governor George W. Bush and Sen. John McCain of Arizona, say they stand by the present policy.

Schmidgall is the author of Walt Whitman: A Gay Life and editor of a new, unexpurgated edition of Whitman's work, Walt Whitman: Selected Poems 1855-1892 as well as the forthcoming Intimate-With Whitman: Conversations With Horace Traubel 1888-1892.

Walt Whitman High Point: A Dallas School for Gay Students Was on Its Last Leg When MTV Taped the New Documentary School's out, but Now Everything Is Looking Up.

Becky Thompson and Pamala Stone, two Dallas-area teachers, found inspiration in a troubling statistic—that over 80% of gay, lesbian, bisexual, and transgendered students are verbally harassed at school—and six years ago established the Walt Whitman Community School in Dallas. The first private school in the nation to specifically serve gay youth, Whitman has served as a haven for youth used to taking some hard knocks and furious punches.

The school has taken some hard knocks too. A new documentary airing April 17 on MTV, School's Out: The Life of a Gay High School in Texas, shows how Whitman has had to struggle with insufficient funding, no accreditation, and low enrollment. Thompson, who works as a teacher, counselor, and principal at the school, has even had to tell students that Whitman may have to close its doors.

But times have changed for the five-classroom school since the documentary was shot. And the 2002-2003 academic year will end with a graduation rather than last rites. The Advocate talked with Thompson one morning before classes got under way. You had a difficult school year last year. What does the future hold?

We're a very small nonprofit, and I think that money is an ongoing demand. We struggle every year. We applied for accreditation in June of 2000 and were turned down for six reasons, but one major one—our sliding tuition.

But we started to reapply in January, and once we are accredited, there are grants we can apply for that will open up a vast array of funding. Do most of the kids come to you after being harassed in public schools?

Yes. Each kid's story, from the day we opened, has been different but similar. There's Angel—she's talked about people gluing her to a chair. And the boys, they talk more about being really roughed up. There's so much need for them, so much need. The kids who end up here—they are so isolated and so alone. They're at a difficult time in life—at a fork in the road.

But does Walt Whitman's trouble with low enrollment suggest that the climate is improving for gay and lesbian students at public schools? Is the need for Walt Whitman diminishing? No, that isn't my sense of it. The stories have been the same for the last six years. Students are still being harassed horribly, and sometimes teachers call and say, "What can I do for this child?" There are not enough resources in the public schools for these kids. These are at-risk kids—95% of the students who come here are all ready to throw school away. How do you stop them from throwing it away?

You try and empower them. And we are doing that with the kids. We empower them to live with the consequences of their decisions—whether it's doing their homework, learning a math problem, or the bigger life issues.

Does Walt Whitman give these kids a good education?

Yes, it's difficult to sit in a classroom here and feel that educational needs are not being met. We've had kids who had spent their lives hiding at the back of classrooms and not learning, and that's not allowed here. We do a good job educating at Walt Whitman.

Why the name Walt Whitman? We thought it fit. We have a quote that we use a lot [from Whitman's Leaves of Grass]: "Each of us inevitable,/Each of us limitless—each of us with his or her right upon the earth;/Each of us allow'd the eternal purports of the earth;/Each of us here as divinely as any is here."

American Renaissance Poetry and the Topos of Positionality: Genius Mundi and Genius Loci in Walt Whitman and William Gilmore Simms.

If the modernist intellectual, fundamentally a deracine, saw literature as a "strategy of permanent exile" and fundamental displacement... the new intellectual rather likes to pose as a topologist: S/he speaks from one specific place of cultural production.... "Positionality"—you might have heard of it-is the magic word, and you'd better take it literally.—Roberto Maria Dainotto, Place in Literature

Ever since f. O. Matthiessen published american renaissance: Art and expression in the Age of Emerson and Whitman, the phrase "American Renaissance" has provided both an organizing principle for the study of nineteenth-century American literature and a lightning-rod for that study's critique. These critiques have challenged Matthiessen's focus on just five authors (Emerson, Thoreau, Hawthorne, Melville, and Whitman), a canonizing gesture that excludes other prominent writers of the "renaissance" period he addresses.

In addition to challenging the exclusion of this period's women writers like Harriet Beecher Stowe and African American writers like Frederick Douglass, critics have more recently questioned the northern bias of Matthiessen's canon, and the author consistently invoked in order to redress this sectional imbalance is the southern writer William Gilmore Simms. In a recent issue of Southern Quarterly, a special issue devoted to Simms, David W. Newton observes that "the construction by Matthiessen and later scholars of the American Renaissance as a critical concept has contributed to the diminishment of Simms's literary reputation," a consequence that "is particularly ironic since the height of Simms's own literary career corresponds precisely with that crucial moment in American letters between 1850-55 which Matthiessen defines as the American Renaissance." Newton's proposed correction, his assertion that "by any measure of literary achievement, poems clearly belong as an important part of the American poetic tradition", underscores the larger point made in the introduction to this issue of Southern Quarterly, where Peter L. Shillingsburg presents Simms as "a literary giant of proportions unacknowledged by—indeed, unknownto—the bulk of Americanist scholars."

For my purposes here, this effort to renew critical attention to Simms is of interest not for the institutional circumstance it seeks to effect—the delayed justice of Simms's literary canonization—but for the historical circumstance it registers: Simms's Poems: Descriptive, Dramatic, Legendary, and Contemplative was published in 1853, a date significant less for its coincidence with Matthiessen's "American Renaissance" than for its proximity to the 1855 publication date of Walt Whitman's Leaves of Grass. Simms, these dates show, was an established figure in belles lettres and a prominent member of the nativist Young America group well before Whitman gave that literary nationalist stance its currently most celebrated articulations. The eclipse of Simms by Whitman might call for more nuanced explanations than Whitman's own populist declaration, in the closing line of his 1855 "Preface," that "the proof of a poet is that his country absorbs him as affectionately as he has absorbed it."

Yet Whitman's affectionate absorption of his country made his work particularly relevant, as Allen Grossman has demonstrated, for a nation on the brink of civil war. Grossman presents Whitman's poetry as a kind of "policy" for preserving union, characterizing the formal innovation of Whitman's line as "an unprecedented trope of inclusion": "Whitman has devised a universal 'conjunctive principle' whose manifest structure is the sequence of end-stopped, nonequivalent, but equipollent lines." At a time of national crisis, the reason a country absorbs a given poet—in this case, the reason the United States absorbs Whitman rather than Simms—has more to do with that poetry's social policy than its literary quality. Compelling as Grossman's analysis continues to be, the question it raises is why—apart, perhaps, from a failure to register Whitman's policy or to grasp its ambitious scope-do we hear new calls for inclusion, calls like the ones that challenge Matthiessen's restricted set of writers? If Whitman's linear catalogues do indeed amount to "a massive trope of inclusion", what are the grounds for challenging Matthiessen and calling for greater inclusion? Should not Matthiessen's emphasis on Whitman—whom he calls "the central figure of our literature affirming the democratic faith" —amount to an assertion of Whitman's own policy, the unavoidable or inevitable inclusion of everyone?

Grossman's work answers this question by identifying a "severe criticism... of Whitman's indeterminate realization of the person—'You whoever you are'". "Whitmanian celebration by pluralization," that is, "extinguishes all personhood which has only singular form", so Whitman's policy—a "reciprocal internality, of persons one to the other ('What I shall assume you shall assume')" —eliminates "the presence of the person as a singular individual; and this Whitman could not restore". But critical resistance to Matthiessen involves more than a defence of "untranslatable individuality"; the individual writers Matthiessen excludes-Stowe, Fuller, Douglass, Simms—imply a much broader exclusion of the constituencies whom these individual writers represent, constituencies-for instance, women, African Americans, and Southerners-larger than a singular person but smaller than Whitman's totality.

Thus if, for Grossman, the criticism of Whitman is that he excludes the individual, the criticism I am identifying is that Whitman—and his champion, Matthiessen—excludes groups. And if Grossman finds this criticism articulated by a contemporary of Whitman, Abraham Lincoln, the criticism I am identifying finds articulation in writings by another of Whitman's contemporaries, William Gilmore Simms. Simms, that is, provides a way to characterize collective entities that—just like the individual persons of Grossman's analysis-would lose their distinctiveness if viewed in Whitman's terms: if

Whitman presents "a taxonomy of which the sorting index is mere being-at-all", as Grossman argues, mere being does not acknowledge different ways of being, such as being a woman, an African American, or a Southerner. These varying ways of being, I want to argue, can be accommodated by the poetry of Simms.

What enables Simms's poetry to achieve this, I will show, is its concern with what Robert M. Dainotto, in the above epigraph, characterizes as "positionality." Simms's poems consistently explore the possibility that one might "pose as a topologist" who "speaks from one specific place" or, as Dainotto has alternately phrased this pose (referencing "Critical Regionalism" rather than Simms), it amounts to imagining "the possibility to return, in short, to a past idea of culture as cultus, of literature as the local crop of a regionalized genius loci". This interest in positionality-or, as it is sometimes described, "situatedness"—is apparent in much recent criticism of gender and race, criticism that has called for a "politics of location" in which subjects, speaking from various "subject positions," express a corresponding "positional consciousness."

This critical embrace of positionality has likewise emerged in recent accounts of the South: in his introduction to the Southern Quarterly issue on Simms, Peter L. Shillingsburg observes that attending to "the 'situatedness' of principles and tastes provides a different picture from the one that has prevailed in this age of judgmentalism", this new picture acknowledging "that there was a national character developing in the literature of America below the Mason Dixon Line... that it was carried forward largely on the broad shoulders of William Gilmore Simms". Unlike Shillingsburg, however, my point is not to extend to Simms or his positional constituency the benefits of suspending "judgmentalism" (that is, ignoring or forgiving his ownership of slaves and his defence of slavery) but, instead, to reveal how this concept of positionality was itself articulated via Simms's particular approach to writing poetry. By attending to Simms, and by doing so in conjunction with Whitman, my goal is to underscore the differences between their poetic theory and practice, differences important not merely for the historical nuance they bring to our understanding of poetry in this "renaissance" period but, in addition, for the light they shed on current critical practice, practice in which positionality figures strongly as a strategy of resistance (for example, in challenges to the exclusionary "American Renaissance") either to the assimilation or to the exclusion of a given positional entity. Hence the positionality Dainotto underscores is a positionality that I want to distinguish from the poetry of Whitman and to link-for the ultimate purpose of critique-to the "renaissance" poetry of Simms. I. Poetic Vocation and Competing Forms of Genius

In associating the recent critical focus on "positionality" with the view of "literature as the local crop of a regionalized genius loci," Dainotto references a concept-the genius loci-central to an earlier discussion of literary history by Geoffrey Hartman. This is apparent in Hartman's "Toward Literary History," the concluding chapter of his Beyond Formalism: "The artist's struggle with his vocation-with past masters and the 'pastness' of art in modern society-seems," Hartman asserts, "to be a version of a universal human struggle: of genius with Genius, and of genius with the genius loci."

Hartman's move beyond formalism and toward literary history, then, involves placing this ultimately formal concept, the genius loci, in association with the struggle for vocation that a variety of artists, each in their own way and in their own historical moment, have found themselves confronting. "To begin with the genius/Genius contest," Hartman continues, "in every period there is an ingenu to be tested by vision, to be lead out of the state of natural light by a Muse who opens an 'everlasting scryne' where the 'antique rolles' lie hidden". In addition to being drawn toward this Genius mundi, the artist-genius may also experience a different vocational call:

The dramatic encounter of genius with Genius is accompanied by the commonplace quarrel of genius with genius loci: of art with the natural religion or dominant myth of its age. To the burden of vision which rouses the poet's sense of his powers is added a combat with insidious habits of thought.... The genius loci can rival Genius as an influence, for it suggests the possibility of a more natural participation in a preexistent or larger self. England as Gloriana and America as Virgin Land are visionary commonplaces indistinguishable from an "idol of the tribe."

Hartman's account of this second struggle associates it, in particular, with the modern age of national identity: "The genius loci is especially significant for modern—that is, vernacular—art, for it is then that the assertion of a national genius becomes vital and a Dante, Ariosto, or Milton turn to the 'adorning of their native Tongue.'" "Native and national," Hartman continues, "are not always identical, of course, and in the Renaissance this is part of the general problem of constructing a 'national universal' from the genius of different localities". This "general problem" persists beyond the Renaissance to include, Hartman shows, not only British writers from Milton through Wordsworth but also writers in the antebellum United States.

A writer like Ralph Waldo Emerson, for instance, will overtly resist the effort to pose as a topologist, insisting instead on a placeless Genius mundi: "I believe in Eternity. I can find Greece, Asia, Italy, Spain and the Islands,—the genius and creative principle of each and of all eras, in my own mind". But in another example, this Genius mundi is placed in apposition to the topologist's pose of the genius loci; this is apparent, Hartman observes, when we see "Bronson Alcott, Thoreau's friend, praising A Week on the Concord and Merrimack Rivers as 'purely American, fragrant with the lives of New England woods and streams, and which could have been written nowhere else,' then because 'the sod and sap and flavour of New England have found at last a clear relation to the literature of other and classic lands...

Egypt, India, Greece, England'". Here the apposition implies indecision regarding these two approaches to artistic vocation, the genius loci or the Genius mundi. In setting out this literary history, Hartman applies this pair of options to his own moment, one in which "the rise of the national literatures" gives predominance to the genius loci: "In our own day this model is often dangerously simplified. Art, we are told, seeks to revitalize and if need be to rebarbarize man.... Yet, simplified or not, this model for creativity becomes an animating force, a psychic silhouette with which the artist strives to coincide"; the artist, in other words, speaks from a position, expressing positionality: "genius, in expelling a false or discovering a true genius loci, discovers itself and enlarges us". For Hartman, however, this dynamic can lead to extremes which he associates with Nazism in Germany and the differently problematic assimilationism of America: "Now that assimilation has proved to be not false but certainly an imperfect reality, we are facing the agony of pluralism all over again—conflicts of allegiance, cultural transvestitism, a splintered national identity".

Hartman's response is to embrace this pluralism, despite its agony: "In reevaluating the prevalence of so many national, religious, or geopolitical ideals-superstitions we still live with despite the universalisms around us-the genius loci concept may help to prevent our collapsing national into nationalistic.... If art is the offspring of a precarious marriage between genius and genius loci, the place of which it is the genius is not necessarily a nation-state. Art can express a people... a region... or a speech-community". Hartman's openness to these "superstitions we still live with" sets him against a notion of universalism associated with Emerson and a corresponding notion of globalism associated, here, with Auerbach:

Erich Auerbach's Mimesis... surmised that we were moving toward a nivellement which would reduce the autochthonous element and gradually eliminate both local and national traditions; and for him this beginning of conformity augured the end of history. When one sees an airline ad with the motto "Introducing the Atlantic River" or hears Andrd Malraux speak of technology creating an "Atlantic civilization," the forerunner of a worldwide humanistic culture, one is almost inclined to agree with Auerbach that historical time and space may be fading into the uniformity of landscapes seen from the air. Hartman, however, prefers to have his feet planted firmly on the ground: "a pentecostal ideal of the plurality of tongues seems preferable to a one-dimensional, deracinated language". Casting his hopes with pentecostal plurality, and thus with the positionality of the genius loci, Hartman ends "Toward Literary History" with a note of prophecy, anticipating future artists aligned not with Genius but with the genius loci: "Surely in that dubious cultural millennium, in that predicted mass-cult era, a Gloriana will appear once more to a Colin Clout, like another angel to another Caedmon, and say 'Sing to me'". The scenario that Hartman envisions—a genius loci calling upon a poet-genius to "Sing to me" —would seem to link this closing sentence of Beyond Formalism with the opening lines of a poem that Walt Whitman wrote a full century before:

By blue Ontario's shore, As I mused of these warlike days and of peace return'd, and the dead that return no more, A Phantom gigantic superb, with stern visage accosted me, Chant me the poem, it said, that comes from the soul of America, chant me the carol of victory. If the "Phantom gigantic" would seem to occupy the position of Hartman's "Gloriana" or "angel," Whitman's speaker would then be that phantom's addressee, thus suggesting that the speaker's response—that of a genius wedded to the genius loci of Lake Ontario—would exemplify Hartman's "pentecostal ideal of the plurality of tongues." But tempting as this reading may be, we should consider an alternative account, one in which the "Phantom gigantic" is Hartman himself, an outsider whose ideal of pentecostal plurality leads him to seek knowledge of the locale.

Whitman's speaker, in turn, becomes the Phantom-Hartman's addressee, a figure generally familiar with such requests for locally anchored speech: sing for the outsider what you sing for the locals. Whitman's speaker, it turns out, has grasped the general commitment animating the Phantom-Hartman's request, the view that "a pentecostal ideal of the plurality of tongues seems preferable to a one-dimensional, deracinated language". Whitman's speaker, from this perspective, turns out to be a broker of such requests-a middle man through whom all responses to the request must pass: "I eject none, accept all, then reproduce all in my own forms". By the poem's close the Whitman gatekeeper role exceeds the scope of the "Phantom gigantic superb":

Not to call even those lofty bards here by Ontario's shores, Have I sung so capricious and loud my savage song. Bards of my own land only I invoke, Ample Ohio's, Kanada's bards-bards of California! Inland bards-bards of the war! You by my charm I invoke. On the way to this ending Whitman's speaker references "America," but "America" only emerges as the product of many bards whose songs he himself will fuse together: I heard the voice arising demanding bards, By them all native and grand, by them alone can these States be fused into the compact organism of a Nation, To hold men together by paper and seal or by compulsion is no account, That only holds men together which aggregates all in a living principle, as the hold of the limbs of the body or the fibres of plants. Of all races and eras these States with veins full of poetical stuff most need poets, and are to have the greatest, and use them the greatest. If America speaks through many bards, it does so only after Whitman has put them to their proper use, fusing these many bards' local statements into "my own forms".

Or, as Cesare Parvese observes of Whitman, "he wrote poetry out of poetry writing." Any expression of the local must be—through him—tallied with the national, a requirement that resolves the local/national conflict that Hartman observed above. Thus for all his insistence on the local, Whitman's speaker would ultimately seem to be distanced from the genius loci, serving as a monopolistic purveyor of the plurality Hartman desires. Simms, by contrast, does not function as this focal point for rendering local bards national, but rather ascribes that rendering to another agent, one whose advent he eagerly anticipates. In an 1842 lecture later published as "The Epochs and Events of American History, as Suited to the Purposes of Art in Fiction," Simms writes:

No nation of our magnitude... can long remain without its Genius loci!. It is in our hearts, that, even now, he breathes and burns.... That genius, thus feebly striving now, and with a faint torch burning in his infant grasp, is yet destined to grow mighty-yea, mightiest among the mighty. Already we behold his chosen altar—place on the blue summits of Apalachy!... We may see his worshipers, as they march in ceremonial procession from our kindred republics, bringing tribute and music, and incense to his shrine! Nor, last araong these-nor least-we may count among the proudest of these shining hosts, our own dear brothers of the south-our offspring-the blessed sons and daughters of the muse.

Here the phrase "on the blue summits of Apalachy" recalls "By Blue Ontario's Shore" in its centralization of national poetry. But if Whitman's speaker was the agent and locus of that centralization, himself assembling the work of the various local bards, Simms, despite the bombast of this passage, occupies a less prominent position: not only is he distinct from the central entity he foresees, but he is also more locally identified—in this case, with the "south" as one of several "kindred republics." If all of these republics are subordinated to the central "altar-place," they are nevertheless "kindred" to each other, suggesting comparable subordination to the national "Genius loci."

In addition to restricting himself to one of these kindred republics, Simms also deviates from Whitman's focus on the present and future: "Others take finish," Whitman writes, "but the Republic is ever constructive and ever keeps vista,/Others adorn the past, but you O days of the present, I adorn you,/O days of the future I believe in you" ("By Blue Ontario's Shore,"). For Simms, by contrast, the genius loci emerges through recovering narratives of historical events specific to his various kindred locales, an archival activity apparent in the title of his lecture—"The Epochs and Events of American History, as Suited to the Purposes of Art in Fiction":

We know that we shall yet behold the advent of this genius of place;—that, penetrating the antique forests, he shall drag the old tradition from his Druid cavern, and compel him to deliver up his secrets. We shall yet hear the incantation uttered by some mighty voice, not unworthy of the great masters who have spelled the departed in their urns. We shall see the cavern unsealed... we shall number the great spirits of the past, issuing forth and trooping in review before us! Simms associates this raising of ghosts with the actions of a "priest" at an "altar" whereas Whitman—asserting, "There will shortly be no more priests, I say their work is done" ("By Blue Ontario's Shore," p. 351)—views the poet as someone whose concern is those who live in the present, those among whom he circulates: "Land of lands, and bards to corroborate!/Of them standing among them" ("By Blue Ontario's Shore,"

Simms and the Genius Loci

Simms's distinct understanding of the genius loci is apparent in both his prose criticism and his poetry. A recent discussion of Simms's poem "The Streamlet" by David W. Newton points to the struggle faced by the poem's speaker, who can "hear the sacred words" the streamlet speaks: "They rise melodious, sad, but softly clear,—/My heart receives the music, not mine ear". Presented with the musical qualities of the streamlet's voice, "the speaker must assume his responsibilities as poet and translate the voice of the stream for others to hear and understand", the translation attempting, Newton argues, "to represent in language the living voice of the stream":

"I am thy guardian genius,-from the first My waters still have slaked thy spirit's thirst. "When thou shall be forgotten I shall be, And to the race that shall succeed thee on, I will repeat my counsel, as to thee And like thy footsteps now, shall theirs be won, From the thick gathering-from the crowded street With me, within the solitude, to meet." While the "quotation marks... indicate that the voice does not belong to the poet", "we are also aware," Newton notes, "that the words—as well as the entire poem—belong to the poet. They represent his attempt to capture the voice of the stream in a poetic language that can only hope to approximate his original experience". Resistant to symbolic representation, the streamlet's musical voice instantiates a positionality that is resistant to translation and thus immune to displacement: experience of that voice—a voice Newton labels generally as "the sublime language of nature" and that I, instead, am calling a particular instance of a genius loci-requires one to visit the site itself. Such an intimate relation to a specific locale arises frequently in Simms's poetry, and critics have attributed this to the influence of Wordsworth, particularly Wordsworth's notion of "spots of time." Exploring how Wordsworth himself came to employ these "spots of time," Geoffrey Hartman asks, "How did Wordsworth raise himself from his obsession with specific place to the key notion of spots of time?

I suspect the intermediate concept to have been that of genius loci, or 'spirit of place.' The renovating energy flowing from the spots of time is really spirit of place reaching through time with a guardian's care." Wordsworth and Simms, then, each started in the same place, but for Wordsworth, Hartman argues, this was a transitional concern: "'Wordsworth refuses to renew archaic modes.... There are no ghosts, no giant forms, no genii in the mature Wordsworth. He is haunted by a 'Presence which is not to be put by,' but it is a ghost without a ghost's shape, not a specter but an intensely local and numinous self-awareness". Simms, by contrast, appears to have avoided this shift from haunted place to self-awareness, so the voices that inspire his speakers-like that of "The Streamlet"—remain situated upon the landscape, imposing their positionality upon the artist-genius they inspire. Simms's commitment to the genius loci is apparent not only in his poetry and prose criticism but also in his best-known work of fiction, The Yemassee.

One of some forty novels that Simms wrote, it occupies a position within an elaborate plan to write historical romances chronicling the entire history of the Americas, from European colonization to British settlement, through the Revolutionary War, and up to Simms's present. The Yemassee falls in the second of these historical periods, its title referring to the Native American tribe indigenous to South Carolina but, by Simms's time, clearly doomed to displacement by people like Simms himself. In the narrative Simms tells, however, the demise or eclipse of the Yemassee is only partial, for even as it narrates their military defeat, the novel also values and seeks to celebrate their beliefs and practices—an impulse apparent in naming the novel after the defeated tribe rather than their conquerors. These European conquerors are portrayed in one of three lights, as a nationless band of profiteering pirates, as Puritans proselytizing for universal Christianity, or as weak-willed subjects needing to be led by the "decisive character" of a colonial Governor—"the Lord Palatine of Carolina" — who, true to his decisive character, imposes martial law on his colonial subjects. The Yemassee, by contrast, are a "nation" organized-like the United States-as "something of a republic" and "ruled by the joint authority of several chiefs" who "were elective, and... were accountable to the nation".

For a Yemassee, to be "expatriated" from the nation (by the removal of the totem tattoo) is a fate worse than death, because it makes him/her "dead to Manneyto", the protective spirit who presides over "the blessed valley" of the afterlife. Manneyto also presides over the Yemassee nation's central city (not unlike the goddess Columbia presiding over Washington, the District of Columbia). Although this nation is defeated in war, their values are clearly the virtues that Simms favors: "confederate nations" fight better than Europeans —in part because of their commitment to their nation, which is simultaneously a commitment to the land and their ancestors: "The lands came from our fathers—they must go to our children. They do not belong to us to sell-they belong to our children to keep". What Simms is trying to convey of this predecessor tribe is a kind of persistence or permanence that we saw in "The Streamlet," where the "guardian genius" asserts, "to the race that shall succeed thee on,/I will repeat my counsel, as to thee".

To defeat the Yemassee, then, is ultimately to usher in the successor "race"—Simms and his fellow Carolinians, and the larger republic of the United States—to whom the guardian genius will offer the same wise counsel. To convey this point, Simms's novel makes extensive use of interpolated poems. In one instance a Yemassee woman "carolled forth in an exquisite ballad voice, one of those little fancies of the Indians.... The strain, playfully simple in the sweet language of the original, must necessarily lose in the more frigid verse of the translator", a translation which he nevertheless produces in full. Simms's point about translation is dramatized in this poem's title—"The 'Coonee-Latee,' or 'Trick-Tongue'"—which must be further translated as "the mocking-bird":

As the Coonee-latee looked forth from his leaf, He saw below him a Yemassee chief, In his war-paint, all so grim—Sung boldly, then, the Coonee-latee, I, too, will seek for mine enemy; And I'll take off their scalps like him. But the initial intention to scalp other birds changes once the mockingbird notices "that with open mouth they slept":

And from bird to bird, with a cautious tread, He unhook'd the tongue, out of every head, Then flew to his perch again;—And thus it is, whenever he chooses, The tongues of all of the birds he uses, And none of them dare complain. In this myth of origins the issue ultimately dramatized is not language and its resistance to translation but song and its susceptibility to appropriation. It is just such an appropriation to which Simms aspires even as he insists on the local and linguistic specificity of the Yemassee poems. The implication is that successful appropriation—rather than poor translation or mere imitation—requires the appropriator also to be a local successor. A drama of failed succession—from chief Sanutee to his son Occonestoga—figures prominently in the plot of The Yemassee and is responsible for the tribe's demise, but Simms's attention to the Yemassee and their poems places himself and his fellow South Carolinians in a position to remedy this failure by becoming, themselves, the local successors of the Yemassee. Another instance of interpolated poetry features the Yemassee "prophet" who "poured forth, in uncouth strains, a wild rhythmic strain, the highest effort of lyric poetry known to his people". In this case, the poem is channeled through the tribal prophet by the malign deity, "Opitchi-Manneyto," whom Simms's footnote calls "The Yemassee Evil Principle":

"Let the Yemassee have ears, For Opitchi-Manneyto-'Tis Opitchi-Manneyto, Not the prophet, now that speaks, Hear Opitchi-Manneyto." In another case a Yemassee warrior's "wild and barbarous chant" catalogues his own achievements in battle and then, shifting to a "less personal, and more national character, a more sounding and elevated strain", the warrior tells of the virtues of the tribe: "Mighty is the Yemassee,/Strong in the trial,/Fearless in the strife". There is also the "scalp-song of the Yemassee" and "the battle-hymn of their nation". Perhaps most notably, the Yemassee chief dies with one of these songs on his lips, and his wife is led away by her captors speaking lines from another of the tribal poems. Through the poems in this novel Simms has, in effect, accomplished the task he assigns the bard in "The Epochs and Events of American History, as Suited to the Purposes of Art in Fiction": to "drag the old tradition from his Druid cavern, and compel him to deliver up his secrets."

But as the novel's popular success suggests, the songs can be distributed as print media, and this mobility is something Simms comes increasingly to view as inconsistent with the place-bound genius loci. This view is apparent in the section of his Poems called "Tales and Traditions of the South," a section in which Simms poses more as topologist than poet, and his poems serve the role not of capturing, in themselves, the genius loci but, instead, of identifying the locale to which this genius loci is inextricably linked. One such poem is "The Syren of Tselica; A Tradition of the French Broad," which narrates in poetic measure what the prose headnote describes: "The tradition of the Cherokee asserts the existence of a Syren, in the French Broad, who implores the Hunter to the stream, and strangles him in her embrace." This same tradition would become the basis for a much longer poem, completed in 1849 but unpublished in Simms's lifetime, which is tellingly divided into two main sections. The first, "The Mountain Tramp," provides an account of walking through the mountains and wondering about the genius loci of the locale:

I guessed the red man's fate, or those Who first upon those mountains sway'd, And sank beneath the red man's blows, Too fiercely savage to be stay'd; Oh! For the spell of magic pow'r To burst the casements of the dead, And bid the sage or hero rise To tell us, why his people fled Or how they toil'd and fought, and bled, And what their triumphs, ere the doom, That shut them in the speechless tomb. No voice to answer!

All is still. The echoes die along the hill, And mock me with my words again! Yet shall the genius of the place In days of potent song to come Reveal the story of the race, Whose native genius now lies dumb. Yes, Fancy by Tradition led Shall trace the streamlet to its bed, And well each ancient path explore The perish'd trod in days of yore. The rock, the vale, the mound, the dell, Shall each become a Chronicle. This frustration followed by optimism leads to the poem's second section, "Tselica; A Legend of the French Broad," where the speaker arrives at a locale whose genius loci is, it turns out, known to his guide:

"He had his gods—though weak indeed,— Yet such as answered to his need, And spirits, well suited to his race, Dwelt with him in this very place!" The story reveals that "The river knows a form of grace,/A spirit maid.../Still haunting every spot she trod", the very spot where the speaker himself stands. The manner in which Simms expanded this manuscript-narrating a traveler's visit to the haunted and storied site—is consistent with his assertions in the later, published work Southward Ho!. "What a pity," one of the characters laments, "that handbooks for the South are not provided by some patriotic author!":

In the old countries of Europe, the... handbook which you carry distinguishes the spot with some strange or startling history. In our world of woods, we lack these adjuncts. If we had the handbook, we should doubtlessly discover much to interest us in the very scenes by which we hurry with contempt. Dull and uninteresting as the railroad rout appears through North and South Carolina, were you familiar with the facts in each locality-could you couple each with its local history or tradition-the fancy would instantly quicken. Here the genius loci is so thoroughly embedded in a place that, in lieu of an anthology of poems narrating these traditions, one must have a guide or guidebook that leads one to the haunted site itself. By calling these texts "adjuncts," Simms indicates the secondary status of the narrative—whether verse or prose—to the experience of the locale itself. In this way, Simms's definition of poetry comes increasingly to favor the voice of a given streamlet over the rendering of that voice-however skilled—in the lines of a poem. III. Whitman and the Genius Mundi Simms's call for guidebooks appeared in the same year that Whitman published a second, expanded edition of Leaves of Grass, so at the same moment that Simms was turning away from written poems in favor of places themselves, Whitman was continuing to write many new poems. In the third edition of Leaves of Grass, Whitman began the volume with a new poem called "Proto-Leaf," which he had initially called "Premonition" and which, from 1867 onward, bore the title "Starting from Paumanok."

Each of these various titles registers beginnings, so they not only reference the poem's placement at the opening of the 1860 edition, but they also announce the speaker of that poem and those that will follow: "Starting from fish-shape Paumanok where I was born.../Solitary, singing in the West, I strike up for a New World". But this poem of beginnings goes on to register a prior moment that enabled this one, a moment that prompted the poet to begin his journey away from Paumanok. The registration of this earlier moment appears in section 11 of "Starting from Paumanok":

As I have walk'd in Alabama my morning walk, I have seen where the she-bird the mocking-bird sat on her nest in the briers hatching her brood. I have seen the he-bird also, I have paus'd to hear him near at hand inflating his throat and joyfully singing. And while I paus'd it came to me that what he really sang for was not there only, Nor for his mate nor himself only, nor all sent back by the echoes, But subtle, clandestine, away beyond, A charge transmitted and gift occult for those being born. This reference to "being born" introduces a moment prior to this poem's "Starting...," a moment depicted in another of this volume's new poems, "Out of the Cradle Endlessly Rocking." In this poem we understand the "gift occult" to be a "charge transmitted" to the speaker himself who, prior to receiving this charge and gift, is firmly rooted in one place, his birthplace in Paumanok. He will be able to embark from this locale only after he is "born" as a poet or bard, the speaker of "Starting from Paumanok." This moment prior to poetic speaking involves another voice, the mockingbird whose singing is referenced in the stanza quoted above. In "Out of the Cradle Endlessly Rocking" the bird's singing is likewise overheard, but in this case the auditor—the speaker as a young boy, before he has become a bard—has an experience that Simms, thinking on the model of his "The Streamlet," his Yemassee songs, or his "The Syren of Tselica," might call an encounter with the genius loci of Paumanok (which is the Native American name for Long Island):

Once Paumanok, When the lilac-scent was in the air and Fifth-month grass was growing, Up this seashore in some briers, Two feather'd guests from Alabama, two together, And every day I, a curious boy, never too close, never disturbing them, Cautiously peering, absorbing, translating. Home, or rivers and mountains from home, Singing all time, minding no time, While we two keep together. The italics are the boy's translation of song the two birds sing, but the song soon changes when the she-bird vanishes, leaving—as the boy translates—only the he-bird to call for her: "Loved! loved! loved! loved! loved!/But my mate no more, no more with me!/ We two together no more".

Having heard this solitary "aria," the boy undergoes the "being born" mentioned by the speaker in "Starting from Paumanok": he is transformed into an "outsetting bard". The force responsible for this birth of the bard—what "Starting from Paumanok" calls "A charge transmitted and gift occult" —is characterized, in "Out of the Cradle Endlessly Rocking," in a manner different from what we have been led to expect from Simms: rather than being charged with responsibility for transmitting this story to subsequent visitors of this place, thereby giving those visitors the guide-book gift of narrating the locale's occult genius loci, it is the boy who discovers this occult gift within himself:

Demon or bird! Is it indeed toward your mate you sing? or is it really to me? For I, that was a child, my tongue's use sleeping, now I have heard you, Now in a moment I know what I am for, I awake, And already a thousand singers, a thousand songs, clearer, louder and more sorrowful than yours, A thousand warbling echoes have started to life within me, never to die. O you singer solitary, singing by yourself, projecting me, O solitary me listening, never more shall I cease perpetuating you, Never more shall I escape, never more the reverberations, Never more the cries of unsatisfied love be absent from me. Realizing that it is "really to me" that the he-bird sings (just as, in "Starting from Paumanok," the singing is "for those being born"), the boy is transformed by having an obligation or "charge transmitted" to him, that of "perpetuating" the "thousand warbling echoes" that have "started to life within me, never to die."

While this may seem like a form of possession by the he-bird "Demon" (as might be suggested by the "never more" referencing Poe's "The Raven"), the particular bird turns out to be less important (there are "a thousand singers, a thousand songs, clearer, louder and more sorrowful than yours") than the experience it triggers, not possession by a particular demon but instead an awakening from the prior state of his "tongue's use sleeping." This phrase recalls the sleeping birds whose tongues were stolen for the use of "Cooneelatee," the Yemassee mockingbird. Thus despite the humility of the phrase "never more shall I cease perpetuating you," the speaker approaches this song in a manner that, ultimately, is more instrumental than deferential, more global than local: by "projecting me," the he-bird's song awakens the speaker to his itinerant vocation as an "outsetting bard." Hartman's discussion of poetic vocation imagined, as we have seen, an artist torn between Genius and genius loci.

In Whitman's case, these two early poems suggest his choice of the former over the latter, a choice confirmed by the remainder of "Out of the Cradle" in which the speaker, awakened to his vocation, asks the sea to reveal to him "The word final, superior to all." In reply, the sea "Lisp'd to me the low and delicious word death,/And again death, death, death, death". The boy hears this while standing at the dividing line between land and sea, "with his bare feet the waves, with his hair the atmosphere dallying". From this vantage the boy can align the division between land and sea with that of life and death, the sea and death providing the limit to the kinds of positions he can occupy. But unlike other such circumstances, where knowing that a limit exists entails knowing there to be something beyond that limit (and, hence, entails transcending or exceeding that limit), in this case the limit exceeds conceptualization—death, the sea, "the fierce old mother incessantly moaning," all suggesting versions of the dynamical sublime.29 If the speaker is in this way circumscribed, it is difficult to think of this as a limit since his range includes all non-sublime positions, which are all the positions he might conceive of occupying.

So although he stands "On the sands of Paumanok's shore gray and rustling," that location—like the he-bird's song—matters less as a particular place than as an alternative to the sea and death, an alternative to be found not only on Paumanok's shore but also at any of a thousand other places he might-starting from Paumanok—choose to go. It is this moment, prior to starting forth, that "Starting from Paumanok" recalls, and it is this beginning—having been limited only by the limitless-that enables the speaker to visit and become a resident of all positions and locales, even Simms's South Carolina: Far breath'd land! Arctic braced! Mexican breez'd! the diverse! the compact! The Pennsylvanian! the Virginian! the double Carolinian! O all and each well-loved by me! my intrepid nations! O I at any rate include you all with perfect love!. If Whitman is posing as a topologist, he is also showing the topologist's positionality to be—from his own more global vantage—a mere pose. In doing so he reveals his vocational commitment to the Genius mundi over the genius loci.

This commitment would become all the more clear in Whitman's subsequent works, including his "Song of the Redwood-Tree". As in "Out of the Cradle Endlessly Rocking," this poem features the poet's voice framing an internal song, one set off by italics: "A murmuring, fateful, giant voice, out of the earth and sky,/Voice of a mighty dying tree in the redwood forest dense". Joining this tree is a "chorus of dryads... or hamadryads," and "the wood-spirits came from their haunts of a thousand years to join the refrain". The occasion for the tree's "death-chant" is the work of foresters, "With crackling blows of axes sounding musically driven by strong arms". Rather than object to this assault, Whitman's tree accepts and even welcomes it:

Nor yield we mournfully majestic brothers, We who have grandly fill'd our time; For them predicted long, For a superber race, they too to grandly fill their time, For them we abdicate, in them ourselves ye forest kings! While this poem has all the transitional force of Milton's "On the Morning of Christ's Nativity," where the pagan deities—like Whitman's tree (which asserts, "I bear the soul befitting me, I too have consciousness, identity"), as well as the "dryads" and "wood spirits"—are dismissed to make way for Christian monotheism, Whitman shows none of the reluctance to see those local deities depart. The contrast with Simms is apparent when we consider his poem "The Memorial Tree": unlike Whitman, who subordinates the ancient trees to the newly arrived settlers, Simms inverts this priority, expressing reverence for the tree's persistence even as human generations-like each year's dying autumn leaves-pass into oblivion:

A famous tree Was this three hundred years ago, when stood The hunter-chief below it, bold and free Proud in his painted pomp and deeds of blood. His hatchet sunk With sharp wound, fixing his own favourite sign, Deep in the living column of its trunk, Where thou may'st read a history such as thine. And others' signs, Tokens of races, greatlier taught, that came To write like record, though in smoother lines And thus declare a still more human flame. Like Whitman's redwood, this tree is elaborately personified, its "outstretched arms,/ Paternal, as if blessing" and its "great white beard" recalling "Moses on the Mount."

Indeed, as with the genius loci, this tree serves as a guardian of the place, "A sire of wood and vale, guardian and king /... Whose memories grasp the lives of every meaner thing". This "record-tree" provides the occasion for the community to gather and, prompted by the markings it bears (themselves a veritable guidebook), recall the local stories that

Simms associates with the genius loci: And still at noon, Repairing to its shadow, they explore Its chronicles, still musing o'er th' unknown, And telling well-known histories, told of yore! Entrusting this tree to record these chronicles, Simms—in clear contrast to Whitman—expresses deference not only to the deeply rooted particularities of a locale but also to the tightly-knit community that is rendered cohesive as they ritually participate in sharing among themselves their knowledge of such local traditions. IV. Positionality and Identity In conveying such deference to rootedness—both that of the tree and of the community it subtends—Simms advances a view consistent with a recent critical topos that has urged similar deference and respect for such tightly-knit communities—communities otherwise known as "identities." Seeking a way to characterize such restricted collectivities while also resisting any recourse to various forms of essentialism, recent critics have employed spatialized language similar to Dainotto's term "positionality."

For instance Michael Awkward's book Negotiating Difference: Race, Gender, and the Politics of Positionality sets out "to examine academic discourse in the humanities within which employment of a politics of positionality has become a significant aspect of our critical behaviors." "Indeed," Awkward continues, "we might say that sincere responses to the injunction, 'Critic, position thyself,' are seen by many as among the most effectively moral and significant gestures of our current age." A key source of this gesture, according to Mary Eagleton, is the work of feminist Adrienne Rich, particularly her 1984 essay "Notes Toward a Politics of Location." The ongoing significance of this early work is apparent in the feminist writings of Linda Martin Alcoff.

More recently, Alcoff has extended this topos of positionality to discussions of race, her essay "Philosophy and Racial Identity" opposing "notions of the self which formulate it primarily as an abstract form without content, a decontextualized ability to reason without any interested positionality." In her essay "Who's afraid of Identity Politics?" Alcoff presents positionality as "a key component of the rationale behind the original concept of identity politics. It should be obvious that one's identity in this full sense, one's positional consciousness, will play a role in one's actions, particularly as these involve political contestations." 35 Most recently, in the essay "Against 'Post-Ethnic' Futures," Alcoff asserts that, "if we were to understand social position in a fuller sense, as involving a structural location, a historical experience, and a set of practices, then this is not a bad beginning for a formulation of what persons are."

Given this endorsement of formulating "what persons are" in the terms of a topos of positionality, it makes sense to consider how it is that positions become available to be occupied. What is the streamlet or memorial tree that anchors these positions, setting them apart from other positions one might inhabit? Are the voices and histories that help demarcate these positions consistent with what Simms would call the genius loci? That is, are these voices and experiences of place built into the structure of a location (thus, like the genius loci, anthropomorphizing that location) and requiring newcomers to be initiated—via handbooks—to the history and voices of that place? And does the anthropomorphism underwriting the place—its haunting by a genius loci—provide an alternative that is any less essential, in the end, than the essentialism it seeks to escape?

Finally, is it not the case that an awareness of multiple positions—like so many places in a guidebook—has the effect of not only separating positions from each other but also, and more importantly, assembling them as stops on a grand tour? In such a scenario, the tourists may end up—as James Clifford has observed-exemplifying "the globalizing condition of postmodernity, [a condition in which] local communities are reconstituted within a superficial shopping mall of identities" where they exist in "nostalgic, commodifiedforms." It is a different aspect of globalization—not its marketplace commodities but its institutional structures—that has prompted Robert Eric Livingston to voice a different note of caution: invoking Geoffrey Hartman's account of the genius loci, Livingston underscores that concept's utility for the project of undermining local variety (Hartman's pentecostal plurality of tongues) and producing institutional standardization within nation-states: "In this form of reimagined community, Hartman suggests, the genius loci could come to be understood as primordial allegiance and mobilized under the banner of nation and race." Indeed, quoting Whitman's "Passage to India", Livingstone suggests that the genius loci is a contributor to, rather than an alternative to, the Genius mundi of globalization. Or, to put this in Simms's terms, a mockingbird may steal several tongues and then choose to sing using only a few or, indeed, just one.

The problem these observations raise is that, at least with respect to positionality, critical practice has been moving in circles rather than charting a new course. This is perhaps most clearly evident in Linda Martin Alcoff's recent essay, "What Should White People Do?" Asserting that "Every individual... needs to feel a connection to community, to a history, and to a human project larger than his or her own life," Alcoff asks, "what are North American whites to do?" "Southern whiteness," Alcoff asserts, "has had a high degree of racial self-consciousness," so it has existed as "a substantive racial identity". The dilemma these whites face, however, becomes apparent to Alcoff as she wonders how one would "substantively define whiteness except in terms of racism and unfair privilege". If "white people's sense of who they are in the world, especially in this country, depends deeply on white supremacy," Alcoff argues, this is because "they are themselves oppressed; that is, because their immigrant relations were a humble lot without other cultural resources from which to draw a sense of entitlement.

White supremacy may be all that poor whites have to hold on to in order to maintain a sense of self-love". Whites are "oppressed" because not only did they suffer a lack of "cultural resources" to serve as a basis for their identity, but also, once they are confronted with the fact that whiteness involves not "cultural resources" but "white supremacy," the task of "facing the reality of whites' moral culpability threatens their very ability to be moral today, because it threatens their ability to imagine themselves as having a socially coherent relation to a past and a future toward which anyone could feel an attachment" —it threatens "the sense of historical continuity that moral action," Alcoff asserts, "seems to require". Without white supremacy, whites have no positionality.

Critics of Simms, however, would beg to differ with Alcofi's conclusion, if not her premise. Not only, as we have seen, is Simms a conceptual architect of the very positionality Alcoff endorses, but his voluminous works also provide an opportunity to position him as a central cultural figure—someone whose "pivotal role as a kind ancestral father to modern literature of the South is beginning to be acknowledged"—within a revitalized account of southernness. Would not southerners, as Alcoff—and Simms—imagine them, prefer to invoke such a guardian genius as the basis of an autonomous southern positionality?

Indeed, in light of recent critical challenges to a coherent American nationality, why seek to include Simms within an embattled American Renaissance at all? Given the positional autonomy Simms enables, would it not seem more sensible (as Dainatto's discussion of "Critical Regionalism" demonstrates) to replace one's national identity as an American with one's positional identity as a southerner? Viewed in this light, the topos of positionality would seem to function—as have many prior rhetorical innovations—merely to reproduce, in the form of an autonomous "position" with its own resources and memories, the racial privileges of whites.

Walt Whitman: He Was a Liberator of People and Culture, Using a Liberated Poetic Form.

By Richard Gambino

In 1848, 29-year-old Walt Whitman was for three months a reporter for the Daily Crescent in New Orleans, writing fluff pieces about local colour and charm as seen through Yankee eyes. But he also saw darker spectacles there—streetside auctions of slaves—and six years later put his emotions into ironic verse. I help the auctioneer, the sloven does not half know his business... Have you ever loved the body of a woman? Have you ever loved the body of a man? Do you not see that these are exactly the same to all in all nations and times all over the earth? If any thing is sacred the human body is sacred. When he returned to New York, he became the editor of the Brooklyn Daily Freeman, the nation's foremost voice of the Free Soil movement, whose motto was, "Free soil, free labour, free men!"

He continued his advocacy of the movement, because of which, just before going to New Orleans, he had been fired as editor of the Brooklyn Daily Eagle. But intimacy with those in the movement had its effect. Whitman came to hate, on the one side, the abolitionists for their fanaticism, most of which went into infighting among themselves, and on the other, the hypocritical and corrupt men of the Democratic Party, all of them "born freedom sellers of the earth." He resigned from the Freeman, despondent. His faith rested in the sympathy of the human heart, which had failed.

I have said that the soul is not more than the body, And I have said that the body is not more than the soul, And nothing, not God, is greater to one than one's self is, And whoever walks a furlong without sympathy walks to his own funeral drest in his shroud. Whitman's faith in democracy flowed from the same source. It was not a faith resting on constitutionalism, legalisms, political science schemes, natural law or laws of history. It was rooted in a belief in the best of the human souls of ordinary citizens, often dismissed as his "mysticism."

But when he was answering the challenge of whether the soul exists, his response did not depend on abstractions or esoterica but on the perceived experience of personal and historical growth. "No reasoning, no proof has establish'd it,/ Undeniable growth has establish'd it." His faith in democracy rested on a distinctly American populism of pragmatic human experience. So in a twentieth century obsessed with ideological convictions that politics, and especially economics, determine human behaviour and history, he was brushed aside as a quaint American naif whistling in the dark.

Another common error is to take Whitman's faith in free humanity as a bombastic pollyannaism, or softheaded narcissistic, mystical messianism. Yes, he tells us that as a boy he was electrified by hearing a sermon by Elias Hicks of the Quaker Church on Joralemon Street in Brooklyn. (Hicks's faith in the human spirit was so radical that even his fellow Quakers denounced him as a heretic.) Whitman was captured by the idea that "the fountain of all...truth... namely in yourself and your inherent relations," and that in this, Hicks was "a brook of clear and cool and ever-healthy, ever-living water." But young Whitman, who'd been pulled out of school at age 11, developed his own pragmatic, experiential populism, so would not become a Quaker. "Logic and sermons never convince,/The damp of the night drives deeper into my soul." His mature populism was not of a Mary Sunshine kind.

Whitman's Democratic Vistas should be read by all Americans. It is a lengthy, scathing critique of American democracy's flaws at the time, and in ours—the flaws being the failings of its people and culture. I would alarm and caution...against the prevailing delusion that the establishment of free political institutions, and plentiful intellectual smartness, with general good order, physical plenty, industry andc., (desirable and precious advantages as they all are,) do, of themselves, determine and yield to our experiment of democracy the fruitage of success.... I say we had best look our times and lands searchingly in the face.... The spectacle is appaling. We live in an atmosphere of hypocrisy throughout. The men believe not in the women, nor the women in the men. A scornful superciliousness rules in literature....

The great cities reek with respectable as much as non-respectable robbery and scoundrelism. In fashionable life, flippancy, tepid amours, weak infidelism, small aims, or no aims at all, only to kill time. Whitman's enduring lesson about American democracy: "O I see flashing that this America is only you and me." No better, no worse. "The genius of the United States is not best or most in its executives or legislatures, nor in its ambassadors or authors or colleges or churches or parlors, nor even in its newspapers or inventors...but always most in the common people." Whitman's brand of populism mandated that he seek the liberation of people and culture, in a liberated poetic form. He did not invent free verse but embraced it and advanced it, against the ornamental, parade-ground regularities of meter and rhyme, which constrained his early poems to the point of banality.

Rhymes and rhymers pass away, poems distill'd from poems pass away... America justifies itself, give it time, no disguise can deceive it or conceal from it, it is impassive enough. In naturalism, freed from pie-in-the-sky otherworldliness: And a mouse is miracle enough to stagger sextillions of infidels. In exquisite sensuality: Out of the rolling ocean...came a drop gently to me, whispering I love you, before long I die, I have travl'd a long way merely to look on you to touch you. In sexuality: Without shame the man I like knows and avows the deliciousness of his sex, Without shame the woman I like knows and avows hers. And in sexual orientation. Although he resisted admitting his homosexuality, even to absurdly claiming he had six illegitimate children, he did so to avoid, as with regard to all matters, being pigeonholed, and thus vulnerable to easy dismissal.

But his "Calamus" poems are frankly homosexual, even celebratory in the sexual orientation (Calamus is a plant with a phalluslike head): O here I last saw him that tenderly loves me, and returns again never to separate from me, And this, O this shall henceforth be the token of comrades, this calamus-root shall, Interchange it youths with each other! let none render it back! Whitman's sexual poems, like many others, were courageous. He was fired from a badly needed job as a clerk at the Interior Department in Washington by none less than the Secretary of the Interior himself. Secretary James Harlan stole Whitman's personal copy of Leaves of Grass from his desk, and noted, ironically, some of the heterosexual poems of the "Children of the Adam" section as "obscene."

The female form approaching, I pensive, love-flesh tremulous aching... The face, the limbs, the index from head to foot, and what it arouses, The mystic deliria, the madness amorous, the utter abandonment. Whitman's courage, and humour, extended to his last days. Wheelchair-bound, sleeping on a waterbed "like a ship or a duck" to relieve constant pain from multiple ailments, including bodywide TB and strokes, he described himself as "some hard-cased dilapidated grim ancient shellfish or time-bang'd conch (no legs, utterly non-locomotive) cast up high and dry on the shore-sands." (Years before, after suffering a stroke that left him paralyzed except for his head and one arm, he had brought himself back to complete mobility through his own efforts, including wrestling with saplings in woods.) He struggled against pain and paralysis to complete a ninth edition of Leaves. And succeeded.Whitman saw in the risky experiment of a free people possibilities for a great polity, culture and morality. Three years before his death, in 1888, when he was 69, he wrote that there had been in his life one "purpose enclosing all, and over and beneath":

Ever since what might be call'd thought, or the budding of thought, fairly began in my youthful mind, I had had a desire to attempt some worthy record of that entire faith and acceptance... which is the foundation of moral America. His challenge to us, again typically American, is that the faith is to be fulfilled with each person and generation in the future.

Dear camerado! I confess I have urged you onward with me, and still urge you, without the least idea what is our destination, Or whether we shall be victorious, or utterly quell'd and defeated.

Four Basic Archetypal Ways Found in

Shamanic Traditions
Angeles Arrien
The Earth is the centre of the universe
The house is the centre of the Earth
The family is the centre of the house
The person is the centre of the family
Basque Song

To survive in the twenty-first century, people must become more capable of handling change than ever before. Alvin Toffler elaborates on this idea in his visionary book Future Shock, when he states, "We have the opportunity to introduce additional stability points and rituals into our society, such as new holidays, pageants, ceremonies, and games. Such mechanisms could not only provide a backdrop of continuity in everyday life but serve to integrate societies, and cushion them somewhat against the fragmenting impact of super-industrialism." Essentially, the challenge in the next century is to become "the change master," a term Rosabeth Moss Kanter introduced. Kanter identifies ways in which we cope, manage, resist, or creatively approach change. Angeles Arrien, anthropologist and Basque folklore specialist, is on the faculty at the Institute of Transpersonal Psychology and at the California Institute for Integral Studies. She is author of the Tarot Handbook—Practical Applications of Ancient Symbols and of numerous articles. This article is an excerpt from Dr. Arrien forthcoming book, The Four-Fold Way: Indigenous Wisdoms Applied in Contemporary Times, to be published in spring 1992 by Harper and Row.

Indigenous and Eastern cultures have long recognized that the only constant is change. Among tribal peoples, medicine men, chiefs, shamans, teachers, or seers are called "change masters." The shamanic traditions practiced by agrarian and indigenous peoples remind us that for centuries, human beings have used nature and ritual to buffer change and to support a life event, rather than denying or indulging in it. Individuals support change and states of health through dreams, images, play, relationships, and acts of creative work. Cultures support change and states of health through these mythic structures and through the institutionalization of art, science, music, ritual, and drama.

In the introduction to Arnold Van Gennep book Rites of Passage, Salon Kimbala said that "one dimension of mental illness may arise because an increasing number of individuals are forced to accomplish their traditions alone and with private symbols." In cultures that are alienated from mythological roots, renewal requires a return to the basic source from which all personal and cultural myths are ultimately forged—the human psyche. Cross-cultural research reveals that shamanic traditions consistently access four major ways of maintaining connections to the mythic structures that support creative expression, health, and adaptation to change. The majority of shamanic traditions practice the following archetypal mythic themes: The Way of the Warrior, The Way of the Teacher, The Way of the Healer, and The Way of the Visionary. The appendix at the end of this article is a visual synthesis of the material incorporated in each of the ways discussed below.

THE WAY OF THE WARRIOR

We convince by our presence.

Walt Whitman

Carl Jung, the psychologist who specialized in the identification of archetypes and how they apply to personal and collective experience, stated that "myth is more individual and expresses life more precisely than does science. Science works with concepts of averages which are far too general to do justice to the subjective variety of an individual life". Through the mythic theme and archetypal expression of the warrior (an oldfashioned term for leader or leadership), indigenous societies connect to the process of empowerment and to the human resource of power. Various words have been used synonymously in both ancient and modern times to describe the Warrior's Way of accessing power.

After Hours: Acclaimed Author Michael Cunningham Channeled His Love of Virginia Woolf in the Hours. in Specimen Days, He Considers the World after Walt Whitman.

By David Bahr

"I try to model myself on artists most heroic to me," says Michael Cunningham, "people who ignore their obvious gifts to try something new and see what happens." After the success of his Pulitzer Prize-winning novel The Hours, Cunningham certainly takes quite a few risks with Specimen Days (Farrar, Straus and Giroux, $24). Cunningham's new book is a trio of interrelated, genre-bending novellas set in New York City and involving Walt Whitman. The first, "In the Machine," is a ghost story set at the height of the industrial revolution; the second, "The Children's Crusade," is a contemporary crime thriller about a kids' terrorist ring; and the third, "Like Beauty," is an interspecies romance circa 2150 between a lizard lady and a male robot who traffics in homoerotic S/M fantasies. In an Advocate exclusive, Cunningham discusses his long-awaited book. With The Hours you took on Virginia Woolf. Why now Whitman?

I hadn't planned it. I'm sure there are people who'll say "He cashed in on Woolf, and now he's cashing in on another one." Actually, the first part was always set in New York City around 1865. Doing research, I realized that New York then was an extremely difficult place for everyone but the rich. People worked 12 hours a day, six days a week at factories. There was a coal-laden sky above everybody's head. I thought how interesting that out of this blighted environment sprang Whitman, the greatest American poet. So I put him in the lust and then thought, If he is going to be in one, he should be in all three.

In "The Children's Crusade," a character refers to Whitman as "a lover of boys." Do you think he was gay? Any doubt about Whitman's homosexuality is heterosexist. Many passages in Leaves of Grass refer to his love of men. Why did you decide to write three novellas instead of one novel? I was interested in what ghost stories, thrillers, and science fiction are telling us about human life and mystery. My favourite is "In The Machine," which is more like your lyrical, realist fiction. I felt that it was especially important after the surprise success of The Hours not to write that book again, like some literary castrato who sings the same song to the delight of the court. Of course, what I'll hear from the next person is, "I'm so glad you finally dumped all that endless relationship crap."

In "Like Beauty," America is Christian-dominated and feudally governed. Is this the future you see?

The idea of a feudal, fundamentalist future is hardly implausible. I wish it were. But it seems to me one of many possible futures. Personally, I've never felt so stuck between skeptical paranoia and profound optimism.

Specimen Days has no gay characters, yet "Like Beauty" is one of your queerest stories. I'm glad you noticed. I've always thought of myself as a queer [rather than gay] writer.

Before The Hours, you were a midlist gay author, and

now—I'm a crossover writer! How do you view your new Whitmanesque reach? My hope is that being pulled out of the "gay readers only" section and deposited in a larger section indicates that the world is just getting bigger. My fear is that I'm the token gay writer who gets to cross over on a provisional basis. What do you most want to say?

The most effective political act for any gay man or lesbian, especially if you lead a public life, is to be completely open. Although, as a gay writer, I refuse to participate in a system that requires me to write only about gay people, the one obligation that I will more than happily meet is to never be discreet, to never let that book club in the Midwest imagine that I have anything to hide.

Walt Whitman to Come to Life Actor to Portray Poet at Naper Settlement.

Walt Whitman may be best-known for his poetry, but during the Civil War, he also was known for the compassion he showed wounded soldiers.

"Walt Whitman was a volunteer hospital nurse during the Civil War," said Donna DeFalco, marketing coordinator at Naper Settlement.

The settlement, a 19th-century museum village that annually hosts Civil War re-enactments, will present a programme about Whitman on Sunday as part of its ongoing History Speaks Lecture Series.

Chicago actor R.J. Lindsey, who gives one-man portrayals of notable historical figures including Abraham Lincoln, Thomas Edison and Franklin D. Roosevelt, will portray Whitman and share biographical highlights about the writer, schoolteacher, journalist and Civil War volunteer from 7 to 8 p.m. Sunday in Century Memorial Chapel.

DeFalco said Lindsey is a settlement favourite.

"He's done a lot of our History Speaks," she said.

The series, which runs October through May, was started about three years ago, she said. Last fall, Lyman Shephard portrayed architect Frank Lloyd Wright; in January, actor Terry Lynch impersonated Benjamin Franklin.

Lindsey said Whitman was a pioneer among poets: "He is the premier poet of the 19th century. He made American poetry go in an entirely different direction," he said.

Until Whitman's arrival on the literary scene, Lindsey said, poetic verse rhymed. Whitman dared to introduce free verse. He also wasn't afraid to address sexuality in his poems, a habit that caused consternation among critics. "They called his poetry obscene and dirty and filthy," he said. "Many people were shocked." Whitman went on to write "Leaves of Grass," his best-known book of poetry. "He would be rewriting it the rest of his life," Lindsey said.

When his brother, George, a Union soldier, was injured, Whitman traveled to Virginia to find him. He discovered his brother's wounds were superficial, Lindsey said, but the scene Whitman encountered inspired him to offer his aid. "He saw how the soldiers were living. He saw the amputations. He saw the piles of legs and arms that had been sawed off the wounded," Lindsey said. "It had such an effect on him. He stayed three years. He said he just couldn't leave these boys."

Lindsey said he'll talk about Whitman's dysfunctional family, his admiration for Abraham Lincoln, his years as a newspaper reporter and schoolteacher, and his clergy-less funeral. "He didn't like ministers very well at all," Lindsey said, adding that Whitman's sister insisted, on his behalf, that no clergy be present at his burial. Lindsey promises that interspersed with biographical notes will be snippets of Whitman's poetic verse. "It's the most beautiful poetry," DeFalco said.

A Dream of Reform? the Eager and Often Inconsiderate Appeals of Reformers and Revolutionists Are Indispensable, to Counterbalance the Inertness and Fossilism Making So Large a Part of Human Institutions.

Walt Whitman: WHETHER Senator-elect Antonio Trillanes could attend Senate sessions to discharge his constitutional duty has obviously been decided by the AFP chief of staff: He may not. The parallel cited is Romeo Jaloslos' continued incarceration even when he was elected congressman.

The strange thing about these "parallel lives" is that they were allowed to run for public office instead of being banned from the start.

In both cases, the authorities saw nothing illegal in their candidacies. They submitted Jaloslos and Trillanes to the will of the electorate despite the knowledge that, in differing circumstances but in the same context, they were "outlaws."

It's not, of course, their guilt or innocence under the law that was submitted to the people but their fitness to serve them as legislators. Jaloslos' local constituency said he was fit while Trillanes, elected at large, has a convincing majority of the national constituency behind him.

Here's where you have a conundrum, a conflict, perhaps an incompatibility, between the sense of justice (albeit still to be proved in the case of Trillanes) and the sense of democratic politics.

It will be recalled that Erap's ouster was "judged" in the streets and not through due process, then upheld later, though the jury is still out regarding its legitimacy.

In Trillanes' case, the electorate acted as the "jury" upholding his right and fitness to "serve as a senator"-not just "be" a senator-if there's any difference between the two.

But the really deep and important question is why "outlaws" like Honasan and Trillanes were elected by the people? Have the people lost their sense of law and order? Are the people so perverse as to elect persons who threatened the government?

However, the popular approval of rebels-certain rebels at least, like Rob Roy and "Brave Heart" Wallace-has, historically, something to do with discontentment and disillusionment with the corruption of power.

It's a sign of a dream for reforms.

War's Emotions, Images Inspired Walt Whitman

Were it not for his brother, George, who was 10 years his junior, Walt Whitman might have spent the Civil War years scratching out a living as a free-lance writer in Brooklyn.

Instead, George's experience drew the author of "Leaves

of Grass" close to the war and had a profound effect on his career for, as he would later recognize, the Civil War was at the heart of his poetry.

Six days after the bombardment of Fort Sumter, George Whitman, then 32 and a cabinet maker, joined the Brooklyn 13th Regiment and later re-enlisted in the 51st New York Volunteers.

As Whitman watched his brother's regiment assemble, he saw exuberant troops "with pieces of rope ied to their musket barrels o bring back prisoner from the audacious South, to be lead in a noose, on our men's early and triumphant return!"

With the defeat at Bull Run, Whitman became less sanguine about the North's prospects and penned a recruiting poem exhorting the North to rise up, "Beat! Beat! Drums," for Harper's Weekly on Sept. 28, 1861.

During the war, George would participate in 21 engagements under Gens. George McClellan, William T. Sherman, Ulysses S. Grant and others; see most of his comrades killed at Second Bull Run, Fredericksburg and Antietam; and spend four months in a Confederate prison.

George wrote vivid accounts in his many letters home and kept a diary that Walt considered one of the most powerful records of the war. On Dec. 16, 1862, George's name, garbled as "First Lieutenant G.W. Whitmore," appeared in the New York Herald list of regimental casualties. Walt set out for the front and, once in Washington, searched the hospitals looking for George.

A friend from Boston, now an assistant to the Army paymaster, got him a pass to Falmouth, Va., where George's regiment had regrouped. One of the first things Whitman saw outside an Army hospital was a heap of amputated limbs, large enough to fill a horse cart. He found George, alive and well, one of the luckiest of the 10,000 Union wounded at Fredericksburg; he had been cut on the cheek by a shell fragment.

For 10 days, Whitman shared his brother's tent and mess. Living so close to the dressing stations, makeshift hospitals and burial grounds, Walt felt an intimacy for the men doing the fighting, which he recorded in detail. At Falmouth, Whitman wrote the prose draft of one of his finest Civil War poems:

Sight at Day Break-in camp in front of the hospital tent on a stretcher, each with a blanket spread over him-I lift up one and look at the young man's face, calm and yellow,-'tis strange! (Young man: I think this face of yours the face of my dead Christ!)

Whitman returned to Washington on Dec. 28 with a trainload of wounded. During the trip he walked about the stretchers, carrying water and taking messages from the men for their families. Whitman wrote to his friend, Ralph Waldo Emerson, the next day that his "New York stagnation" had ended and, as he acknowledged later, he had found his great work.

Though he planned to remain in Washington for only a short time, his stay, interrupted by periodic visits home, would last a decade.

Whitman rented a room at 14th and L streets, and the following year moved to Sixth Street near Pennsylvania Avenue. He got a job as a copyist in the paymaster's office, which paid only a few dollars a week but left time during most of each day to visit the hospitals. With meager funds sent from his friends and the sale of a few articles to the newspapers, Whitman bought tobacco, fruit, stationery, books and magazines, and other small items that the men wanted, which he distributed on his many trips through the wards.

The spirit of his work and change in attitude about the war are captured in the "Wound-Dresser": Arous'd and angry, I'd thought to beat the alarum, and urge relentless war, But soon my fingers fail'd me, my face droop'd and I resigned myself, To sit by the wounded and soothe them, or silently watch the dead;

By 1862, Washington had nearly 50 military hospitals, most converted hastily from churches, schools and taverns. Even the Capitol served as a refuge for the wounded. Whitman also found wounded lying between display cases in the Patent Office, the "noblest of Washington's buildings." The improvised hospitals held as many as 70,000 sick and wounded, roughly equal to the city's peacetime population.

Whitman reckoned that by the end of the war he made more than 600 hospital visits, often lasting for several days and nights. The emotional and physical strain affected his own health; sometimes he had to return to Brooklyn for rest.

But he always went back to his rounds, visiting the men, reading to them, cheering them, and washing and dressing wounds. Whitman developed a deep paternalistic affection for the men, some of whom were amputees he had nursed through the danger of hemorrhage. Many never forgot the large, graybearded man who selflessly gave of his time, energy and kindness.

While in Brooklyn, Whitman learned that his brother had been captured on Sept. 30, 1864. Except for two letters in October, Whitman had no idea whether his brother had perished inside a Confederate prison. Meanwhile, Whitman's friends in Washington got him a job as a clerk for the Department of the Interior and he reported for work in January.

He was assigned to the Office of Indian Affairs located in the Patent Office, the same building where he had ministered to casualties and which was soon to host President Abraham Lincoln's second inaugural ball.

Whitman poignantly contrasted the "beautiful women, perfumes violins' sweetness" at the Inaugural Ball to the "odor of wounds and blood" of the building when used as a hospital.

He continued to inquire after George and, according to one account, an editor at the New York Times pressured Grant to arrange a prisoner exchange if George was still alive.

George's luck held; he was released from the Danville, Va., prison just before Lincoln's second inauguration. Whitman took leave to join his brother in Brooklyn and there began printing his wartime poems, "Drum-Taps."

He was at home on April 14 when Lincoln, whom Whitman had come to revere, was assassinated. Realizing that his poetic record of the war could not be complete without a memorial poem on Lincoln, Whitman hastily inserted a poem,

"Hush'd be the camps today," and appended a subtitle, "A.L. Buried April 19, 1865," the date of the funeral in Washington.

But as time passed, Whitman brought together the emotions and images of that spring in his immortal elegiac poem: When lilacs last in the dooryard bloom'd, And the great star early droop'd in the western sky in the night,

I mourn'd, and yet shall mourn with ever-returning spring. Whitman returned to Washington shortly after the war ended. In May, he had a splendid view of the grand review of the Union armies.

He watched the massed brigade, an unbroken line of 200,000 soldiers, pass. Now a major, George Whitman again marched with his regiment, this time across the bridge from Arlington, past the Capitol to the train station bound for civilian life.

In early autumn, Whitman wrote a sequel to "Drum-Taps," the theme of which is a memorial tribute to the war dead, in which he added his best known poem, "0 Captain! My Captain!" In 1875, he recorded his hospital visits in "Memoranda During the War," which came from the soiled, penciled notes he took as he walked among the wounded with his gifts and consoling presence.

Until his death in 1892, Whitman remained mindful of his own debt to the war and the days that changed his life. Ken Kryvoruka is a Washington lawyer who also teachs writing at George Washington University School of Law.

Bibliography

Reader's Guide by G.W. Allen (1970);

Critical Essays on Walt Whitman, ed. by J. Woodress (1983);

Language and Style by C.C.Hollis (1983);

Walt Whitman by James E. Miller Jr., Helen Regenstein (1990);

From Noon to Starry Night: A Life of Walt Whitman by Philip Callow (1992);

Masculine Landscapes by Byrne R.S. Fone (1992);

The Growth of Leaves of Grass by M. Jimmie Killingsworth (1993);

Walt Whitman; The Centennial Essays, ed. by Ed Folsom (1994);

The Cambridge Companion to Walt Whitman, ed. by Ezra Greenspan (1995);

Walt Whitman by Catherine Reef (1995);

Walt Whitman & the World, ed. by Gay Wilson Allen, Ed Folsom (1995);

Walt Whitman: A Gay Life by Gary Schmidgall (1997);

Walt Whitman: An Encyclopedia, ed. by J.R. Lemaster, Donald D. Kummings (1998);

Walt Whitman: A Comprehensive Research and Study Guide, ed. by Harold Bloom (1999);

A Historical Guide to Walt Whitman, ed. by David S. Reynolds (1999);

Walt Whitman, ed. by Jim Perlman (1999);

Walt Whitman by Jerome Loving (1999) other studies among others by J. Kaplan (1980);

H. Aspiz (1980);

W.H. Eitner (1981);
P. Zweig (1984);
D. Cavitch (1985);
M.W. Thomas (1987);

Museums: Walt Whitman's birthplace, 246 Old Whitman Road, Huntington Station, Suffolk.

Note: Edgar Lee Masters, who wrote Spoon River Anthology, published a biography of Walt Whitmanin in 1937.